George Santayana's Philosophy of Religion

For Tom —

Read and learn from an Agnostic Catholic.

All the Best

[signature]

George Santayana's Philosophy of Religion

His Roman Catholic Influences and Phenomenology

Edward W. Lovely
Foreword by Robert S. Corrington

LEXINGTON BOOKS
Lanham • Boulder • New York • Toronto • Plymouth, UK

Published by Lexington Books
A wholly owned subsidiary of The Rowman & Littlefield Publishing Group, Inc.
4501 Forbes Boulevard, Suite 200, Lanham, Maryland 20706
www.rowman.com

10 Thornbury Road, Plymouth PL6 7PP, United Kingdom

British Library Cataloguing in Publication Information Available

Library of Congress Cataloging-in-Publication Data

Lovely, Edward W., 1938–
George Santayana's philosophy of religion : his Roman Catholic influences and phenomenology /
Edward W. Lovely ; foreword by Robert S. Corrington.
p. cm.
Includes bibliographical references and index.
ISBN 978-0-7391-7626-9 (alk. paper) — ISBN 978-0-7391-7627-6
1. Santayana, George, 1863–1952. 2. Religion—Philosophy. I. Title.
B945.S24L68 2013
210.92—dc23
2012029425

℗™ The paper used in this publication meets the minimum requirements of American
National Standard for Information Sciences Permanence of Paper for Printed Library
Materials, ANSI/NISO Z39.48-1992.

Printed in the United States of America

Contents

Acknowledgments

I gratefully thank Professor Robert S. Corrington, a leading American Naturalist, for his help, constructive critique and encouragement while I was writing this book. Much of my initiation into American philosophy has been an outgrowth of a deep reading of his Ecstatic Naturalism and sharing in Robert's insights into the philosophy of C. S. Peirce, William James, Josiah Royce and other iconic figures in the American canon. I also thank Dr. Herman Saatkamp, Jr., for his encouragement and early reading of the manuscript and guidance while I was writing my doctoral dissertation on Santayana. I am grateful as well to Professor John Lachs, who read the early version manuscript, provided many helpful suggestions and encouraged me to consider publication. The anonymous reviewers of the manuscript for this book provided an excellent critique with many important suggestions, and I thank them for their thoroughness, scholarship and time. I am also indebted to Janet Menkes for her editorial help.

I dedicate this book to my wife Barbara without whose persistent encouragement it would have remained fallow in the face of much excellent scholarship already published which is bringing Santayana's philosophy into the contemporary light of recognition that it deserves.

Edward W. Lovely
Kinnelon, New Jersey

Foreword

At first blush, Santayana appears to be a fairly easy philosopher to read and to understand. But deeper acquaintance reveals that he is both radical and complex. His writing style is often moving and beautiful, but it can also be intense, densely packed and layered. Some of the paragraphs in his 1923 *Scepticism and Animal Faith* brook comparison with similar difficult passages in Hegel or Heidegger. He often weaves several distinct ideas into a single sentence compelling the reader to pause to unravel the threads. Here is a typical example: "The ultimate reaches of doubt and renunciation open out for it [a mind], by an easy transition, into fields of endless variety and peace, as if through the gorges of death it had passed into a paradise where all things are crystallized into the image of themselves, and have lost their urgency and their venom" (chapter 9).

Like a number of other philosophers, I have come to Santayana later in life. Dewey and Peirce first captured my imagination and helped to shape my world. Indeed, I can say that Dewey is part of my philosophical DNA. My first serious encounter with Santayana came when reading his brilliant critique of Dewey's *Experience and Nature*. Santayana drew blood and Dewey knew it. Suddenly I was compelled to acknowledge a bigger naturalism, one less shaped by a midworld of instrumentalities, and one which took finitude as seriously as had the existentialists. I note in passing that Santayana mastered Heidegger's *Sein und Zeit* and felt its influence on his implicit phenomenology.

Putting it differently, Santayana's works are always a stretching experience for me with the result that more tribal perspectives leave me cold and hungering for the truly generic. I saw this impulse in my mentor Justus Buchler who had a high regard for Santayana, having coedited some of his essays. In a way, Buchler's masterpiece, *Metaphysics of Natural Complexes* (1966 and 1990), continues in the tradition of Santayana's generic conception of foundational work in philosophy.

Consider the characters in Santayana's mature metaphysics: essences and their intuitions, animal faith, substance and matter, free-floating spirit, rugged psyche, deep scepticism, anti-idealism (read Josiah Royce here), anti-empiricism, symbols, memory and existence. These primal concepts amplify each other to produce one of the most challenging and unique perspectives in philosophy, East or West. It takes strong hermeneutic skills to open out Santayana's full perspective.

This is why I am pleased that we now have Ed Lovely's masterful book on Santayana which shows these hermeneutic skills in action. His primary focus is on Santayana's philosophy of religion and the phenomenological aspects of his approach. This is the first book to bring these explicit foci together. At the same time, these foci illuminate Santayana's mature metaphysics, especially his distinctive concept of spirit.

Lovely anchors his account in Santayana's complex relationship with Roman Catholicism, noting the alliance of atheism with a kind of spirit-infused poetic piety with no literal divine referent. Religion is best seen as high poetry operating in the realm of spirit, a realm of essences where there is no causal connection to the hidden and sundry activities of substance/matter. We are in a realm of imagination using symbols and signs of the sacred. On the other side, Santayana had little patience with the Boston Protestantism with which he grew up, partly for its lack of the imaginative and poetic spirit. This is especially clear in the character of Oliver Alden in Santayana's novel, *The Last Puritan*, who is hampered by a lingering Puritanism that won't let him experience the *jouissance* that is fully experienced by Lord Jim and Mario Van de Weyer.

Moving to Santayana's philosophy of religion, Lovely provides an exhaustive analysis of the major thinkers whose work played a role in shaping Santayana's views. The Greeks and Germans are foremost, while Spinoza receives treatment for his critique of the idea of a personal god. Santayana was especially hard on the psychic inflation (egoism) found in German Romanticism, singling out Fichte and Hegel for special critique. Absolute knowing runs roughshod over the finitude that marks the "tethered" creature that has knowledge in fits and starts.

Schopenhauer comes off a little better (as he should). Santayana wanted to write on Schopenhauer for his doctoral dissertation under Royce at Harvard. However, Royce persuaded him to write on Lotze instead. Regardless, there are traces of Schopenhauer in Santayana's mature philosophy. In particular, I sense a parallel between the type of "knowledge" operative in animal faith, tied to the psyche, with Schopenhauer's understanding of our knowledge of the Will through the immediacy of the will-infused body. In both cases, that of matter and Will, there is a kind of epistemic agnosticism that cannot be erased by the quest for first principles or conceptual grounding.

Lovely carefully works through the edifice of *The Realms of Being*, showing the internal correlations among the regnant concepts in the four realms. Even Santayana sophisticates will find much that is novel and valuable in his treatment. Lovely uses Buchler's major category of "ontological parity" to show the equality of being in *Realms*. Perhaps most valuable in this book is Lovely's thorough and brilliant treatment of the phenomenological elements of Santayana's stance, especially as applied to the traits in the realm of spirit. Similarities and differences with Husserl are uppermost, while comparisons are made with Peirce, James,

Whitehead and Heidegger. Santayana had heard Peirce lecture but, unlike Royce, was not a Peirce scholar. His relationship with James was multilayered and genuine.

Lovely concludes with an exhaustive analysis of the social and religious thought of Santayana in the larger field of philosophy of religion *per se*, dealing with such themes as Catholic modernism, dogma, semiotics, the Good, contemplation, domination, beauty and consciousness.

Ed Lovely's book is among the very best written on Santayana and will advance Santayana scholarship to new levels of inquiry, especially in the area of phenomenology, that discipline that works slowly and carefully to let essences come into radiant intuitions with no extrinsic causal claims. Phenomenology is first philosophy insofar as it is the method of methods for letting what is prevail in its own modality beneath the manic reach of what for many philosophers is an unwitting imperial ontology. Lovely has given us a rich and multilayered Santayana, and we are in his debt for his having done so.

Robert S. Corrington
    Drew University
    Madison, New Jersey

Introduction

As an undergraduate student, I "discovered" George Santayana in a relatively comprehensive few pages of Will Durant's popular *The Story of
Philosophy*. I became particularly intrigued with his approach to the Roman Catholic Church, its symbols, doctrine and mystery, while still sustaining a naturalistic and materialistic philosophical vision. A short time
later I learned that Santayana, as a young boy only recently emigrated
from Spain with scanty knowledge of English, had vacationed in the
house at Nahant, Massachusetts, owned by the Sturgises, a prominent
Boston merchant family and his mother's in-laws from her first marriage.
This occasion had been the first time in his life that the youth had made
an overnight "stay" from Boston for a vacation visit. Nahant, an island-
town north of Boston, is the town where I grew up and where three
generations of my family had lived since the turn of the century. During
the nineteenth century the Lowells, Cabots, William James, Louis Agassiz
and intellectuals of the period summered in Nahant, only a short ferry
ride from Boston. Louis Agassiz had in fact done his foundational work
in marine biology at East Point in Nahant and died in 1873, the year of
George's first visit there. Santayana also visited Nahant again while at
Harvard and somehow his former presence there on my home ground
further stimulated my interest and my undertaking a study of his philosophy of religion.

BIOGRAPHICAL SUMMARY OF GEORGE SANTAYANA

George Santayana (1863–1952) was baptized Jorge Augustin Nicolas and
later in life would appeal well enough to his professional and literary
contemporaries and the general flux of human opinion to appear on the
cover of *Time* magazine in 1936, one of the few philosophers ever to have
been so honored by *Time*. Born into a traditional Spanish family of Deistic
and anti-clerical leanings in Madrid, he was baptized into the Roman
Catholic Church, and in 1872, after living in Avila from 1864 to 1872,
Santayana emigrated from Spain to Boston, Massachusetts. He was nine
years of age and was to live on with his mother Josefina and the three
children of her widowed first marriage to George Sturgis, a ninth son of
Nathaniel Russell Sturgis, a merchant of Boston. Josefina had been widowed at a young age and at the age of thirty-three married George's

father Augustin Santayana, a retired middle-level official in the Colonial
Service of Spain who had spent his career in the Philippines and returned
to Spain to retire due to his fragile health.

The conditions of Josefina's move to Boston in 1869, leaving young
George to remain with his father, was purported to fulfill her promise to
her former husband and the Sturgis family that the three children of that
marriage would be educated in the Boston area. Young George remained
with his father until 1872, neither his father nor he seeing Josefina until it
was decided that George should be nearer to his mother in order to enjoy
the benefits of schooling in America and the social privileges of the Sturgis family which were not available to him with his father in Avila. However, the seeds of a permanent separation of Augustin and Josefina were
there, and following Augustin's trip to Boston to deliver young George,
despite declared intentions to remain with the family, he returned to
Avila less than a year later in 1873. Despite this, Augustin clearly loved
his stern and imperious Josefina and pleaded with her unsuccessfully to
return with the family to Spain and Avila. Josefina, however, was drawn
to the waning social prominence of the Sturgis clan and her hermitic but
comfortable life on Beacon Street and declined to leave. Augustin and
Josephina were to remain separated but on amiable terms. George Santayana would remain close to and influenced by his father and emotionally drawn to Avila for the balance of his life although, despite warm
correspondence, his first visit to see Augustin in Avila after 1873 was
almost ten years later upon completion of his freshman year at Harvard
in 1883.

George Santayana never gave up his Spanish citizenship, learned English while attending primary schools in Boston, went on to Boston Latin
School and then Harvard University where he distinguished himself as a
gifted scholar. With the exception of periodic visits to Avila, some graduate work in Germany and England and frequent European sojourns and
scholarly trips, he remained at Harvard his entire professional career. At
forty-eight years of age, after establishing an international philosophical
reputation and benefiting from a modest inheritance from his mother's
estate by virtue of the Sturgis family connection, Santayana resigned
from his tenured professorship and departmental chair of philosophy at
Harvard and left teaching and America forever. For the next forty years
until his death in Rome at eighty-nine years old in 1952 while under the
devoted care of the Blue Sisters of the Little Company of Mary, he would
live a philosophical and contemplative life in Europe and consolidate his
philosophical canon.[1]

METHODOLOGY

My methodology in this book may be characterized as a "sympathetic" hermeneutic rather than a critique of Santayana's philosophy. I have imposed a limited historical perspective in chapter 1 to demonstrate the period of transition in American philosophical and theological thought in the late nineteenth century and the academic milieu of romanticism and doubt that constituted the environment in which Santayana wrote his early works. Intending to provide a sense of Santayana's views on religion in his old age, I have chosen an anecdotal approach in chapter 1 which is consistent with my effort to address his mature philosophy of religion rather than, as other authors have effectively done, the historical development of his thought from early manhood until his death. In chapter 2, however, I discuss Santayana's influential philosophical antecedents. Ultimately my purpose is to systematically address, in "a piece," Santayana's philosophy of religion which has been done in part or in brief so well by Henry Samuel Levinson, George W. Howgate, Anthony Woodward, J. H. Faurot and others. I begin by associating the influences of Santayana's Roman Catholic background with his philosophical "disposition," and go on to demonstrate the consistency of his "technical" philosophy in relation to his philosophy of religion. Throughout my treatment, the tension in Santayana's project between the orthodoxy of the Roman Catholic Church and the "compromise" of liberal Protestantism becomes evident as does the philosophical foundations of this tension. I argue that Santayana's philosophical method has phenomenological aspects, although idiosyncratic in relation to the classical phenomenology of Edmund Husserl. My characterization of Santayana's philosophy of religion and the rationale for its development utilizes his essay "Ultimate Religion" as a pathway for exploration. Finally I address the uniqueness of Santayana's philosophical "profile" and identify some aspects of his project that are pertinent to contemporary religious studies and issues. My sources are primarily Santayana's published works and letters and secondary Santayana scholarship published in the twentieth century.

Consistent with this approach, in chapter 1, "A Paradoxical 'Catholic' Naturalist," I characterize religious and cultural influences upon Santayana's core beliefs and his philosophical disposition that have influenced his philosophy of religion. In chapter 2, "The Philosophical Basis for Santayana's Philosophy of Religion," I outline Santayana's "technical" philosophy and his theory of *essences* and indicate some antecedent philosophical figures that influenced his thought. I recognize that I am asking for some patience to be brought to bear by more sophisticated Santayana scholars as this chapter may seem as a primer. However, I am hopeful that for the less informed scholar, particularly those peripheral to

American philosophy, this will provide a helpful basis for moving forward to his philosophy of religion. In chapter 3, "The Phenomenological Character of Santayana's Philosophy of the Spirit," I address my theory of phenomenological aspects in Santayana's approach and indicate its importance in relation to his philosophy of religion. I compare Santayana's approach particularly to the phenomenology of Edmund Husserl and also to other philosophers of a phenomenological bent such as Alfred North Whitehead, Charles Sanders Peirce and William James. In chapter 4, "The Coherent Nature of Santayana's Philosophy of Religion," I integrate Santayana's philosophy of religion in its essential aspects and relate it to his concept of the religious and spiritual elements of his life of reason. I conclude in chapter 5, "Aspects of Santayana's Legacy to Religion in the Third Millennium," with a characterization of Santayana's particular relevance to contemporary religious thought, inclusive of his preemptive constructionist theology, views on religious and spiritual *praxis*, and I provide some examples of radical application of his philosophical vision.

In writing this book I found myself frequently resorting to quotations from Santayana's works instead of summarizing his ideas in my own words. There seems to be no one better than Santayana himself to provide a built-in hermeneutic for his own philosophy, and his rich descriptions and clear and insightful writing are hard to surpass in stating his position. Since my claims for the phenomenological aspects of Santayana's philosophy are somewhat off the beaten track of scholarship to date, I anticipate and look forward to critique and further scholarship to arrive at a more systematic understanding of the extent of his phenomenological bent.

NOTES

1. John McCormick, *George Santayana: A Biography*, (New York, Knopf: Dist. by Random House, 1987.) Biographical material was also substantially obtained from Santayana's autobiography, *Persons and Places: Fragments of Autobiography*, ed. W.G. Holzberger and H. J. Saatkamp, Jr, (Cambridge, MA: MIT Press, 1986), as well as "A General Confession," by George Santayana, *The Philosophy of George Santayana*, ed. Paul Arthur Schilpp, La Salle, IL: The Open Court Publishing Co., 1971).

ONE
A Paradoxical "Catholic" Naturalist

Perchance when Carnival is done,
And sun and moon go out for me,
Christ will be God, and I the one
That in my youth I used to be.

George Santayana, "Easter Hymn"

George Santayana (1863–1952), Spanish born, Harvard University–educated materialistic-naturalist philosopher, poet, cultural observer
and critic, has charmed me as he has others by his character, profound
philosophical wisdom and the poetic flow of his literary style. At inter-
vals, he reaches an epiphany of insight in his philosophical project and
then may descend into delightful critique, even of a "catty" and razor-
like sharpness. He gives one a glimpse of the "steel" and philosophical
"cruelty" that belies the gentleness and vulnerability of this seemingly
gentle soul. Here is a philosopher uniquely disposed toward a paradoxical religious and philosophical perspective, complex and ironical, yet
who remains resistant to the transcendent and is incapable of belief in a
divine *telos*. Any empathy we may have for Santayana could surely not
be based upon a lament for the apparent godless plight of this gentle,
stoic poet-philosopher, whom Anthony Woodward has called a very
much "self-gathered" man.[1] After all, in his maturity, there is no clear
evidence of suffering or melancholia in his stand for a life of *disillusion*
and acceptance of this world as a dark perspective on the "flux of matter"
that leaves physical life "blind and groping."[2] For Santayana seems a
happy person even in light of his vision of a contingent, naturalistic
world with no expectation or hope for a better, less cruel life beyond.
However, like Democritus, his major Greek influence in regard to the
scientific intelligibility of his naturalism, Santayana, in the face of a harsh
realism, still seems "the laughing philosopher." Scholars are drawn to

1

seek out aspects of Santayana's philosophy that lie beneath, under his harsh realism (who is the *real* Santayana?), for surely there is spiritual acumen, wisdom of the ages, remarkable social and sociological insight and the sense of a priestly resource for enhancement of contemporary visions of our world. Is there something yet hidden, some discovery that would provide the key to the attractiveness of Santayana's paradoxical spirituality? As an initiate to Santayana's world, I join other scholars who envision contemporary value in Santayana as he addresses the dilemma of religious orthodoxy, the moral issues associated with pluralism, the need for salvation in the world and the epistemological limits on the human penchant for absolute resolution.

There is a notion that Santayana's philosophy transitioned with his aging into one more spiritual, significantly distanced from the purported critical realism and humanism of his more poetically productive years at Harvard University.[3] Were the seeds of his theory on *essences* already sprouting in *The Life of Reason* (1905–1906) that were fully developed in the later works *Scepticism and Animal Faith* (1923) and *Realms of Being* (1937)? This question seeking evidence of change or evolution in Santayana's thought is an example of some inquiries regarding the question of "two Santayanas" I will briefly address in chapter 2. Consistency in Santayana, despite his own insistent claim for it, has been questioned by some scholars, that is, in regard to a perception of an "early and later" stage of philosophical thought such as in Plato, Wittgenstein, C. S. Peirce, Schleiermacher, and Husserl, and indeed, there seems to be at least one order of transition which I will discuss as we progress.[4]

My current interest in Santayana the philosopher comes from a conviction that his paradoxical religious nature, derived on behalf of his own personal salvation from a harsh world and its contingent nature may have lessons for contemporary philosophy, philosophy of religion and religious life. Many others, for example, notably, in my view, Lachs, Dilworth, Levinson, Kerr-Lawson, Saatkamp, Woodward and Seaton, have expressed similar notions. I venture that Woodward's assessment that "Santayana has suffered unmerited neglect" may be somewhat less so at this late writing, but there seems to be a growing consensus on this point among Santayana scholars. Understandably, such an assessment of Santayana's worth in this respect—after all, here is a man who fell short of theistic belief—may have been justifiably questioned, particularly by more orthodox Christians during his lifetime, as we will see, and today, by those sympathetic with the contemporary wave of both orthodox and evangelical Christianity in America. A useful perspective can be gained from Santayana's responses to the criticism he engendered in his Christian orthodox interlocutors by considering examples of some personal encounters occurring especially in his old age, when his philosophical project had reached a level of maturity to be limited only by his lifespan.

In my view, it is particularly important as well, at the outset, to claim for Santayana a particular abiding interest in the doctrines, discipline, symbols and *Kultur*[5] of the Roman Catholic Church since this will have substantial bearing on the formation of his philosophy of religion and his view of the world. Therefore, in this chapter, I will propose the consequences and importance of this influence (i.e., of his Spanish origins and disposition and his consequent nurturing in a Roman Catholic tradition). I will claim that an understanding of this formative influence is essential in arriving at an understanding of his philosophy and the dispositions of his view of the world and the problems of living in it.

There are impressions of Santayana by his admirers and critics that are vivid, telling and important in appreciating the philosopher, his character and his views. I have also taken the tack here that his response to various encounters in his later years, particularly with Roman Catholic interlocutors, is a helpful method to illuminate his very personal attitude toward organized religion. Although some of these encounters are anecdotal, they are still very revealing. My intention in this chapter is to briefly but adequately ground the reader in Santayana the man, in the paradoxical nature of his philosophical perspective and in the influence on his philosophy from Roman Catholicism. Other than periodic biographical comments throughout this book as they apply to my argument, and the brief biography in the introduction, I have considered only later intellectual and philosophical antecedents and influences on Santayana's project.

IMPRESSIONS OF THE PHILOSOPHER

There is a sympathetic view of George Santayana entertained by some scholars that seems to ride on a wave of protectiveness and advocacy for his soul and his deserved salvation from the categorical curse of materialistic-atheism. Then there are Santayana's gentle demeanor and courage in the face of earthly contingency, his later years of writing, solitariness and reflection in a anchoritic, but not altogether ascetic existence following the self-proclaimed *metanoia* (conversion, turn-around) of his early middle age. Somehow he engenders a quest in scholars to probe deeper for that holiness, even saintliness, that lies hidden beneath the cool frame of his materialism.[6] I'm not quite sure that my own project is not entirely innocent of such a quest. Santayana's complex personality evoked sharply contrasting responses from many of his contemporaries, most of whom were likely otherwise to admire his genius. William James, his mentor and contemporary at Harvard, suggested that Santayana had "put his heart on ice," and that he reflected the "rarified indifference of an aesthete."[7] Santayana's friend at Harvard and longtime interlocutor on art and aesthetics, Bernard Berenson, suggested that there was "something

philistine about him . . . without pity, without humanity"; and Edmund
Wilson commented on his "insensitivity."[8] Santayana's personality to
this day has been variously construed as spiritual, aesthetic, overly fas-
tidious, passionless, remote, stoic and characteristically homosexual. Santayana himself, by his own vocalized reflections, lent some credence to
such observations but strongly contradicted others; for example, he
claimed a general antipathy toward aestheticism as a lifestyle despite his
acclaimed treatise on aesthetic theory, *The Sense of Beauty*,[9] and affirmed
that "in philosophy I recognize no separable thing called aesthetics."[10]
On the other hand, the implication of Santayana's possible homosexual
bent could be supported by his own observation in 1929, in a conversation with his long-time assistant and friend, Daniel Cory, that "I think I
must have been that way in my Harvard days, although I was unconscious of it at the time."[11] Charles W. Eliot, president of Harvard during
Santayana's tenure, and his nemesis throughout ("the awful cloud of
Eliot"),[12] expressed the view that "this withdrawn contemplative man
who takes no part in everyday work of the institution, or of the world,
seems to me to be a person of very uncertain future value."[13] Santayana
would later inflict, in *The Genteel Tradition at Bay*,[14] an admonishing critique on the Protestant view of a world of material "progress" in America, a view of the world that the autocratic President Eliot's industrial-
technocratic and "anti-humanist" disposition propagated at Harvard.[15]

At the same time, the acute intellectual awareness, companionability
and even lovability of Santayana has been depicted by many who knew
him. Some of the most telling and poignant of these characterizations
occurred in Santayana's old age. Edmund Wilson, while claiming the
"insensitivity" of Santayana, on one hand, while visiting the aging philosopher at the end of World War II at the Convent of the Blue Nuns in
Rome, where Santayana spent the last ten years of his life (1941–1952),
dignified him on the other. Wilson described Santayana as wearing "a
brown bathrobe which made him look rather like a monk . . . his drab
Franciscan dressing gown [which] was not perhaps altogether an accident." Having been received by Santayana with great courtesy, he indicated that Santayana was highly conversational on many subjects and
possessed a remarkable dignity—as befitted a philosopher.[16] Anthony
Woodward reflects on further comments by Wilson whom he considered
"a man not easily fooled." Wilson perceives Santayana as a "perfectly
fulfilled organism," and suggests that "one is, if anything, even more
impressed by him after meeting him than one had been in reading those
books." Woodward also directs us to the dramatic elegy by the American
poet Wallace Stevens (1879–1955) where Santayana lies in "a kind of total
grandeur at the end."[17] One of the most revealing verbal characterizations of Santayana, reflecting his complex and ambiguous nature, is related in an interview of him by Max Eastman a year before his death, also at

the Convent of the Blue Nuns in Rome. This was published in the *American Mercury* and I quote below in small part Eastman's reflections.

> In that quick and easeful way he answered every question I asked. I never knew a man whose thoughts flowed out of him like liquid — nothing stiff or contained — no guards up against inconsistency or misunderstanding. In his books you sometimes feel that this is a fault . . . but in conversation it is a pure delight and makes him winning at first encounter, and if you keep on going to see him, lovable. [18]

Woodward, Howgate, McCormick and others quote laudatory commentary and anecdotes from philosophers and literary personages of some fame who reflect on Santayana, his works and his unique melding of literary style, critique and clarity of language in his philosophical project. Wallace Stevens, an underclassman friend of Santayana's at Harvard profoundly influenced by his Lucretian interpretation of Epicureanism, envisioned the philosopher shortly before his death as "in his old age, he dwells in the head of the world, in the company of devoted women, in the company of familiar saints, whose presence does so much to make any convent an appropriate refuge for a generous and human philosopher." [19] Stevens, further in his elegiac poem *To an Old Philosopher in Rome*, confers praise and honor upon Santayana in his cloistered last days in a modest room and depicts the attractive humanity of the man:

> So that we feel, in this illumined large,
> The veritable small, so that each of us
> Beholds himself in you, and hears his voice
> In yours, master and commiserable man,
> Intent on your particles of nether-do. [20]

Here we have Santayana, a philosopher, poet, and litterateur who was characterized in so many ways that the paradox of his character and personality seem to parallel the paradoxical nature of his *epiphenomenal* [21] materialism, his attitude toward religion and the world and particularly his elusive spirituality. In chapter 4 I will explore some of these paradoxical contrasts, in particular as they are reflected in Santayana's philosophy of religion. Frederick Conner's observation that the phenomenon of Santayana as a "deeply religious materialist" may be certainly seen as a paradox — but further even as an oxymoron — captures the difficulty of a seemingly incompatible philosophical complex. [22] However, in Santayana we find evident a kind of balance, an accepting stoicism, an existential courage and "willed" disposition toward happiness of the individual over against the contingency of nature. His proclivity toward piety and awe in his naturalism, as we shall see, is reflected both in his personal character and philosophy of religion. Further, his unique philosophical goal is, in fact, happiness itself, and while still having attained a state of *disillusion* from supernatural expectations, also a kind of "salvation." But it is salvation he seeks, not a "solution," in the face of what Woodward, capturing Santayana's naturalistic pessimism, has called "the momentous contingency of existence."[23] Even in such a stark materialism as Santayana's, in stoical detachment and resignation with the abandonment of illusion, he prescribes a way to happiness through awareness, and under the bright aura of consciousness, a drawing near to the eternal. Is such a prescription only for the elite, the truly Platonic initiate finding consolation in worship of the ideal "good?" Can "everyman" be happy on the brink of the abyss with no hope for a "better life" in the cosmic beyond offered by conventional religions? Santayana's realistic notion of the human response to contingency acknowledges "that spiritual minds should appeal to the supernatural is not to be wondered at. Few are courageous enough to accept nature as it is, and to build their spiritual house on the hard rock of truth."[24] Such questions will surely bear on the value of Santayana's project to contemporary philosophy of religion and religious practice, and I will explore this as we move forward.

Here I wish to make a point regarding the apparent contradictory nature of Santayana's philosophical declarations as they apply to understanding his philosophy. It becomes evident early to the reader of Santayana's works that there is, with some notable exceptions (e.g., industrial "progress" or Protestantism), a generally congenial perspective in considering all sides of an issue. Santayana addresses the polarities in regard to considerations in the quest for ontological balance and happiness with uncanny equanimity. As a result we encounter paradox, apparent antinomial declarations and irony despite a sense of the general coherence in his work. He observes, for example, that there are both benefits in religious orthodoxy as well as abhorrent aspects, and he addresses both; a spiritual life of *disillusion* constitutes the preferable life of reason, but a religion based upon supernatural beliefs may be most beneficial for a large portion of mankind; the individual must be free to develop unconstrained, but departing from orthodoxy or tradition may compromise one's true nature and even threaten the coherence of a life of reason. On and on the dualities are revealed, until reaching a near "Derridian equilibrium," a "true" reading of Santayana's philosophical trajectory can become exceedingly difficult. Morris Grossman has proposed both that "there are no arguments or doctrines in Santayana" and what he, Grossman, has coined as "the double moral grid" results in the apparent irony in Santayana's declarations and the consequent difficulty in interpreting his philosophical position.[25] Further, in this case referring to *Interpretations of Christ in the Gospels* but implying the same holding true variously in Santayana's works, Grossman suggests that "Santayana characteristically gives us not arguments for viewpoints, which would be lean and insufficient, but intellectually passionate cases for them; as he also makes intellectually passionate cases for their opposites."[26] Such seemingly healthy relativism could lend itself, as we might expect, to a positive example for contemporary views on religious dogma and religious pluralism in general.

Following the general characterization of Santayana above, I will now continue with the depiction of an atmosphere close to the end of his life, as in this way the reader may gain a preliminary impression of both Santayana's position on Catholicism and also an appreciation for the weight of its influence. In the balance of this chapter I will also demonstrate the importance of Santayana's Roman Catholic background in influencing his philosophy of religion and finally propose some specific theoretical associations traceable to this influence. In the course of this narrative we can also perceive the frustration of some of his Catholic interlocutors who wished not only the honor of involving him in a philosophical dialectic, but also fervently desired his return to Mother Church.

IN PURSUIT OF A LOST SOUL

A particularly vivid depiction of Santayana's frame of reference in regard to the Catholic Church is provided again by the poet and essayist Max Eastman following his visits to Santayana at the Convent of the Blue Nuns:

> Although a materialist, Santayana considers himself devout and worshipful. He loves the rites and ceremonies of the Catholic Church. He loves its dogmas, knows them to the last detail, and dwells on them with unreserved emotion. But he does not think they are true. He thinks they express in a symbolic way ideals that are needful to spirits in finding their way through the material world.[27]

Eastman's summary representation is, for now, an adequate summary statement for one to begin to understand in a preliminary way the perspective of Santayana, the Catholic materialistic naturalist. Not surprisingly, it was due to not a little frustration suffered by the more orthodox of Catholics that his seemingly untenable and contradictory position atop this paradoxical platform was assaulted. In chapter 4, I will develop an argument regarding the truly Christian but radical character of Santayana's own "orthodoxy." While it was to a significant extent Santayana's stated position on how he viewed religion as a materialistic naturalist that invited aggressive critique by his Roman Catholic challengers, more was at stake for them. Here was the increasingly respected philosopher of international reputation who widely claimed Catholicism as "my religion," despite his lack of "true belief" or practice, while still proclaiming the value of Catholicism before any other religious form. At the same time, he was making the more helpful proclamation that a disastrous fragmentation of Catholic tradition and culture—of what he considered an ideal synthesis—was attributable to the Protestant Reformation, and we were now left with the barren legacy of the Protestant world and its free-ranging derivative philosophies.[28] I will return to elaborate on this important viewpoint of Santayana in chapter 4. Then, again raising a "red flag," was his ultimate conclusion, as Faurot has suggested, that "the future of Christianity as a cultural source . . . has had its day."[29] To compound the dilemma, beyond these factors, was his charmingly open and courteous reception to all who came to overtly or subversively "convert" him in the seemingly accommodating and auspicious religious atmosphere of the Convent of the Blue Nuns. Certainly these seemingly contradictory or ambiguous claims of Santayana are lures for curiosity and they beg for resolution. Grossman has suggested that "Santayana without dramatic disguise is not Santayana,"[30] reflecting the image of irony and ambiguity that belies what I hope to demonstrate as the logical systematicity of Santayana's thought.

There are some indications that the more blatant religious conversion efforts did wear on Santayana's patience, and a few such incidents are presented in anecdotal fashion by the Dominican priest, Father Richard Butler, OP, of whom I will say more below in regard to his own personal interaction with Santayana.[31] One blatant but somewhat humorous incident described by Butler was on the occasion of the French neo-Thomist philosopher and Roman Catholic convert Jacques Maritain and his wife taking Santayana for a ride in the countryside as a respite from his room at the convent. At some point in the drive something was said by one of the Maritains in regard to Santayana returning to the Church. Santayana purportedly responded by suggesting that the subject of the conversation be changed or he would return to Rome on foot![32]

John McCormick's rendition of Santayana's interaction with Richard Butler, the Dominican priest I refer to above, who ultimately parlayed his doctoral dissertation on Santayana's philosophy into a book, *The Mind of Santayana*, is of particular interest. My own impressions of Father Butler's approach from his platform of Thomistic rigor and Dominican pastorality were quite similar. Santayana himself, in a letter to Father Butler just prior to Santayana's death, suggested that Butler learned nothing from reading his books and likely interpreted them through the eyes of St. Thomas. Beyond Butler's philosophical critique, on which I will comment further, he also claimed, referring to Santayana, "Religiously, I was his spiritual father anxious to help a lost child find his way home. Personally, I was his friend." McCormick suggests that "the notion of George Santayana as a lost child trying to find his way home would be comic if it were not so comically erroneous."[33] I substantially concur, as Santayana in his maturity gives no evidence of uncertainty or fear, which reflects a healthy and even happy attitude despite his inherent pessimism regarding human vulnerability in the face of impersonal nature and seems free of neurosis or depression near the end of his life. A conversation between Daniel Cory and Santayana a few days before he died is particularly telling in this regard. Santayana had already graciously declined the last rites of the Roman Catholic Church and commented on his state of mind. "What comes before or after does not matter . . . and this is especially so when one is dying. It is so easy for me now to see things under the form of eternity—and in the particular little fragment called my life."[34] The day before Santayana died, Cory inquired as to whether he was suffering. Santayana replied, "Yes, my friend. But my anguish is entirely physical. There are no moral difficulties whatsoever."[35]

I have no question that there were earlier religious conflicts experienced by Santayana, but I believe that Butler found some of them in the wrong places; for example, he suggests that Santayana's attending a Unitarian church as a boy was an incident of conflict. In fact, aside from distaste for the starkness of the formal service and the self-consciousness of the congregants, Santayana was never tempted in this direction. As Butler suggests, Santayana's own sense of belonging was immutably Catholic. The personal conflict arises, as I will show below, not from the dilemma created by Catholicism and Protestantism, but rather from Santayana's arriving at an intellectual affirmation that he would ultimately depart spiritually, fully and completely, from the irrational elements of literal belief in Roman Catholicism. Even when intellectually precluded on a rational basis, and theism itself having been long rejected as a personal consideration, the visceral-level attraction to this holy structure would still hold sway.

McCormick further portrays the repeated efforts to gather Santayana "into the fold."[36] Santayana fended off these attempts, for the most part, courteously and with good humor, and sustained his cheerfulness in firm conviction of his rationally derived *disillusionment*.[37] Not the least of the appeals for a return to the fold came from his "guardian angels," the Blue Sisters of the Little Company of Mary, who must have suffered the irony of having him reside in the convent, a crucifix over his bed and constantly under siege by a series of scholarly clerical guests. One anecdote surrounding this situation was that Santayana much preferred repose and deliverance in the state of limbo rather than in heaven. There in the underworld, he could carry on in person a dialectic with his beloved ancient Greeks: Democritus, Socrates, and the Aristotelian, Avicenna— some of the foundational sages of influence on his philosophical thought.[38]

If, in Father Butler's case as well as in that of another young priest-scholar, the Jesuit Thomas N. Munson,[39] the conversion wasn't forthcoming, then a "reductive" philosophical process seemed to follow. Complementing the process would be a saddened relegation of Santayana to the intractable state of a dottering and confused old professor who was too far gone to be saved. Such a characterization was provided to Father Munson by Terrence O'Conner, OSM, who had offered to interview Santayana and convey some responses from Santayana to some of Munson's inquiries. I quote in part:

> I saw Mr. (Dr., Signor, Professor—he responds to all stimuli, he told me) Santayana on several occasions . . . He stays in his room twenty-four hours a day, and confines his exercise to jumping at conclusions. His responses to just about all of your questions seemed to verge upon family history, the philosophers he studied under, his ideas of the U.S., Italy, Spain, wine . . . and diverse other topics. For the first hours or so of each bout I conscientiously took notes, but invariably found myself moodily studying the pattern of the rug he affects across his lap.[40]

O'Conner's annoyance is apparent in his humorous but sardonic depiction as he takes on the difficulty "that lies largely in the difference behind your philosophy and *ours*."[41] It was indeed "theirs" since Pope Leo XIII, in *Aeterni Patris* (1899), set the modern stage for sustaining Catholic doctrine through the reestablishment of Thomas Aquinas as the sole magisterial beacon of philosophy in the Roman Church. At the time of both Father Butler's and Father Munson's post–World War II and pre–Vatican II interaction with Santayana the influence of these guidelines from the Magisterium was still unquestionable. Father Butler's philosophical platform was fixed and contra-Cartesian and opposed to most of those ensuing modernists who succeeded Descartes in questioning the scope of human epistemological possibilities. In Father Butler's view, "The *cogito* of Descartes ripped philosophy away from its moorings in reality and set it adrift in the hazardous flux of individual conscious experience."[42] He would have likely also affirmed that Kant only further perpetuated the "error" separating the mind from matter and object. In this way Father Butler and other critics and petitioners of a Thomistic bent entered the arena with the aging Santayana. Their expectations for gaining Catholic fellowship with the evasive philosopher went often to philosophical antagonism, personal criticism and a patronizing sympathy. There were also further grounds for frustration reflected in Butler's surprising realization that Santayana was one of those "individualistic" philosophers, those practitioners of "subjective" philosophy, who generated "as many philosophies as philosophers."[43] For the Thomist, philosophy is of an ever-perfecting piece. The unbroken continuum from the Greeks—the inheritable philosophic fruit of the ages—in direct touch with material evidence attained through an impersonal speculative method culminating in the medieval scholastics was the canonical trajectory of thought. Descartes, Kant, Hume, Hobbes, Nietzsche, the American Transcendentalists and now Santayana had rended the connection with tradition. But Santayana, who harkened back to the Greeks for inspiration, especially from Heraclitus, Democritus, Plato and Aristotle, could disclaim any notion of *his* disconnection with foundational Western philosophy. At the same time, he would likely acknowledge that Aquinas's position on the finitude of human intellect and the consequent limits of knowledge were akin to his own thought as well. Santayana, in the preface to *Scepticism and Animal Faith*, famously claimed his philosophical system to be "not mine, nor new" and further that "for good or ill, I am an ignorant man, almost a poet, and I can only spread a feast of what everybody knows."[44] His debt to the Greek naturalists, the "first" philosophers, was always persistently but modestly proclaimed as was his debt to Spinoza and the Roman poet Lucretius (these important antecedent relationships will be expanded upon in chapter 2). To Father Butler's likely further chagrin, Santayana *also* rejected the "scramble" of modern philosophy in its mistaken notion of the relationship of man's spirit to the universe. Therefore, although Father Butler and others would claim that Santayana's personal and introspective philosophy helped sever the succession from a "healthy intellectual objectivity," it is important to fully appreciate Santayana's view that despite this individuality, there was still an overwhelming incorporation and influence of antecedent teachings and traditional philosophical and theological concepts throughout his project.

> I had no thought of constructing any rival system; yet my sincere reaction to one system after another gradually revealed to me the unformulated principles that guided my judgement; so that my system was not so much formed by me as discovered within me. I should hear the tramp of the next system on its heels. This philosophy that I have unearthed within me is ancient philosophy, very ancient philosophy.[45]

I don't wish to belabor Father Butler's dilemma here but only to provide some sense of the tension evident between Santayana's Roman Catholic "disposition" and the Magisterium-dominated philosophical attitude of the formal church and these few of its priest-scholars. Santayana's vision incorporated a Catholic cultural disposition, a theological fluency and a pluralistic tolerance of all religious inclinations and individual views to the extent they did not detract from human wellbeing. Such a congenial complex, ungrounded in theism or for that matter in any other metaphysical *Grund* that Santayana would admit to his thought, would pose a conundrum to anyone of a Roman Catholic absolutist bent. James W. Lane, for example, complained in his essay "The Dichotomy of George Santayana" that "thus no matter how broad Mr. Santayana's system manages to be, no matter how pointedly pointless, something is wanting. Faith has been left out!" We cannot be too hard on Lane, because he has a point there. On the other hand some demonstration of coherence in Santayana's project must be forthcoming in this treatise to confront Lane's lament in the same essay that "Santayana is a combination of the irreconcilable!"[46]

RELIGIOUS FOUNDATIONS OF THE PARADOX

Despite Santayana's path beginning in adolescence toward *disillusion* in regard to the supernatural and absolutist claims of religion, the influence of Santayana's Roman Catholic background would continue to manifest itself throughout his philosophical and critical writings. Although he essentially ceased writing poetry, with some few exceptions, at the end of the nineteenth century, the voluminous collection of verse written throughout his youth and during his twenty-three-year teaching tenure at Harvard University (1889–1912) can be a startlingly synoptic reflection of his philosophical path as well as of the transitional benchmarks of his emotional and intellectual life. Santayana once objected to G. W. Howgate that possibly his poetry received too much attention in Howgate's book *George Santayana*, but then ironically suggested that "the function of my verse is simply to betray the undercurrents of my mind in the formative period."[47] Consider, for example, Sonnet 29 written in 1895 when he was thirty-two years old:

> To me the faiths of old are daily bread;
> I bless their hope, I bless their will to save,
> And my deep heart still meanith what they said,
> It makes me happy that the soul is brave,
> And, being so much kinsman to the dead,
> I walk contented to the grave.[48]

Here is a stoic, but still admiring, perspective on "faiths of old" with the evident resolution reached that abides with blessing of their promise but declines all but fellowship with humanity, facing death with no illusion. In Sonnet 11, Santayana reflects a position on the edge of things, apart: "And some are born to stand perplexed aside, From so much sorrow — of whom I am one.[49] But one also recognizes in Santayana's stoicism a rejection of the suffering and worldly concerns of those (priest, prophet or saint) who can sustain an illusion of hope and play their part in life under the umbrella of faith. Santayana's philosophical and living objective never varied from finding happiness while participating in the material world.

Santayana himself, in retrospect, affirmed his "apartness," which although acknowledged to have been apparent since his youth, was particularly evident as a component of change that came over him in mid-life — his self-characterized *metanoia*.[50] This "apartness" should be thought of as more a selective or chosen aspect of Santayana's manner of living as opposed to his sense of alienation or "aloneness" which was a given element in his life from an early age. Santayana perceived himself as *always* apart, in his childhood, adolescence and days as a student at Harvard, and certainly throughout his teaching career at Harvard. His poetic nature, individuality, Spanish and Roman Catholic background and general distaste for, and alienation from, the "progressive" drive of Protestant industrial America reflected at Harvard during the period, contributed substantially to his attitude. I have suggested that his friends and critics often observed this as a "flaw" in his nature, as a detraction from his essential humanity, and a contradiction to his claimed sensitivity and credence accorded to the intuitive wisdom of the common man.[51] Despite Santayana's social and amicable disposition when required of him, and a definite skill in making and sustaining friendships, this "apartness" would persist, and would have significant bearing on his prolific reflective writing both in his propensity for solitude and personal freedom and, as we will see, his phenomenological outlook.

Mossie Kirkwood astutely observes that Santayana's Platonic poetry, composed when a young professor at Harvard, gives all indications of reflecting his suffering in the clear rift that had been opening for some time between "faith's divine moonlight" within the Latin orthodox frame of the Catholic Church, and a consolidation of his hard-earned naturalistic philosophy. That Santayana is torn between his disposition toward the religious *Kultur* of his youth and his maturing thought seems clear. Kirkwood quotes him as claiming, "I breathed more easily in the atmosphere of religion than that of business, precisely because religion, like poetry, was more ideal, more freely imaginary, and in a material sense, falser."[52] In the opening line from Sonnet 5 written in 1884, one senses an almost schizoid dilemma, an antinomial pattern, that at first impression seems unique in philosophical thought: "Of my two lives which should I call a dream?"[53] Out of this inherent polarity in Santayana will arise a broad and catholic acceptance of the world and a striving for individual happiness, only to be held in check by the limits of its positive effect on the welfare of civilization. Harmony is paramount then between the good of the individual and that of society and is achieved as Henry Samuel Levinson suggests, *e pluribus unum*.[54] Nevertheless, Santayana sustains a pessimism that entertains few expectations that humanity can influence the unbridled contingency of the world. This is the outcome for Santayana of what is, in fact, a momentous disappointment in his life as the idealistic illusion in Catholic Christianity becomes an irretrievably idealistic *disillusion*. As Kirkwood indicates, the pangs experienced by Santayana at decisively abandoning orthodoxy are clearly evident in his poetry. Contiguous lines in the transition from sonnets I and II (1882), for example, seem to reflect the departure from orthodoxy to naturalism:

> So came I down from Golgotha to thee,
> Eternal Mother; let the sun and sea
> Heal me, and keep me in thy dwelling-place.
> Slow and reluctant was the long descent,
> With many farewell pious looks behind,
> And dumb misgivings where the path might wind,
> And questioning of nature, as I went.[55]

There were, however, short of any inherent psychological disposition in Santayana, some important extenuating circumstances. These are especially pertinent, given his lifelong love and attachment to the Roman Catholic tradition, even in what I will call a "religious" sense, while all the while denying the supernatural Absolute and divinity of Christ or, for that matter, as discussed above, the supernatural claims for the Divine unseen power in any religious faith. J. H. Faurot emphasizes a somewhat obvious but likely important influence relating to Santayana's exposure to the weak, mixed, somewhat indifferent and even hostile attitudes of his parents toward Catholicism and the clergy. Referring to his devout sister Susan's later strong influence when he was a young boy in America, Santayana observes that the church claims if given a child until he is six, the child will be theirs forever, "but they didn't get Santayana until he was eight—with a mental age of perhaps fourteen."[56] Indeed, even then, it was the emotional, doctrinal and aesthetic sides of Catholicism that occupied him. Moreover, a certain despair or helplessness, a *Weltschmerz*, possessed Santayana from an early age in that he was not certain that life was worth living; even stating that the material world was like "ashes in my mouth."[57]

In *A General Confession*, Santayana relates that he had never been a practicing Catholic in an environment where both mother and father generally agreed that "God was too great to take special thought for man: sacrifices, prayers, churches, and tales of immortality were invented by rascally priests in order to dominate the foolish."[58] Although he learned his catechism and prayers and loved the Christian epic, he was not of the opinion, as his Deist parents were, that although religion was a manifestation of the imagination that this was necessarily bad! Despite Santayana's claim that he was never a practicing Catholic, as a young man in Boston under the influence of Susan, he gave all evidence of being dedicated to a devout and enthusiastic but faithless practice.[59] Nevertheless, a natural intellectual commitment to *disillusion* from an early age was still not as yet the emotional wrenching experience of a more decisive abandonment of all possibilities for belief in and adherence to Catholic doctrine, vestigial as it may have seemed by then. To one degree or another, Santayana suffered the pangs of apostasy, although likely more as mourning than through feelings of guilt. He had already long acknowledged intellectually the illusory aspect of religion. A popular romantic poet of the generation earlier, Alfred de Musset (1810–1857), had considerable influence on Santayana, who seemed to empathetically identify with the poet's "regret and tenderness for a faith he had entirely lost."[60] Woodward insightfully suggests that Santayana is left as a "priest" without a church.[61]

George W. Howgate captures the critical importance and long-lasting effect of Santayana's existential dichotomy when he suggests that "pessimism born of conflict between one's preferences and one's convictions is deep-seated; neither the intellect or the heart will yield."[62] This experience of "disinheritance" from a grounding in an objective association with symbols of a supernatural realm, but still leaving a remnant need to draw near to its mother-lode, the church, has been manifested in others caught in the maelstrom of religious dilemma. Even Kant, Santayana suggests, had dared to reason and arrive at the consequences of the synthetic *a priori* and the categorical imperative, but the residue of his Protestant Christian belief was not so easily scuttled in old age. Santayana speculates that "doubtless in his private capacity Kant hoped, if he did not believe, that God, free-will, and another life subsisted in fact, as every believer had hitherto supposed."[63]

THE POST-DARWINIAN GLOOM

The pervasive environment of progressive materialistic thought of the late nineteenth and early twentieth centuries in America set the stage for romanticism and doubt as the challenge to traditional Christian views. This created a vacuum of pessimism and despair as an anti-modernistic response to the deterioration of religion and associated tradition. Darwin had left an apparent yawning gap between the biblical teachings of the creation and the welling of interest and enthusiasm for science and its fulfillment of the Enlightenment promise. Howgate suggests that like many sensitive souls, "Santayana was experiencing that malady of his age, that nostalgic soul-sickness caused by the retreat of Christianity and the void it left behind."[64] William Graham Sumner, an Episcopal priest at Yale College during Santayana's tenure at Harvard, suggested that having once put his religious beliefs in a drawer, he found them missing when he opened it later.[65] The helpless determinism that can be sensed in Santayana's project under the overwhelming "flux" of contingency in the world was deeply felt by Sumner and others as the yoke of Puritanism and the metaphysic of the idealists was falling away along with hope for another world. Sumner, reminiscent of Santayana's own perspective of a contingent world, depicts humanity caught in the sway of nature.

> The great stream of time and earthly things will sweep on just the same in spite of us. It bears with it now all the errors and follies of the past, the wreckage of all philosophies, the fragments of all civilizations, the wisdom of all abandoned ethical systems, the debris of all institutions, and the penalties of all mistakes. It is only in imagination that we stand by and look at and criticize it and plan to change it. Everyone of us is a child of his age . . . He is in the stream and swept along with it.[66]

Such was the underlying pessimism and sense of the human helplessness in the face of the "sweep" of nature and culture that characterized the *enfants du siècle* of which Santayana was certainly one.[67] Santayana was informed by the Enlightenment and by the post-Darwinian world (*The Origin of Species* was first published in 1859) just as Sumner, James, Royce and earlier, Emerson and other New England theologians and philosophers were. All were likely to have been influenced by the mood of reflective solitude, natural piety and individualism practiced by Thoreau in a realization of the "clear and ancient harmony," to be attained outside the strictures of any institution.[68] For a sensitive mind at this time was to be immersed in a culture of intellectual and spiritual accommodation arising from a new awareness of epistemological limits and a need for ontological resolutions. Living one's life in a certain way was to become more important than seeking knowledge of any underlying metaphysic of life and the cosmos. Science would gradually reveal truth in increments, but the foundational wonder of life and the universe would be ever inaccessible to humans. The prevailing Protestant ethic of the Victorians, of which Santayana's Harvard in the late nineteenth century was an institutional upholder, provided the environment for putting one's back to the wheel of commerce or a profession and unreflectively falling in behind the assured progress of the new industrial science. The confidence of the Enlightenment drove progress. Santayana, as I suggested earlier, deplored the world of progress and business that influenced the atmosphere at Harvard under President Eliot. Very simply, he felt, it was a distraction from thought and personal freedom. However, for a reflective and poetic soul who discovers his kinship with other animal life and has reached a new awareness that he is subject to being swept up in the "stream" of natural forces, there is a need to both live in the world of affairs and witness the truth.

There is most of all a need for an alternate approach to salvation of the spirit and a way to live out one's life without the assurance of a better place, of a supernatural realm. There was in this milieu of religious crosscurrents a new humanism born of romantic idealism hearkening back to Greek and Renaissance models. Santayana, despite immersion in the humanistic incubator at Harvard, subjected humanism early on to severe criticism, associating it with Transcendentalism and finding it "contrary to Christian humility and Catholic discipline."[69] Although humanism "begins in the moral sphere," he suggests in *Realms of Being*, "we may easily slip into equivocations that will land us in moral chaos."[70] In a 1928 letter to Daniel Cory, Santayana depicted the environment at Harvard in 1885, near the end of his undergraduate studies as follows: "You must remember that we were not very much later than Ruskin, Pater, Swinburne and Matthew Arnold: our atmosphere was that of poets and persons touched with religious enthusiasm or religious sadness."[71] In reference to these comments, John McCormick writes that Walter Pater's novel *Marius the Epicurean* had substantial influence on Santayana's poetry and philosophical writing. Its analogous depiction of a post–Darwinian-like pessimism, aestheticism and asceticism set in ancient Rome and appealing to aesthetics and ideals of the old religion facing the incursion of Christianity, appealed to the poetic nature of those caught up, in spite of themselves, in the transition to modernity.[72]

A COMMITMENT TO DISILLUSION

Santayana, as a Spanish Catholic in his innermost being, although granted a "non-believing" one, was still essentially alone and alienated from the American Protestant tradition even until he departed America and Harvard in 1912. In order to place the proper emphasis upon what may be construed as Santayana's struggle in departing emotionally from the ideal world of Roman Catholic belief, it is helpful to briefly make mention of similar struggles by other artists and philosophers. Fellow sufferers, mostly of the Victorian period, that Howgate mentions are writers and poets Ernst Renan (1823–1892), Matthew Arnold (1822–1888), the French poet Alfred de Musset (1810–1857) and the Spanish writer, poet and philosopher Miguel de Unamuno (1864–1936).[73] Of particular interest is Unamuno both as a contemporary and Spanish compatriot of Santayana whom Santayana never met but whose poetry and critical work he likely read.[74] Unamuno's troubles with the Catholic Church were more volatile than Santayana's but his works, as well as Santayana's, were banned under the Franco regime in post-revolutionary Spain.[75] Both men were considered heretics and atheists, and Santayana was further considered an American who had abandoned Spain.[76] The cases of Unamuno and Santayana are different in many aspects. Unamuno lived in Spain all his life and was accorded laudatory recognition as an artist, but suffered severe political suppression and persecution from both the church and the state. He also, in the face of his lifelong unrepentent heretical teachings, continued his devotions in the Catholic Church, despite strong Protestant leanings and anti-dogmatic sentiments for most of his life. Finally he was buried a Catholic without overtly claiming whether he was either Catholic or Protestant. Unamuno could well have been correctly characterized by Santayana as one who had not made a true transition from illusion and faith and who still clung to the solace of the supernatural. Further, Unamuno attended retreats, advocated celibacy as the ideal for the true Christian, was obsessed with the idea of immortality and admired the Christian mystics.[77] Santayana, on the other hand, in regard to mystics, sardonically suggested that they were not practicing religion but suffering from a "religious disease" and "confusion of the faculties."[78] Paradoxically, a significant caveat was implied when in *The General Confessions* he proclaimed, "I have always disliked mystics who were not definite in their logic and orthodox in their religion."[79] One can gather here some mitigation in Santayana's views toward mystics if they were Catholic and scholastic in their philosophy.

What then, given these important differences, can we learn from any comparison between the two men? What I will demonstrate is simply that there is a basis, both from the cultural environment of his upbringing and the temper of the period from Santayana's birth in 1862 through the turn of the century, for the profound influence of Catholicism on his later thought. Moreover, the *Zeitgeist* was conducive to religious and philosophical struggles of one degree or another in Santayana's contemporaries.[80] Santayana and Unamuno were both of Spanish character and origin. Both were poets and philosophers in an age of religious doubt, of Spanish and Catholic origin, philosophically oriented individualists and in conflict with the teachings of the Church. Particularly, for the purposes of my argument, they were both in love with Catholicism, and despite their heresies and apostasies (actual in Santayana's case and accused in Unamuno's), both clung to Catholicism's aura of ideality in their own individual fashion throughout their long lives. Both reflected the consequent conflict in their poetry and writings. Most important is the demonstration that, as Howgate suggests, the heart clings to the faith the mind is unwilling to accept. He proposes as well that the enhancing character of the Spanish cultural environment for such a dichotomous attraction is of importance and quotes the Spanish writer Salvador da Madariaga: "The eternal conflict between faith and reason, between spirit and intellect, between life and thought, between heaven and civilization is the conflict of Spain herself."[81] Herman Saatkamp, Jr., reminds us of the Spanish character of Santayana's life as he quotes Santayana's reflections of his life as a youth in Boston.

> Still, our family life in Boston was wholly Spanish: I never spoke any other language at home: and you can't imagine what a completely false picture comes to mind that my mother was an American. Then, too, she and my sisters would have been Protestants, and my whole imagination and moral background would have been different.[82]

One can appreciate that Santayana, at a time when the Roman Catholic population in the Boston area was substantial, although college-educated Catholics were relatively few, had good cause to draw up rather rigid cultural demarcations and limitations as a function of religion. Certainly there were few Catholics as classmates or friends attending Boston Latin School, and a similar situation existed at Harvard. Fully justified or not, Santayana would perceive the Western world to be seen through these two separate perspectives of Protestantism and Roman Catholicism throughout his life, and his philosophy of religion would be consequently influenced. His general contempt for all modern philosophical derivatives, with few exceptions, of the Reformation and Protestantism, particularly German Protestantism, is clear evidence of this tension. Further, despite his philosophical vector of materialism and rejection of a supernatural realm, in his thought he would never stray far from the issue of religion "which is the head and front of everything."[83]

CATHOLICISM AND SANTAYANA'S PHILOSOPHICAL DISPOSITION

The influences of Catholicism on Santayana's philosophy of religion is more evident in some aspects than in others and in more than one aspect, susceptible to counter-argument. However, to bypass consideration of these Catholic influences, or to give them short shrift on the basis of Santayana's "atheism," is to neglect the *sine qua non* of his philosophical trajectory.[84] Therefore, an early consideration of these influences on Santayana's thought is essential and enormously revealing when considering later the grounding tenets of his philosophy of religion. I have proposed below what I believe are the key influences from Roman Catholicism on Santayana's thought and will continue to refer to them and expand on my comments in later chapters. The Platonic influence on his Catholicism is implicit and I will discuss this influence in chapter 2. Howgate, particularly, has put more emphasis on the aspect of Catholic influence than other authors, and I will suggest at this point, before proceeding with my own associations of Catholicism and Santayana's philosophical disposition, that many of Howgate's associations seem too confidently asserted. In addition, his book was more literary and biographical than philosophical; hence, for my purposes, I will refer to him more frequently for biographical or even intellectual historical material.[85] One of the more important possible conflicts between Howgate's perspective and Santayana's later works, in my view, lies in some of Santayana's mitigating remarks in *Persons and Places* regarding his lack of emotional involvement with the religion of his youth.[86] One thing is clear: the Catholic influence was there and substantial.[87]

THE VALUE OF ORTHODOXY AND TRADITION

The doctrinal and dogmatic framework of Catholicism had substantial influence on Santayana's philosophical outlook. Despite his own authentic apostasy, his paradoxical observations, antipathies and cautionary note regarding the pitfalls of a departure from religious orthodoxy, his negative view of mysticism practiced outside of an orthodox framework and heresies of any kind is particularly telling. The consistency and uncompromising aspect of Catholic doctrine has a logic and beauty that reflects a soundness and excellent expression of the ideal of human expectations. This consistency must be conserved, only as poetic expression of the ideal, not as literal truth, and as Woodward suggests, "as a help to steering a steady course amid the currents of existence under the tutelage of hallowed ideals that are the fruits of ancient spiritual insight."[88] Santayana's expressions of distaste for the whimsy and self-serving logic of Protestantism and its departure from the traditional Christian faith are almost "harping" in their persistence.[89] He viewed orthodoxy as valuable and worthwhile in providing a systematic and uncompromising structure for thought, and a discipline on mind, but not one that either rested in an affirmation of its own absolute truth or denied equal human rightness to other orthodoxies. In philosophy he recognized the orthodoxy of Indian philosophy and Greek philosophy before and after Socrates as "being right in their own sphere."[90] I find a striking example of Santayana's respect for orthodoxy as well as an expression of his profound affection for the orthodoxy of the Roman Catholic Church in *Winds of Doctrine* (1913). Santayana reflects upon the influence of modernism on the church:

> And under the name of modernism they [social instability, reconstructions of history, etc.] have made their appearance even in that institution which is constitutionally the most stable, of most explicit mind, least inclined to revise its collective memory or established usages—I mean the Catholic church. Even after this church was constituted by the fusion of many influences and by gradual exclusion of these heresies . . . which seemed to misrepresent its implications of spirit, there still remained an inevitable propensity among Catholics to share the moods of their respective ages and countries, and to reconcile them if possible with their professed faith.[91]

I will return to discuss again at length the issue of orthodoxy and modernism in chapters 4 and 5.

THE IMPORTANCE OF THE "IDEAL"

There is a direct connection between Santayana's rejection of religious dogma and doctrine as based upon history and cosmology and his ultimate attribution of value to these precepts. If indeed these were the products of human imagination, they were not willy-nilly in their intent, although they could not safely be based upon anything approaching fact. Santayana begs our indulgence for any "error and follies" and suggests that our sympathy must lie with the intent behind the doctrine—that is, "to interpret and to use the materials of experience [reflected in the doctrine] for moral ends, and to measure the value of reality by its relation to the ideal."[92] The hypostatization of these ideals (e.g., the Forms of Plato) is seen by Santayana as the great error both in philosophy and religion. However, it is the value-judgment of Santayana that religious doctrine and dogma, when grasped as moral examples of the *ideal*, are both pleasing as poetry and reminders of moral tenets for the individual and society. As we will discuss in chapter 4, even the most severe of religious doctrines (e.g., the doctrine of hell) have profound meaning and value in their uncorrupted but seemingly harsh form and only suffer from compromise (e.g., in liberal Protestantism). What Santayana salvages from orthodox religion, then, is the *ideal* reflected in its teachings, and it is this concept of the *ideal* that enables him to harvest a spiritual philosophy from a "harsh realism." His inclination is never to compromise regarding traditional expressions of moral absolutes as these are universals or ideals. Howgate proposes, I believe correctly, that Santayana's inclination was toward the "sterner side" of Christianity in his work, continually claiming the inviolate nature of the moral ideal. The idealistic character of Catholicism, therefore, inoculated his naturalism with the ideal, giving it also the uncompromising "dogmatic" character that I mention earlier, but with the suffering human free of intimidation and fear of supernatural consequences.

AN UNCOMPROMISING AND "DOGMATIC" ATTITUDE

This has a negative connotation, raising images of the rigid dogma and doctrinally governed theology and philosophy of Roman Catholicism. It also connotes a prescribed discipline and *praxis* that fosters a culture of same-thinkers and intolerance. Santayana was intimately familiar with this atmosphere as part of the *Kultur* surrounding Spanish Catholicism but was never in its grasp. His distaste for dogmatism was more in its manifestation than the fact of its formulation. A religion or philosophy obsessed with a single criteria for truth, its own formulated dogma, and imposing its will in a way that distracted from a person's individual response to the world was anathema. Dogmatic emphasis for Santayana, as Kirkwood suggests, can "turn bigotry into a principle."[93] There is however the "residue" of the systematic method of Aristotle adapted by Thomas Aquinas into the scholastic foundation of Catholic doctrine that engenders an expectation of method, always logical, always consistent — ultimately uncompromising. This uncompromising and dogmatic viewpoint was transferred to Santayana's own naturalism,[94] not in the least so as to impose it on others, but in demanding rigor in general from those engaged in the philosophical pursuit of understanding the world. In his essay "A Brief History of My Opinions," Santayana reflects on the influence of Professor Palmer, one of his undergraduate professors at Harvard, who opened his mind to being more sympathetic toward the views of other philosophers. However, Santayana suggests that "even this form of romanticism, amiable as it is, could not put to sleep my scholastic dogmatism."[95] And for Santayana philosophy, not unlike dedicated Christian practice, is a vocation — a consecrated way of life.[96] It is then in

philosophical rigor, honesty and discipline that Santayana is not willing
to compromise. It is in this rigor, whatever consistent philosophical discipline that one were to follow, that Santayana is uncompromising and
dogmatic.

For Santayana, there were no "cop-outs." As we will further discuss in
chapter 4, he associates religious dogma with the *ideal* in man's contemplation of the life and cosmos. One strives toward the *ideal* through an
appreciation for the *essences*, that grammar of the *ideal* that presents itself
to us. All of Santayana's philosophy rests upon the value of the *ideal*.
Herein lies contempt for "cheating" in thought, taking the easy way in
accommodation, diverging from what Santayana saw as the model of an
ideal or compromising in seeking of it through rigorous *praxis*. He proclaims this disposition in summary in the final chapter of *Scepticism and
Animal Faith*, revealing the scrupulous rigor and conscience of a scholastic:

> My criticism is not essentially a learned pursuit, though habit may
> sometimes make my language scholastic; it is not a choice between
> artificial theories; it is the discipline of my daily thoughts and the ac-
> count I actually give to myself from moment to moment of my own
> being and of the world around me. I should be ashamed to counte-
> nance opinions which when I'm not arguing, I did not believe. It would
> seem to me dishonest and cowardly to militate under other colours
> than those under which I live.[97]

THE TROUBLE WITH PROTESTANTISM

Santayana's contra-Protestantism disposition can be considered a corollary to the previous dispositions of orthodoxy, tradition and an uncompromising and dogmatic attitude. These are obviously closely inter-
twined. However, it deserves separate attention at this juncture, not only
in relation to Santayana's uncompromising attitude but especially to emphasize the dominance of this individual aspect as it relates to his philosophy of religion. First off we can recognize that Santayana, as a cultural
Catholic and admirer of the Catholic orthodox structure as an ideal,
would likely be less disposed to Protestantism of any stripe. It is rather
the extremism of his disposition that draws our attention. Close to the
root of the problem is the fact that Santayana considers the Protestant
Reformation a fragmenting and destructive event of ongoing impact on
both the morality of Western civilization and the spiritual life of both the
Christian community and individual. The continuum from the Platonic
construct through the naturalization of Plato's thought by Aristotle, the
neoplatonic reforms and the adaptation of Greek thought to Christianity
by Augustine and Aquinas was ruptured. Protestant Christianity turned
from tradition more to Hebraic roots and away from the spiritual truth of

the neoplatonic adaptation. The "dramatic wholeness" that Santayana sought was lost in this rupture as was the orderliness of that "whole body of influences that can render civilized life noble and good; influences which they [the Greeks] beautifully pictured in the forms and worship of the gods."[98] In Protestantism were lacking the pagan roots that Santayana became increasingly sensitive to after attending the lectures of Professor Paulsen at Berlin.[99] In a letter to Daniel Cory in 1936, he states, "The source of what you call the Catholic view is really Aristotle and quite pagan, except that the early fathers who were Platonists may have worked out Catholic doctrine in those terms."[100] Fathers Butler and Munson, whom I discussed earlier, perceived Santayana and other "modern" philosophers as extending the rift in Christian and philosophical tradition beginning with Descartes, and of course saw the Protestant Reformation to be as disruptive as he did. In the ironical tension we have come to appreciate in him, Santayana, in general agreement with this viewpoint, only excluded his own project and possibly Spinoza's from culpability. Despite the distance one might project between Santayana and the Thomistic priest-scholars, there would likely be at least initial consensus that as the philosopher proposes, "The three R's of modern history, the Renaissance, the Reformation, and the Revolution [French], have left the public mind without any vestige of discipline."[101] We can safely gather, then, that Santayana recognizes one holy Catholic Church, and it is Roman, and anything else or less, such as the English Church, which engenders "a sham front of moral solemnity,"[102] is an abominable compromise.

THE VALUE OF SELF-DISCIPLINE

In the conclusion of *The Idea of Christ in the Gospels*, Santayana proposes, "The idea of Christ thus represents the intrinsic ideal of the spirit; that is to say, the acme of disinterested intelligence and disinterested love."[103] One can associate such an idea of an objective and impartial ideal with Santayana's own philosophical and religious viewpoint, as well as gather from this Santayana's assignment of value to ideals. In my view, the extension of the idea of Christ as an ideal is in the implicit inference of Santayana that one can choose to partake of "an imitation of Christ" and thereby attain a transcendence, and even a form of "union," with the ideal through self-discipline, becoming thereby a disciple in a more traditional framework than Santayana would be expected to propose. In this way the "harmony" of the life of reason can be attained in which the distractions of the passions are sacrificed. Levinson refers to Tillich's observation that Santayana's idea of Christ is "Catholic for its emphasis on the disciplines allowing people to imitate, even incarnate, divinity."[104] When one considers the concept of self-discipline in the framework of the Catholic (or Orthodox) Church, the practice of monastic structure and discipline, the self-discipline of prayer, the Holy Office and the self-discipline of spiritual growth from a novice to perfection may come to mind. Santayana's origins and nurture in the *Kultur* of Spanish Catholicism and the deep identity of the Spanish people with the Catholic Church, which he shared, imprinted upon him irreversibly a sensitivity to the deep spirituality and piety of the environment. For example, the parallels in the self-discipline and methodology of St. Ignatius's mental prayer and meditation from his *Spiritual Exercises* to attain freedom in Christ and Santayana's self-discipline in attaining the transcendence necessary for the freedom of spiritual life can be easily discerned.

Spiritual discipline for Santayana is the transcendence from world, passions and even values in order to achieve freedom as opposed to distraction.[105] The exercise of spiritual discipline may be no better exemplified by Santayana than the following from *Platonism and the Spiritual Life*:

> Spirituality has material conditions; not only the general conditions of life and intuition . . . but subtler and more special conditions such as concentration of thought, indifference to fortune and reputation, warmth of temperament disciplined into chastity and renunciation. These and other such conditions the master of novices does well to consider.[106]

THE VALUE OF PIETY AND PRAYER

In his naturalism, Santayana never abandoned the concept of piety and prayer so much associated with traditional religion. We will discuss at length in chapter 4 the inclusion of the elements of piety, spirituality and charity in *Reason in Religion* and the perpetuation of the importance and value of these elements in Santayana's naturalistic religion in his later works. Santayana has confessed his own piety as a Catholic youth in Boston, but this as a fully engaged aesthetic or poetic fascination with the rituals and symbols of the Catholic Church rather than with a living faith.[107] Only in Catholic or Orthodox tradition does one associate the importance and practice of piety, that is, veneration, reverence or profound respect toward holy objects, images, sacred events, saints or God, with the very essence of the tradition. Santayana, with Spinoza's reverence for the *Deus sive Natura* as a powerful example, extended the practice of piety beyond nature to morality and the "good." Without piety, Santayana proposes, spirituality deteriorates into madness in its isolation.[108] In the course of the life of reason, the traditions and icons of the times (e.g., in the Roman Catholic Church), the encapsulation of the "reflected light from other ages,"[109] must be held in pious reverence.

In *The Idea of Christ in the Gospels* Santayana addresses the direction of Christ's prayer (The Lord's Prayer) as "open[ing] . . . the inner dialogue of the spirit with itself." [110] From this we may gather that Santayana's privileging of the need for reflection in his philosophy of *disillusionment* also may find prayer consistent with the reflective life as it is in the church. In Santayana's naturalistic, non-theistic spirituality, the role of prayer never is sacrificed in the life of reason, but rather, "strange as it may seem to the rationalist who thinks prayer ridiculous, the only per- fectly rational form of life for a spirit that has attained self-knowledge is the life of prayer." [111] As the psalmists cried out their lamentations to God in the Scriptures, Santayana perceives prayer as "essentially *oratio*, the eloquence of destiny . . . abound[ing] in regrets, praises, aspirations, laughter, and curses" in the face of the contingent world. [112] However, in Santayana's vision put forth in the final chapter of *Realms of Being*, he proclaims his *caveat* that "in his life-long prayer the reflective man need not be especially inclined to address petitions to heaven; rational prayer is not a means, but an end." [113] In chapter 4 we will address further the indispensability of prayer as an "end" in Santayana's achieving a "union with a different infinite Good at first hidden from the eyes." [114]

THE VALUE OF THE IMAGINATION

Karen Armstrong, in the introduction of her book for the popular press, *A History of God*, reflected that while living in a convent as a nun, instead of waiting for God she should have "deliberately created a sense of him" for herself, since "in an important sense God was a product of the crea- tive imagination." [115] The importance of the imagination to Santayana's life and work is evident from his youth and his roots in Roman Catholi- cism. Reflecting on a discussion with his parents, he draws a contrast to their view and his own regarding religion.

> Thus, although I learned my prayers and catechism by rote, as was then inevitable in Spain, I knew that my parents regarded all religion as a work of the human imagination: and I agreed, and still agree with them there. But this carried an implication in their minds against which every instinct within me rebelled, namely that the works of the human imagination are bad. No, said I to myself even as a boy: they are good, they alone are good; and the rest—the whole world—is ashes in my mouth. [116]

Santayana continues in the same essay to remind us that modern philoso- phy considers the world as a work of the imagination and, certainly, religion to be so as well. He asks, "Which imaginative system will you trust?" He proposes that no system is to be trusted, not even science, and "all systems may be used and, up to a certain point, trusted as sym- bols." [117] Santayana despaired as a youth that "if religion was false, every- thing was worthless," [118] and he salvaged the aesthetic quality that ultimately meant most to him in his disillusion (i.e., the imaginative, poetic element at the foundation of all doctrine and art in the church). Indeed, for him, the *Weltanschauung* of Catholicism was pregnant with a catastrophe if one were to see anything but poetry behind the symbolic constructs.[119] Kirkwood's book *Santayana: Saint of the Imagination* is appropriately titled as Santayana's disposition, spirituality and metaphysics are inherently bound in the generative power of imagination. Irving Singer confidently proposes that "in the history of philosophy no one has written about imagination with greater profundity than Santayana."[120]

In chapter 1 of his *Interpretations of Poetry and Religion*, "Understanding and Imagination," Santayana addresses the critical nature of the faculty of imagination. He suggests that when understanding falls short in its demands for verification through the senses, it is only through imagination that it will "draw the wider views, the deeper harmonies which it craves."[121] No other human faculty can serve religion and metaphysics, "those large ideas tinctured with passion, those supersensible forms shrouded in awe, in which a mind of great sweep and vitality can find its congenial objects."[122] Imagination was nothing short of "the great unifier of humanity," and "to repress it is to chill the soul."[123]

THE IMPORTANCE OF SYMBOLS AND SIGNS

A major platform of language for Santayana's phenomenology of the spirit in *Realms of Being* and his philosophical interpretation of the Christian doctrine and dogma in *The Idea of Christ in the Gospels* is the repository of religious signs and symbols from Christianity, and more especially, Roman Catholicism. He justifies the value of these religious myths, legends, fables and theological formulas on the basis of their encapsulation of human experience and traditional moral teachings for continued reverence. The Roman church is Santayana's rich source of symbolic Christian material first evident in his poetry and to which he returns again and again from *Interpretations of Poetry and Religion* and *The Life of Reason* to *Realms of Being* and *The Idea of Christ in the Gospels*. His sensitivity to the power of symbols in the context of their religious tradition and their potential to lose "value" if the traditional context is weakened provides the basis for him to reinterpret the reality behind the metaphor and extend its moral usefulness.[124] In chapters 3 and 4, I will refer periodically to the semiotics, or the application of signs and symbols, to Santayana's project and draw some parallels to the semiotics of Charles Sanders Peirce.[125] There is sufficient evidence in Santayana's writings to attribute some significance to his early absorption in Roman Catholic imagery, doctrine and dogma and his application of signs (i.e., semiotics) to his epistemology and ontological scheme. Note: Santayana's use of the medieval language of Christian theology and its precursor of Greek (Platonic and Aristotelean) terms (e.g., "Soul," "Essence" and "Spirit"), although redefined in Santayana's reconstruction, indicates the terms he was most comfortable with. His theory of *essences* ultimately is founded on the basis of symbols providing possible access of the *Spirit* or consciousness to the material world. For Santayana, *all* perception is through a semiotic stream of images derived from the grammar of *essences*. The church is a repository of symbols in art and words reflecting the ideal as seen through the human imagination. As Howgate suggests, Catholicism brought him "close to essence, for from the earliest he looked upon theology as myth and fable, arresting and beautiful, but unsubstantial."[126]

NOTES

1. Anthony Woodward, *Living in the Eternal: A Study of George Santayana* (Nashville, TN: Vanderbilt University Press, 1988), 9. Woodward took his reference of "self-gathered" from Plotinus, suggesting a certain wise detachment from chance and change. Copleston refers to Plotinus as a man "who made many friends and no enemies, and though his personal life was ascetic, he was gentle and affectionate in character." One might think of Santayana in the same way, although the resemblance should stop there. Frederick Copleston, SJ, *A History of Philosophy*, vol. 1, "Greece and Rome" (New York: Doubleday, 1993), 464.

2. George Santayana, "A General Confession," *The Philosophy of George Santayana*, ed. Paul Arthur Schilpp (LaSalle, IL: Open Court Publishing, 1951), 23.

3. This has been and remains a dynamic controversy, and I will refer to authors and works such as Justus Buchler, "One Santayana or Two," *Journal of Philosophy* 51 (January 1954): 52–56; George W. Howgate, *George Santayana* (New York: Russell & Russell, 1938); Marin Ten Hoor, "George Santayana's Theory of Knowledge," *Animal Faith and Spiritual Life*, ed. John Lachs (New York: Appleton-Century-Crofts, 1967); and Santayana, "A General Confession," Schilpp, 23.

4. Justus Buchler suggested that "it was contended, and primarily by admirers of Santayana, that the later philosophy was incompatible with the earlier, his own protestations to the contrary notwithstanding." Buchler, "One Santayana or Two." Santayana occasionally claimed that *The Life of Reason* (published 1905–1906 in five volumes) was not representative of his mature philosophy which he systematized in *Realms of Being* (published 1927–1942 in four volumes). Daniel Cory depicts Santayana, with Cory's assistance, as revising *The Life of Reason* for a new one-volume edition only a year before Santayana's death and being "rather alarmed at the bold use of his big red crayon in places." Daniel Cory, *Santayana: The Later Years, A Portrait with Letters* (New York: G. Braziller, 1963), 314.

5. George W. Howgate examines the meaning of *Kultur* at length. He relates Santayana's own interpretation: "[*Kultur*] resembles the polity of ancient cities and of the Christian church in that it constitutes a definite, authoritative, earnest discipline, a training which is practical and is thought to be urgent and momentous . . . and demands entire devotion from everybody." Further expansion by Santayana proposes that "it [*Kultur*] is not like culture, a matter of miscellaneous private attainments and refined tastes, but, rather, participation in a national purpose and in means of executing it." George Howgate, *George Santayana* (New York: Russell & Russell, 1971), 178–79. Quotations taken from George Santayana, "German Freedom," *New Republic* 28 (August 1915): 94–96.

6. Some sympathetic examples in this regard are H. T. Kirby-Smith, "Santayana's God," *Overheard in Seville* 20 (Fall 2002): 8–14; and Thomas Alexander, "Beauty and the

Labyrinth of Evil: Santayana and the Possibility of Naturalistic Mysticism," *Overheard in Seville* 18 (Fall 2000): 1–16.

7. Woodward, *Living in the Eternal*, 5.

8. Ibid., 17.

9. George Santayana, *The Sense of Beauty* (New York: Dover Publications, 1955).

10. Santayana, "A General Confession," Schilpp, 20.

11. Daniel Cory, William G. Holzberger and John McCormick all provide us with insight into the possible existence or etiology of a homosexual proclivity in Santayana but no evidence to suggest that he ever physically acted upon it. McCormick refers to the inclusion of Santayana's poems in Robert K. Martin, *The Homosexual Tradition in American Poetry* (Iowa City: University of Iowa Press, 1998), 109–14. See also Robert Dawidoff, "Santayana: Genius of the Closet," *Overheard in Seville* 29 (Fall 2011): 4–13.

12. Letter to B. A. G. Fuller, February 7, 1914. *The Letters of George Santayana*, ed. Daniel Cory (New York: Charles Scribner's Sons, 1955), 136–37.

13. McCormick, *George Santayana*, 97. From a letter, T. S. Eliot to Hugo Munsterberg, Cambridge, Massachusetts, January 25, 1898.

14. George Santayana, *The Genteel Tradition at Bay* (New York: Charles Scribner's Sons, 1931), 18. Eliot's practical bent at Harvard toward support of the world of "big business" was in essential conflict with the anti-modernistic temperament of Santayana and others like him of sensitive or poetic disposition. Through the "amiable monster" of big business, Santayana suggests, "Society has gradually become a rather glorious, if troubled, organization of man for material achievements."

15. George Santayana, *Dominations and Powers* (Clifton, NJ: Augustus M. Kelley, 1972), 334. See chapter 10, "Confusions about Progress." For various comments on Eliot and American business and its influence at Harvard, see George Santayana, *Persons and Places*, ed. William G. Holzberger and Herman J. Saatkamp, Jr. (Cambridge, MA: MIT Press, 1986), 158, 395–96.

16. Jeffrey Meyers, *Edmund Wilson: A Biography* (New York: Houghton Mifflin Company, 1995), 275–76. Wilson's comment on Santayana's monkish "Franciscan" dressing gown recalls an expressed youthful reflection of Santayana's on "how glorious it would have been to be a Dominican friar." George Santayana, "A Brief History of My Opinions," *Contemporary American Philosophy*, vol. 2, ed. George P. Adams and William Montague (New York: Macmillan, 1930), 243. Others have suggested that Santayana's disposition and reclusive lifestyle, particularly late in life living in Rome, could be compared with that of a hermitic monk. Given Santayana's early observations on himself and his trajectory as he aged toward a more contemplative life as well as the obvious model of solitude in Catholic monasticism, I concur that he was likely not unconscious of this anchoritic image.

17. Woodward, *Living in the Eternal*, 20–21.

18. Maxwell Eastman, "Philosopher in a Convent," *American Mercury* 75, no. 335 (November 1951): 35–40.

19. Woodward, *Living in the Eternal*, 20–21.

20. Wallace Stevens, *The Collected Poems of Wallace Stevens* (New York: Alfred A. Knopf, 1955), 508–11.

21. Santayana's theory of the relation between matter and spirit or consciousness is a form of *epiphenomenalism* that accords all mental occurrences to a physical organic base and holds that mental phenomena have no causal power of their own. *Epiphenomenalism* has an implicit relationship to Santayana's naturalistic philosophy and the dependency of reason on biology. See Benjamin Allen's Ph.D. dissertation "Epiphenomenalism in the Moral Philosophy of George Santayana," Drew University, Madison, New Jersey, 1952. I will return to this subject in later chapters.

22. Frederick W. Conner, "To Dream with One Eye Open," *Soundings* 74 (Summer 1991): 166.

23. Woodward, *Living in the Eternal*, 26.

24. George Santayana, *The Idea of Christ in the Gospels: Or, God in Man, a Critical Essay* (New York: Charles Scribner's Sons, 1946), 130.

25.   Morris Grossman, "Interpreting *Interpretations*," *Overheard in Seville* 8 (Fall 1990): 18, 22.

26.   Grossman, "Interpreting *Interpretations*," 25.

27.   Eastman, "Philosopher in a Convent," 35–40.

28.   Santayana, *Persons and Places*, 419.

29.   J. H. Faurot, "Santayana's Philosophy of Religion," *Hibbert Journal* 58 (1960): 263.

30.   Grossman, "Interpreting *Interpretations*," 21.

31.   Father Richard Butler's association with Santayana began two years before the philosopher's death in 1952 with interviews leading to Father Butler's Ph.D. dissertation. In 1955 Butler's book appeared, *The Mind of Santayana* (Chicago: H. Regnery, 1955), and five years later a more biographical and anecdotal volume, *The Life and World of Santayana* (Chicago: H. Regnery, 1960).

32.   Butler, *The Life and World of George Santayana*, 501–2.

33.   McCormick, *George Santayana* , 501 –2.

34.   Cory, *Santayana* , 324.

35.   Ibid. , 325.

36.   McCormick, *George Santayana*, 502.

37.   *Disillusionment* is Santayana's rejection through reason of any expectation for supernatural salvation in a world to come and of the objective truth of any supporting myth, dogma or doctrine in religion. *Disillusionment* also has other philosophical ramifications in regard to epistemological limits in Santayana's system which will be apparent in chapter 2.

38.   McCormick, *George Santayana*, 502. In 1926, Santayana represented these hypothetical post-mortem dialogues in *Dialogues in Limbo* (New York: Charles Scribner's Sons, 1948).

39.   Father Munson had the opportunity to extensively interview Santayana at the Convent of the Blue Nuns during Santayana's last years just as Father Butler did at an earlier time. Fathers Butler and Munson enjoyed repeated visits and correspondence with Santayana as well as his personal critique of their interpretations of his philosophy. They both, at different times, claimed a friendly relationship with him and three publications resulted from their interviews. In addition to Father Butler's books mentioned above, see Thomas N. Munson, SJ, *The Essential Wisdom of George Santayana* (New York: Columbia University Press, 1962).

40.   From a letter dated April 16, 1947, from Father Terence O'Conner, OSM, to Thomas Munson, SJ, from the book jacket of Munson's book *The Essential Wisdom of George Santayana*. Also quoted in full in the appendix of Munson's book, 146–47.

41.   Munson, *The Essential Wisdom of George Santayana*, 147. Taken by Munson from notes of an interview of Santayana by Father Terence O'Conner, OSM, in 1947; italics mine.

42.   Butler, *The Mind of Santayana*, 7.

43.   Ibid., 8.

44.   George Santayana, *Scepticism and Animal Faith* (New York: Dover Publications, 1955), v–x.

45.   George Santayana, *Realms of Being* (New York: Cooper Square Publishers, 1972), xxviii. One can recognize here in Santayana's "unearthing" a Socratic or Platonic recollective process of recovering knowledge preexisting in the individual. However, I do not suggest any conscious association with such a process by Santayana.

46.   James W. Lane, "The Dichotomy of George Santayana," *Catholic World* 140 (October 1934): 20–28.

47.   Cory, *The Letters of George Santayana*, 329.

48.   Holzberger, *The Complete Poems of George Santayana*, 109.

49.   Ibid. , 96.

50.   In chapter 25 of *Persons and Places*, "A Change of Heart," Santayana describes what I believe is the most vivid and authentic representation of his *metanoia* and the influences leading up to it—for example, the death of both his beloved friend Warwick

Potter and his father in 1893 and the late-in-life marriage of his beloved sister, Susan, to an Avila widower with six children. Santayana relates his feeling of intellectual transition, and while acknowledging the religious and spiritual parallels, parses his way through a counter-argument, or even denial; for example, "There was therefore no occasion for me to suffer moral revolutions or undergo any change of heart. My interest in religion had never been agonizing, only speculative and devotional" (*Persons and Places*, 418). There is a natural tendency to "over-spiritualize" this transition, and possibly Woodward's rendition of this "conversion and repentance" does just this. However, I subscribe enthusiastically to the "gist" of his reading that the *metanoia* had too many parallels to that religious staging process of "leaving behind the fleshly self and identifying with a transcendental self, be it Atman, *purusha*, or *nous*" (Woodward, *Living in the Eternal*, 122–23).

51. Bertrand Russell likely thought of him as a "dandy" and Woodward suggests that "earlier his isolation and aloofness had a provocatively flippant edge" (Woodward, *Living in the Eternal*, 13–14).

52. Mossie May Waddington Kirkwood, *Santayana: Saint of the Imagination* (Toronto: University of Toronto Press, 1961), 51–52.

53. Holzberger, *The Complete Poems of George Santayana*, 93.

54. Henry Samuel Levinson, "What Good Is Irony?" *Overheard in Seville* 8 (Fall 1990): 31.

55. Holzberger, *The Complete Poems of George Santayana*, 5.

56. Faurot, "Santayana's Philosophy of Religion," 259.

57. Santayana, "A General Confession," Schilpp, 7.

58. Ibid., 7–8.

59. Santayana, *Persons and Places*, 160–71.

60. George Santayana, "The Present Position of the Roman Catholic Church," *New World* 1 (1892): 659.

61. Woodward, *Living in the Eternal*, 13.

62. Howgate, *George Santayana*, 29. Howgate, a literary critic rather than a philosopher, delves with some risk into the association of Santayana's poetry and his psychological and intellectual state that paralleled his poetic writing over time. Nevertheless, both Howgate and Kirkwood present a helpful guide in assessing the trajectory of Santayana's philosophical development. Santayana was initially enthusiastic, excepting a few details, regarding Howgate's biography of him first published in early 1939, but tempered his enthusiasm when his Harvard friend Boylston Beal suggested that Howgate had "missed the real Santayana—the Santayana of long walks and talks" (McCormick, *George Santayana*, 379–80). My view is that Santayana's initial response of enthusiasm was justified. Later in 1946, Santayana commented to a would-be biographer, Cyril Clemens, nephew of Samuel Clemens, a.k.a. Mark Twain, that "Howgate's biography was accurate although premature" (McCormick, *George Santayana*, 474).

63. Ibid.

64. Ibid.

65. Herbert W. Schneider, *A History of American Philosophy* (New York: Columbia University Press, 1946), 397.

66. Schneider, *A History of American Philosophy*, 396. From William Graham Sumner, *War and Other Essays* (New Haven, CT: Yale University Press, 1911), 209–10.

67. Santayana, "The Present Position of the Roman Catholic Church," 659. Santayana characterizes the writer Joseph de Maistre and his audience as pessimistic *enfants du siècle*.

68. Schneider, *A History of American Philosophy*, 292. "A clear and ancient harmony, Pierces my soul through all its din." From Thoreau's poem "Inspiration."

69. Santayana, *Persons and Places*, 302.

70. Santayana, *Realms of Being*, 530–31.

71. McCormick, *George Santayana*, 84.

72. Ibid. Walter Pater, the Victorian scholar-aesthete (1839–1894), shared the literary and aesthetic stage of the period with Matthew Arnold. Both as poets, writers,

literary and art critics of a humanist and naturalist bent, they substantially influenced Santayana and other budding young humanists. See Paul Barosky, *Walter Pater's Renaissance* (University Park: Pennsylvania State University Press, 1987); and Michael Levey, *The Case of Walter Pater* (Plymouth, England: Thames and Hudson, 1978).

73. McCormick, *George Santayana*, 29.

74. Woodward briefly compares Unamuno and Santayana in relation to the Spanish "archetype," their social pessimism and their common focus on the salvation of the individual. Woodward, *George Santayana*, 53–54.

75. Margaret Thomas Rudd, *The Lone Heretic* (Austin: University of Texas Press, 1963), 209.

76. See Herman J. Saatkamp, Jr., "Santayana: Hispanic-American Philosopher," *Transactions of the Charles S. Peirce Society* 34, no. 1 (Winter 1998): 51–68.

77. Rudd, *The Lone Heretic*. See chapter 17, "Through Doubt to Faith," passim, 149–65, and "Epilogue," 317–21.

78. George Santayana, *Interpretations of Poetry and Religion* (London: Adam and Charles Black, 1900), 240.

79. Santayana, "A General Confession," Schilpp, 27.

80. T. J. Jackson Lears, *No Place of Grace* (Chicago: University of Chicago Press, 1982). Lears writes extensively on the anti-modernistic period around the *fin de siecle*. He describes Santayana's anti-modernistic inclinations and his insightful response to the "general uncoiling of the springs of moral action" as reflected in Santayana's essay "The Poetry of Christian Dogma" (1900) from *Interpretations of Poetry and Religion*. Santayana suggests that "The Christian doctrine of rewards and punishments . . . is in harmony with moral truths which a different [i.e., more liberal] doctrine might have obscured." He argues against the liberalization of doctrine (e.g., hell and punishment), and its appropriate symbolism, by liberal thinkers who would "deprive the fable of that moral significance which is its excuse for being" (*Interpretations of Poetry and Religion*, 103).

81. Howgate, *George Santayana*, 19.

82. Saatkamp, Jr., "Santayana: Hispanic-American Philosopher," 57. Quoted from a letter from Santayana to Ficke, August 15, 1949 (manuscript at Yale).

83. Santayana, "A General Confession," Schilpp, 7.

84. Following Santayana's *disillusion* in regard to Catholicism, there clearly is a "residue" (Santayana, *Persons and Places*, 26). My argument on the nature of the Catholic influence on his philosophy is based upon the presence of this "residue" and its persistent manifestation. There is also a certain lack of self-awareness, an insensitivity to possibly deep-seated emotional drives in Santayana masked under the guise of his harsh rationality. For example, in rationalizing his *metanoic* shift during his tenure at Harvard, he ruminates in regard to his *disillusion* with Catholicism: "There was therefore no occasion for me to suffer moral revolutions or undergo any radical change of heart. My interest in religion had never been agonizing, only speculative and devotional" (*Persons and Places*, 418). He ponders further that "it was more like a bereavement or a total change of surroundings" (419). A bereavement indeed. The specter would persist.

85. Howgate's book was derived from his PhD dissertation "George Santayana: Man of Letters" (University of Pennsylvania, 1933).

86. There are occasions in *Persons and Places* and elsewhere where Santayana disclaims emotional turmoil or substantial existential suffering due to his departure from Catholicism (e.g., 419, 425–27).

87. Santayana, "Apologia Pro Mente Sua," Schilpp, 497. In referring to his view on the nature of ideals, Santayana attributes his sentiments on this subject as "show[ing] an attachment to Platonism and Catholicism (which was the religion most familiar and congenial to me [Santayana]) entirely divorced from faith."

88. Woodward, *Living in the Eternal*, 44.

89. George Santayana, *The Life of Reason* (New York: Charles Scribner's Sons, 1953), 179.

90. Santayana, "A General Confession," Schilpp, 22.

91. George Santayana, *Winds of Doctrine & Platonism and the Spiritual Life* (Gloucester, MA: Peter Smith, 1971), 25.

92. Santayana, *Winds of Doctrine*, ix.

93. Kirkwood, *Santayana: Saint of the Imagination*, 135.

94. Woodward, *Living in the Eternal*, 89. Woodward refers to Santayana's "materialistic dogmatism" in regard to his rigorous epiphenomenalism.

95. George Santayana, "A Brief History of My Opinions," in *The Philosophy of George Santayana*, ed. Irwin Edman (New York: Charles Scribner's Sons, 1953), 7. Earlier in this chapter, I depicted Santayana's dialogue with the two Catholic priests, Fathers Butler and Munson, and their own uncompromising Thomism. Here, Santayana is referring to the method, in its rigor, rather than to the theistic conclusion of Aquinas's natural theology.

96. Woodward, *George Santayana*, 13.

97. Santayana, *Scepticism and Animal Faith*, 305.

98. Santayana, *Dominations and Powers*, 166.

99. Friederick Paulsen (1846–1908) was a member of the philosophy faculty at Berlin. Still short of starting his Ph.D. dissertation, Santayana was in Dresden and Berlin on a study grant to improve his German and take some courses. Recalling Paulsen, he affirms his importance: "Paulsen . . . was simply an excellent professor . . . This semester he lectured on Greek Ethics, and in the next winter semester on Spinoza. In both subjects he helped to settle my opinions for good. The Greek ethics wonderfully supplied what was absent in Spinoza, a virile, military, organic view of life, a civilized view, to keep the cosmic and religious imagination of Spinoza in its proper moral place" (Santayana, *Persons and Places*, 257).

100. Cory, *Santayana*, 171.

101. Santayana, *The Genteel Tradition at Bay*, 8.

102. Santayana, *Dominations and Powers*, 256.

103. Santayana, *The Idea of Christ in the Gospels*, 253.

104. Henry Samuel Levinson, *Santayana, Pragmatism and the Spiritual Life* (Chapel Hill: University of North Carolina Press, 1992), 239.

105. Santayana, *Realms of Being*, 779.

106. Santayana, *Platonism and the Spiritual Life*, 256.

107. Santayana, *Persons and Places*, 419–20.

108. Santayana, "Apologia Pro Mente Sua," Schilpp, 572. Also quoted in Levinson, *Santayana, Pragmatism and the Spiritual Life*, 268.

109. Santayana, "Apologia Pro Mente Sua," Schilpp, 572.

110. Santayana, *The Idea of Christ in the Gospels*, 142.

111. Santayana, *Realms of Being*, 801.

112. Ibid., 800.

113. Ibid., 798.

114. Ibid.

115. Karen Armstrong, *A History of God* (New York: Ballantine Books, 1993), xx.

116. Santayana, "A Brief History of My Opinions," Edman, 5.

117. Ibid., 6.

118. Ibid.

119. Santayana, *Persons and Places*, 419.

120. Irving Singer, *George Santayana, Literary Philosopher* (New Haven, CT: Yale University Press, 2000), 199.

121. Santayana, *Interpretations of Poetry and Religion*, 6.

122. Ibid.

123. Santayana, *Interpretations of Poetry and Religion*, 9.

124. Santayana, *The Life of Reason*, 202–3. When a myth "has lost its symbolic value and sunk to the level of merely false information, only an inert and stupid tradition can keep it above water."

125. Semiotics is generally the study of signs, or anything that represents something else. "Signs take the form of words, images, sounds, gestures and objects," and are concerned with "meaning-making and representation in many forms." Daniel Chandler, *Semiotics: The Basics* (London: Routledge, 2002), 2–5. The basic concepts of semiotics are important in gaining an in-depth understanding of Santayana's theory of *essences*.

126. Howgate, *George Santayana*, 244.

TWO

The Philosophical Basis for Santayana's Philosophy of Religion

Reason, as Hume said with profound truth, is an unintelligible instinct.
George Santayana, *Reason in Common Sense*

Following a broad and brief review of Santayana's "technical" philosophy I will attempt in this chapter to identify those elements of his project that are most basic and essential in deriving his philosophy of religion. Further, since I identified in the previous chapter a number of influences on his philosophical thought that may be attributed to his Roman Catholic upbringing and the cultural environment of his youth, I will refer to some of these associations as I proceed. I will also briefly draw some associations with the primary antecedent philosophical influences on Santayana, especially Aristotle, Plato, Lucretius and Hegel, Schopenhauer and Spinoza. Although in this book I intend to focus upon what constitutes Santayana's "mature" philosophy independent of the time during which the primary source material was written, I will begin by briefly addressing a controversy surrounding a perception of evolution or shift in Santayana's thought. This transition, in the opinion of some, occurred in the time between his days at Harvard and a later, more contemplative period, while living in Europe in retirement from academic life.

THE PHILOSOPHER'S THOUGHT OVER TIME

As other authors have observed, Santayana's integrated philosophical treatment is impossible to derive *in summa* from one or two of his works. One, therefore, must read him rather broadly in order to realize that he is in fact systematic in his approach, despite his proclaimed aversion to the concept of "systems" in philosophy.[1] The following works can, together, indeed leave the reader with an adequate perspective on Santayana's philosophy: his philosophical *opus ultimus*, *Realms of Being* (1927–1938), the introduction to this work, *Scepticism and Animal Faith* (1923), his semi-autobiographical *Apologia Pro Mente Sua: A Rejoinder* (1940), *A General Confession* (1940) and excerpts from his major autobiography *Persons and Places* (1943–1947). However, this cannot be the entire story for Santayana. His earlier and often called "humanistic" period represented by *The Life of Reason* (1905–1906), the slightly earlier *Interpretations of Poetry and Religion* (1900) and his aesthetic work, *The Sense of Beauty* (1896), provide the scholar with a perspective from his earlier works while at Harvard and an opportunity to consider any congruence or discontinuity with his later philosophical integration. In addition, the eight-volume critical edition of *The Letters of George Santayana* is invaluable in assessing the trajectory of his thought.

One therefore has resources and opportunity to plumb any continuity in his essential philosophical themes and the groundwork and early intuitions behind his final synthesis in the categorical and ontological philosophy of *essences*. Justus Buchler, naturalistic philosopher of the Columbia "school" and correspondent with Santayana, observed that the inherent consistency and systematic structure of Santayana's naturalistic project may not be easily discerned for a number of reasons. Not the least of these was his literary, and even poetic, style which could distract from a rigorous analytical reading more easily come by if one were reading a "tight," more conventional philosophical text using philosophical terms. As a result, Buchler proposes, "two Santayanas" came to be identified with "irreconcilable differences" between one more humanistic and rational and the latter more disinterested and spiritual.[2] Buchler goes on to provide evidence that there is one philosopher and one philosophy in Santayana, but one that evolves both in development and mode of expression with substantial coherence between the earlier and later work. Santayana himself, as indicated earlier in this thesis, claimed such a consistency.[3] William Dennes also proposes that there has been no evident shift in Santayana's earlier naturalism as put forth in *The Life of Reason* and his later works of *Scepticism and Animal Faith* and *Realms of Being*. On the other hand, he does observe that significant shifts have occurred in the development of critical realistic-naturalism over the same period, hence suggesting an independent trajectory for Santayana, who has often been identified with this contemporary philosophical movement.[4]

I believe it is reasonable to conclude that the evidence suggests that Santayana's philosophical perspective took a "softer" turn in the second half of his life and the spirituality in his naturalism became more evident. At the same time, it has been suggested by John P. Anton that "scepticism took deeper root in his ripe old age."[5] My own view is that his "method" of skepticism depicted in *Scepticism and Animal Faith* remained quite unchanged as a constant foundational premise for his epistemology. This was dogma for Santayana's project, as was *animal faith*, the only window of human access into the world of day-to-day living. In any case, it is clear throughout his project that the natural world of matter itself was seen to have lost none of its contingency or overwhelming might in the face of human helplessness. Nevertheless, the "turn" was there, consistent with his earlier work but with a more contemplative shift and higher definition, particularly in terms of the grammar of *essences* and their ontological and epistemological role for humans in the world. Taking a slightly more sympathetic side of the argument, Lachs is more ready to justify a perception of a major shift in Santayana's emphasis from humanistic in earlier work to ontological in the later. He particularly notes that the treatment of religion is cast more in ontological terms in the later works. However, despite justifying the rationale for "two Santayanas," ultimately he also concludes that for the most part, Santayana's ideas did not take a major organic turn over time.[6] Irwin Edman manages to capture a contemplative definitive "turn" toward spiritual "goals" in describing Santayana's temper as evident in his later works, *Scepticism and Animal Faith* and *Realms of Being*.

> Santayana remains fundamentally a naturalist through these later books, a naturalist whose own gaze is directed to those forms to which he himself is by temperament, as a poet and a speculative mind, addressed. He worships not existence but such fruitions or discernments as it makes possible. He recognizes universal power and respects it. But he worships other things, the goals of life, insofar as any of them can be defined or attained anywhere, for so defined or attained, they become glory and beauty.[7]

In the second stage of Santayana's philosophical life following a *metanoia* or "conversion" (see chapter 1) begun during his tenure at Harvard in 1893, he was more tolerant in his expectations of people's ability to differentiate between fantasy and fact. J. H. Faurot notes how Santayana's earlier condemnation of Cervantes's Don Quixote and his departure into fantasy shifted to an acknowledgment of the universal "normal madness" in humans. Santayana, in *Dialogues in Limbo*, has Democritus depict the folly of "normal madness" to the youthful Alcibiades and Dionysius. Essentially, this is the inclination of "conventionally sane" humans to associate characteristics through opinion, cultural conditioning or presumption with phenomena as representative of the natural world. The lines of demarcation in our perceptions of the world and objective reality can never be ascertained for the only absolute we can be assured of is in the immediate intuition of an *essence*. For Santayana then, this human inability to be assured of congruence between perception and the real world means that all action is a leap of faith, frequently based upon

illusion. Hence we are in a weak position to be intolerant or overly judgmental of any vision of what is reality, even if it seems "madness."[8]

Another view of a possible shift over time in Santayana is from Anthony Woodward who proposes that Santayana had not "canalized the powerful current of his religious nature" until after he wrote *The Life of Reason*,
and that his later writings (e.g., *Realms of Being* and *Dominations and Powers*) gave more evidence of this spiritual turn.[9] Woodward's treatment of
Santayana's purported transition is rigorous and well demonstrated in a
comparative analysis of Santayana's writing over time. He particularly
contrasts *The Life of Reason*, the early work considered by his contemporaries just after the turn of the century to offer " a classical humanism fit
for consumption in the modern world of post-Enlightenment
progress."[10] Woodward goes on to depict the later disillusionment of
these same contemporaries who had earlier found a model of a rational
philosophy engendering hope in human progress in *The Life of Reason*.
Thus from *Scepticism and Animal Faith* and *Realms of Being* to Santayana's
final major work on politics and society, *Dominations and Powers*, he was
observed to recant significantly on his earlier humanistic vision of more
rational control and depict a human dilemma where we are "playthings
of forces unamenable to human art or wit."[11]

The evidence of a deeply spiritual nature is there from Santayana's
youth and is represented most clearly in his poetry. Also, I related earlier
his experience of some level of despair in emotionally "abandoning" his
tenuous affiliation with the Catholic Church. He had, of course, abandoned it intellectually years before but it seems that the spiritual residue
was not altogether vestigial. One can surmise that his contemplative spirituality in later life emerged from this residue and not from the *disillusionment* that was free of both the harassment of the world and the encum-
brances of self-consciousness and specific allegiances to any one form of
being. He would ultimately, on the grounds of his spirituality and *disillusionment,* achieve a harmony, and even a happiness. Santayana was never
to mitigate the harshness of his realism but a perceived "mystical" bent
depicting a naturalistic "salvation" or "deintoxification" of the world
through a transcendence of cares and anxieties and the contemplation of
the *essences* raised the flag of the critical humanist community. Such a
transcendental approach through the use of the imagination grounded in
the one dimension of nature and matter, would elevate the human spirit
and weave a second, very personal "reality" above the contingency of the
"flux" of the world. This reality would "be," but not exist! Certainly there
can be an impression of something mystical in all of this, despite Santayana's proclaimed distaste for the "absolutism" of mysticism. We will examine in chapter 4 both the nature of Santayana's contemplative spirituality along with his distrust of mysticism.

I am inclined to conclude that the vitality of Santayana's very personal
philosophy allows for such a "tone" shift, a maturation, that may be

attributable to a more spiritual emphasis later in his life rather than an actual modification of his naturalism. However, while I suggest that Santayana's philosophy does not change markedly over time, this is obviously not to say that intellectual and philosophical development was unimportant. In any case, the philosopher himself proclaims his own late-in-life disclaimer for the immutability of his "system."

> My philosophy has never changed. It is by no means an artificial academic hypothesis; it doesn't appeal at all to the professors; it is a system of presuppositions and categories discovered already alive and at work within me, willy-nilly, like existence itself, and virtually present not only in the boy but in the embryo. [12]

THE NATURE OF PHILOSOPHICAL INFLUENCES

Santayana's study of Hellenistic philosophy just prior to his writing of *The Life of Reason*, and his early fascination with the ethics of Plato (427–347 BC) and the de-hypostatization of the moralistic Forms by Aristotle (384–322 BC), are particularly important for his philosophical development. Heraclitus (ca. 500 BC), Democritus (ca. 460–371 BC) and the Roman Lucretius (ca. 95–54 BC) all weigh in as major influences with philosophical concepts that strike the scholar as similar or parallel to Santayana's. The influences of the modern era—of Spinoza, Schopenhauer, Hegel and later, his teacher and colleague at Harvard, William James—came even earlier in Santayana's philosophical trajectory and would persist in their importance to him. [13] Nevertheless, the Greeks are clearly foundational and dominant in their weight of influence. In order that my intent not be misunderstood regarding antecedent philosophical influences, I need to introduce a similar *caveat* to the one I mentioned in chapter 1 in regard to Roman Catholic influences. It is never easy to discern for certain where influences of earlier philosophers result in concepts developed by those that follow, even if the philosopher, as Santayana does, admits to some substantial level of antecedent influence. The other side of this coin is the historiographical "sin" of attributing an evolutionary, "building-block" pattern to succeeding philosophical systems or ideas. Frederick Copleston, SJ, has offered the scholarly admonishment that "one must not assume *a priori* that every opinion of every thinker is borrowed from a predecessor . . . nor can we safely assume that whenever two succeeding contemporary thinkers or bodies of thinkers hold similar doctrines, one must have borrowed from the other." [14] As Timothy Sprigge has suggested, Santayana himself was repelled by the notion of an artist or thinker being valued for a contribution made to "some great human progression towards some future idea . . . across time." [15] Providing an appropriate analogy in the same vein, Santayana further suggests that "to call Berkeley a stepping stone between Locke and Hume is like calling an upright obelisk a stepping stone between two Sphinxes that may be crouching to the right and the left of it."[16] With this caution in mind, in the case of Santayana, given his confessed influence by some specific ancient philosophers, I will point out in this section similarities and some differences of antecedent concepts to Santayana's where it seems helpful. In chapter 4, I will further address some important environmental influences on Santayana (e.g., Darwinism and anti-modernism).

Sometimes, one detects apparent "footprints" in Santayana's project that suggest that he has taken up as his own certain antecedent philosopher's ideas even if there may be as much as a denial. Have adequate attributions been made by the great man in every case? Some scholars have thought not.[17] Justus Buchler referred to "Santayana's innocent factual lapses," observing that Santayana's obvious awareness of Peirce's semiotic theory, based on comments from Santayana in a letter to Buchler, never appeared or were acknowledged in his work.[18] Certainly, in the case of the Hellenic influence (e.g., Plato, Heraclitus or Democritus, the Roman poet-philosopher Lucretius, and later, Spinoza and Schopenhauer), the attributions are sometimes clear and pervasively proclaimed, and I will address these below. The paucity of attributions in footnotes is evident throughout Santayana's project, of which even his doctoral dissertation on Lotze is almost totally devoid. Santayana read Husserl and commented on his phenomenology in the postscript to *The Realm of Essence*, but my sense is that the commentary is nominal in relation to the remarkable parallels in the approaches of the two philosophers.[19] On the other hand, Santayana denied to Justus Buchler that he had ever read Brentano, Husserl's mentor (I will address a comparison of Husserl's and Santayana's phenomenological approach in chapter 3). The phenomenological character of William James's *The Principles of Psychology* strikes me as another possible debt that Santayana may not have adequately acknowledged.[20] In any case, Santayana was a first-rate scholar of the history of philosophy and at the end of the day, provided a balanced synthesis of what he considered important and integral to his total system.[21] Yes, it was his system, but in his own admission, still, not his! His beguiling admission in the telling reflections from his often quoted preface to *Scepticism and Animal Faith* is revealing of the disposition and attitude of his discourse and, in my view, exonerates him from any but cautious criticism.

> Here is one more system of philosophy. If the reader is tempted to smile, I can assure him that I smile with him . . . *My system is not mine, nor new.* I am merely attempting to express for the reader the principles to which he appeals when he smiles. There are convictions in the depths of his soul, beneath all his overt parrot beliefs, on which I would build our friendship . . . I think that common sense, in a rough and

dogged way, is technically sounder than the special schools of philosophy, each of which squints and overlooks half the difficulties in its eagerness to find in some detail the key to the whole.[22]

There were antecedent philosophers that *confirmed* or even significantly formed Santayana's position by revealing concepts in their own philosophical thought in such a way as to allow him to substantiate and formalize his early project with more confidence.[23] While studying with Professor Paulsen in Berlin as a graduate student he "knew henceforth that in the Greeks I should find the natural support and point of attachment for my own philosophy."[24] Edman comments on Santayana's inclination toward "the clear lines of Greek thinking," further hyperbolically suggesting that Santayana, intellectually, "might be called the last Greek."[25] Certainly the parallels are unmistakable from his philosophical themes and even to his lifestyle. As we will see, however, Santayana's philosophical and religious heresies do not exclude a major breakaway from many tenets of the Greek model. The Roman poet-philosopher Lucretius, the Epicurean apologist, also had an early and profound effect on Santayana's thought from the time of his undergraduate days when he carried a volume of Lucretius in his pocket.[26] Later, in 1910, he memorialized this influence of Lucretius in *Three Philosophical Poets: Lucretius, Dante, and Goethe*, exalting his "vividness and smack of reality."[27] I will now proceed to discuss the important parallels of the Greeks, a Roman poet and a few modern philosophers relative to Santayana's naturalistic project. However, we should remain sensitive to his *caveat*-laden reflection that "if a Democritus or Lucretius or Spinoza or Darwin works within the lines of nature, and clarifies some part of that familiar subject, that fact is the ground of my attachment to them: they have the savor of truth . . . [which] I know very well without their help."[28]

I plead some forbearance on the part of the academic reader as, for the sake of continuity, I briefly and summarily cover some familiar ground in order to address some pertinent aspects of the following antecedent figures: Heraclitus and Democritus, both of whom for Santayana represented the onset of the transition from *mythos* to *logos* in the ongoing saga of materialistic-naturalism; Plato, the major influence in regard to Santayana's theory of *essences* and his model for spiritual discipline; Aristotle, the "naturalizer" of Plato's transcendent forms; and the Roman Lucretius, the early spiritual and Epicurean model for Santayana. I will transcend the great middle ground of philosophical striving that is less relevant to Santayana until we arrive at the example of Benedict de Spinoza (1632–1677), who for Santayana was the "sublime prophet."[29]

Heraclitus

Santayana's *The Life of Reason* was substantially influenced by his study of the Greeks and the manner in which they developed rational thought in relation to nature. Howgate suggests that Santayana's foundational materialism "needs only a compound of Democritus and Heraclitus."[30] This is a stretch in my view but there *are* foundational points that will relate closely to Santayana's brand of naturalism. At the foundation of the Greek philosophical trajectory is a dedication to logic and reasoning in a striving to explain natural phenomena. Heraclitus sustained in his *cosmos* a bevy of anthropomorphic humanoid gods with troubles enough of their own so as to be indifferent to human life.[31] Otherwise, Heraclitus proposed that in nature "all things are in a state of flux," and that essentially, substance is process—a process of change.[32] Within this flux existed a conflict of opposites, each in itself beyond goodness or badness therefore, except for human assessments as to effect and value, obviating any absolute moral judgments in an eternal system. Heraclitus posed epistemological limits—for example, "Nature likes to hide," and therefore, the universe may be said to be in "hidden attunement,"[33] and its habits (tropes or repeating events) when perceived by humans may be called "laws." It is generally inaccessible except by hints through symbols and signs. Matter remains as mysterious as ever. The mechanistic-pantheistic "God" is universal reason, and the way humans participate in this universal mechanism for a brief time is through a life of reason and by realizing the futility of rebelling against an indifferent universe. John Anton reminds us that Heraclitus was a transcendentalist by virtue of his "God" of reason being "the guarantor for the recurrence of law, the hidden *logos* behind everything in flux."[34] Still, there are no gods capable of teleological impact, there is no immortality, and man is dependent upon the contingencies of the cosmos. Finally, for our purposes here, Heraclitus was perceived by Santayana to be the first ancient who was sensitive to the idea of *immediacy*.[35] This idea will be important as we progress in relating to Santayana's epistemology and ultimately to his theory of *essences*. It will also pertain directly to my arguments for his phenomenological method in chapter 3.

Democritus

In Heraclitus we have the *flux* of matter and in Democritus we have an altogether consistent theory of "atomization" or the particulate nature of matter—the foundation for Newtonian molecular physics. Although the model of atomism is crude, Santayana emphasizes its symbolic value as a profound early notion of nature's dynamics, and further proposes that "all notions of matter . . . must be wholly inadequate, otherwise the natural philosopher would be claiming a plenitude of miraculous illumination such as no prophet ever thought to possess."[36] One may anticipate what Santayana's response might have been to the penchant of modern physicists for "a theory of everything." Democritus's rational construction of atoms and their forms is really an *ideal* construction in Santayana's view, and as science advances inspired by this basic model, the model is reconstituted in some fashion (e.g., in modern particle physics).[37] All then, is in eternal motion, atoms and void in the flux of nature and, like Heraclitus, the anthropomorphic gods—not immortal but only longer-lived than humans—did not create the universe.[38] Again, there is no defined cosmological teleology in Democritus and, as Santayana affirms in the final chapter of *Realms of Being*, although Democritus and the Epicureans (e.g., Lucretius) would not deny existence to the gods, they assigned to them no dominion over nature.[39]

A perception of the *immediate* is again evident in Democritus with the added "physics" as an aid to understanding it. Hence, it is mechanism (i.e., the kinetics of atoms interacting) that provides him with an explanation of human perception. This aspect of Democritus's primitive particle physics extended to his mechanical interpretation of sensation (i.e., the "effluences" flowing from an object and entering the organs of sense). Of importance is Democritus's conclusion that representations by this atomistic impingement on the senses are false (i.e., subjective) and caused by the object itself, giving us only a sense of reality, not knowledge of it. For Democritus states that "by the senses we in truth know nothing sure, but only something that changes according to the disposition of the body and of the things that enter into it or resist it."[40] It is this concept, substantially modified, that we will later associate with Santayana's own theory of *essences* in relation to his epistemology and the limits of knowability of the existing object. However, Democritus himself offered no resolution in regard to epistemological problems (i.e., gaining real knowledge), but given the "bastard" quality of sense knowledge, he privileged *a priori* reason as the source of legitimate knowledge (e.g., of atoms).[41]

In the face of a contingent world with no divine source of aid, Democritus counseled *euthymia*, or equanimity and cheerfulness. Here, as we shall see, Santayana's view is reflected quite precisely. The objective for humans is happiness, a striving after wellbeing since "the best thing for a man is to pass his life so as to have as much joy and as little trouble as may be."[42] The aspect of happiness is very evident in Santayana's philosophy, and the roots of this notion are also evident in Lucretius and the earlier school of Epicurus. As "the laughing philosopher" Democritus did, Santayana also discovered the value of laughter as "a joyous form of union with our defeats, in which the spirit is victorious."[43]

Plato

Plato's *Dialogues* may be the first instance where the argument for the concept of *universals*, to be known as the Platonic *Forms*, their character and consequences, was brought forward.[44] Santayana's life of reason, moral philosophy and theory of *essences* has obvious parallels with Plato's metaphysical theory of *Forms*, as well as its implications for knowledge of facts and values in the world. As a self-proclaimed "Platonic realist," Santayana reflects a certainty, as Plato did, that we can have positive knowledge of a realm of universals (i.e., Forms or *essences*). However, the hypostatization of these Forms in Plato (i.e., elevation to a transcendental and hierarchal realm) is the point of philosophical departure for Santayana who adheres to his materialistic view of ontological parity, and only then returns to the Platonic view that no object can be known directly.

Plato's epistemology is of particular importance and can only be considered in connection with his metaphysics. It is only Forms or Ideas that are the "strictly" real things—that is, in Plato's system, they are depicted as existents, real and apart, and owe their reality somehow to a universal "one" or "Good."[45] If then the Form of the Good lends *being* to objects of the world, this suggests both ontological power (causation) as well as epistemological properties.[46] It is only through perceiving the Forms that we can have any notion of real objects and their properties which are, expressed in a vulgar mode, in some way "copies" of the Forms. Existence is therefore enabled by another existent which, for Plato, seems to exist apart, outside of space and time—that is, eternally![47] Such an impartation of enabling properties to Forms is a major departure from Santayana's concept of *essences*, which we will find as real but nonexistent *beings* and as nonexistents are not in space and time and therefore have no power over matter. Also of major significance in Santayana's concept, *essences*, therefore, do not impart ontological power but only epistemological properties of perception and possible knowledge.

If Forms did not exist for Plato, perception would only deliver the object (if this can be imagined) without its properties. Again a dualism of what can be seen as two different levels of reality contradict the materialism of Santayana where objects can exist independent of our thought and the *essences* symbolic of these objects only enter upon the playing field when we *attain them in perception*. Having separated the act of perception from that of attainment of the object and its properties, Plato then seems to find the recollection of the absolute Forms, not directly from a realm apart, but rather as an *a priori* presence, brought forth and delivered to us from *recollection*. Plato prescribes for the student a Socratic progression through "levels" of knowledge that represent corresponding levels of reality *via* the dialectical method. The path is upward toward the highest level that is the "rational intuition" of the Forms themselves.[48] Also, in Santayana, we see a kind of "ladder" of spiritual progression finally to reach the heights in perfect contemplation of the eternal *essences*. These heights, for both Plato and Santayana, are only achievable by those especially gifted.

For Plato, the objects representing the perception are the Forms, or properties or accidents of the real object, and the object *per se* cannot be known. Therefore, the perceptibles can be conceptually (dialectically) separable from the Forms but still there is a necessary interdependence for existence.[49] Plato's cosmos is both divined by him to *allow* perception, and therefore human dialogue about objects, but is also two-tiered in the sense of objects in time and space and those abstract objects, Forms, beyond time and space. The abstract level Forms are not subject to the same patterns of regularity as material objects and hence are independent of the senses and all transactions with material things.[50] As I suggested above, we find a great contrast to Plato in Santayana's view on causality which has been the subject of substantial controversy by Santayana's modern critics.[51] Short of Plato's theory on the causality of the Forms, Santayana's analogous *essences* are not only nonexistent but also do not act causally in the world. Further, thought emanating from consciousness, or the *spirit*, is similarly non-efficacious. For Santayana, only from the roots of the biological organism in time and space as part of the realm of matter does animal action result in the world. This view, as we will discuss later in this chapter and further in chapter 3, is the basis for his *epiphenominalism*.

There are two near parallels of many in Plato and Santayana that are important to note. The first is that in both philosophers, the Forms, in the case of Plato, and *essences*, for Santayana, provide the only path to wisdom and attainment of reality in the world. The second relates to the Platonic view of elitism: that is, that the average person may be incapable of achieving this level of contemplation, knowledge and wisdom, and that the attainment of wisdom is left to the philosopher—of an elite, contemplative order in society . At the same time, the idea of an Athenian democracy is rejected by Plato since the average person is not deemed capable of sensibly participating in Athenian democracy. Harsh though they may seem, similar conservative views are expressed by Santayana although in a somewhat gentler vein. He proposes that the contemplation of *essences* may not be for the average man, and that "happiness implies resource and security; it can be achieved only by discipline," and it "is hidden from the free and casual will; it belongs rather to one chastened by a long education and unfolded in an atmosphere of sacred and perfected institutions."[52] Neither does Santayana trust democracy and governance by the "average man," but rather, like Plato, tends toward the elevation of those educated elite and institutionally initiated to decision-making status in the state.

A derivative of the dualistic vision is Plato's idea that our souls are immortal and will be reborn in other bodies after death. An extension of the immortal character of the soul relates to our innate ability, in Plato's view, to comprehend the *ideal* even if we don't experience it in life. This innate ability, for Plato, comes about through our direct contact with the Forms.[53] Such a view can be contrasted to the naturalistic view that we find in Santayana's materialism, wherein there is only one level of existence as matter (Plato's "concrete objects"). There is an "orthodoxy" in ◦

Plato that is best demonstrated in his conflict with the Sophists, and particularly Protagoras, on the sense of truth being relative to the individual. Plato insisted that we must accept an objective truth independent of any notion of it by a particular believer, and that knowledge of truth is at least partially attainable.[54] This same rigor in regard to a ground of truth, unattainable in certainty but absolute if one could attain it, characterizes Santayana's own orthodoxy in this regard. As we have seen in chapter 1, Santayana finds repugnant any compromise or option to step off of the path of reason in accommodation to a systemic coherence (e.g., to resort to sophism). Only life itself, out of our total control, is at best an unwitting compromise.[55]

Aristotle

In Aristotle, a humanistic or human-centered concern dominates and a dualistic vision is evident (i.e., a natural and transcendental realm). Santayana covers the same scope despite his general denial of metaphysical content (excepting his weak admission to it in *Realms of Being*) and a dualistic cosmological view. Just as we have discovered in Plato substantial parallels and influence in regard to Santayana's philosophy, we find a less obvious, but possibly more substantial influence from Aristotle. Louis Harap speculates correctly, I believe, that Santayana's *Life of Reason* has a close parallel in Aristotle's "good life," and that the Aristotelian point of view is implicit throughout his project.[56] John Lachs, while acknowledging Santayana's debt to Aristotle in the adoption of Aristotle's categorical scheme, points out that the "starting point" in his Cartesian-like epistemological path from skepticism is based upon human action and objectivity, and is much closer to Aristotle than to Descartes.[57] I suggest, however, that if we agree that Santayana, in *Scepticism and Animal Faith*, begins his trajectory with a skeptical method, he may be more akin to the Pyrrhonian School and a post-Aristotelean synthesis—for example, by Aenesidemus (ca. first century AD)—than either Descartes or Aristotle.[58] Santayana refers to the skepticism of the Sophist Protagoras ("Man is the measure of all things"),[59] but not, to my knowledge, to the Pyrrhonian school, therefore I leave it as an open question. Aristotle's theory of substance, primary substance and non-substance are closely related to Santayana's corresponding theory of matter, substance and *essence*. Santayana's periodic use of the word *entelechy* to designate consciousness or spirit as a derivative of substance or animal biology is just another example of Aristotle's influence.[60] Lachs further notes that the tone of Santayana's moral philosophy is substantially Aristotelean.[61] This seems to be well supported by their mutual idea that, on one hand, there are no universal moral prescriptions, but on the other, each individual gains by striving toward his or her potential—that is, ideally through the life of reason and implicitly, the life of the spirit.[62] Santayana's debt to

Aristotle lies generally in the synthesis and systemization of Greek thought from the pre-Socratics, through Socrates and Plato and the "naturalization" of the mystical Platonic Forms from a transcendental realm beyond space and time.[63] All of this thought was ontological in nature while Aristotle's project, still essentially ontological, formed a "bridge" to the modern pursuit of knowledge through experience. Santayana sustains the ontological character in his own project, and in his identification with the Greeks, bypasses the metaphysics of experience and mind, and is contra-absolutist in his epistemology. John P. Anton differentiates well the influential roles of Plato and Aristotle, suggesting that both are "moralists of the life of reason. Plato articulates the ideal, [while] Aristotle gives it its objective form." I concur when Anton also suggests that the primary influence of Aristotle on Santayana is in delineating the "natural basis for the spiritual life," but "not in the understanding of nature, nor in that of the immediate, but in revealing the conditions of the Life of Reason."[64] For Aristotle and Santayana both, the "good life" is happiness and what constitutes happiness depends upon the nature of their *being*, upon their characteristic function.[65] If humans function well they optimize the characteristic human feature of reason by living the life of reason.[66] Here, then, is the guiding principle, initially for Santayana's *The Life of Reason*, and remaining so for his mature philosophy exemplified in *Realms of Being*. Aristotle, therefore, can be seen as the "organizer" and integrater and Plato as more the spiritual inspiration for Santayana. The concept of *essence*, the *a priori*–derived eternal Forms in Plato and those attained through objective observations in the world by Aristotle, are also of particular importance as background for Santayana's analogous, but much broader theory of *essences*. Aristotle's concepts of *Soul, Psyche, Form* and *Substance* are all important terms respectfully adopted by Santayana which are analogous but have somewhat different meanings for him. I will cover these definitions when I outline Santayana's "technical" philosophy later in this chapter. It is important to acknowledge that Santayana and Aristotle are not in accord regarding their basic definition of the natural world as the totality of its objects in space and time. Since only matter has any power of causality, nature as congruent is then seen to be that which stands as real and independent of mind and is affective of all that happens to animal life and the human spirit. It is only Aristotle that hypostatizes in his natural theology, deductively through the concept of matter and form, an immaterial and eternal "unmoved mover." This "mover" is outside of nature and as unconscious of life and the world as Whitehead's primordial god-head, a "prime mover" who "moved" creation of an already eternally existing world into being, enabling it through motion, and then left it subject to the regenerative powers of nature.[67]

Lucretius

I referred earlier to the influence of the Roman poet and Epicurean apologist Lucretius on Santayana, beginning in his student days at Harvard. Lucretius's influence may be the most profound of all the ancients as a lure to Santayana during a period of searching out rational alternatives to the Roman Catholicism of his birth. What Edman termed the "vividness and smack of reality" in Lucretius's materialism was a gospel of salvation for the young poet-philosopher when *die Zeitlichkeit* circumscribed all human hope. As a student, Santayana had committed passages of Lucretius's long poem *De Rerum Natura* to memory. Later he would say, "The great master of sympathy with nature, in my education, was Lucretius."[68] The Epicurean vision, with some significant exceptions, is strikingly similar to Santayana's, not only within the elements of his system, but also in the translation to lifestyle. A major exception in Democritus, Epicurus, and Lucretius is their belief in a "physics" of direct but impartial access to objects in the world through the senses (i.e., through the emanation of the *eidola* from the object impinging on the senses), and furthermore, they hold the view that the truth of this sensory input is incontrovertible.[69] Hence, their view and Santayana's were, on both counts regarding access to the reality of external objects, widely disparate. In Santayana's view, however, Lucretius gave form and body to the Epicurean motifs, and through the vehicle of Epicurean thought, carried forward the naturalism and physics of Democritus to an early model of scientific-materialism.[70] Of particular interest is Lucretius's view that the Epicurian trust in sensation is the only "hold-fast" against slipping into the "abyss of scepticism."[71] One could think of Santayana's *Animal Faith* as a recovery from the "slide" on the other side of skepticism (i.e., upon "testing" skepticism as a potentially viable approach to life and finding it untenable, resorting to life through faith in reality).

When one considers Lucretius's melancholy character, his poetic nature, an inclination to skepticism, love of friendship and intellectual pleasures, a disinclination to sexual love, denial of suffering, pain as a barrier to happiness, and passionate opposition to the destructive nature of fear of death imposed by religion, we can't avoid noting the similarity to Santayana. It would seem that even Lucretius's poetic expression of the Epicurean axiom *"Nil igitur mors est ad nos"* (Therefore death is nothing to us) is reflected in Santayana's grim acceptance of the materialistic rejection of suffering after death (e.g., in hell).[72] The franchise for a philosopher as once-removed "observer" standing safe above the fray and observing all beneath is characteristically accurate for both Santayana and Lucretius as is their respect and piety toward nature and matter.[73] But life is perilous for the "accidental" man, and only in wisdom is one less vulnerable.

> But nothing is sweeter than to dwell in peace

> high in the well-walled temples of the wise,
> Whence looking down we may see other men
> wavering, wandering, seeking a way of life,
> ....
> O wretched minds of men, O poor blind hearts,
> how great the perils, how dark the night of life
> where our brief hour is spent![74]

In emotional withdrawal from the harshness of the world and their view of ethics, both Santayana and Lucretius are on similar ground. Santayana suggests that "materialism, like any system of natural philosophy carries with it no commandments and no advice."[75] The "living of life," following the focus on ontology rather than cosmology, is the focus of Santayana and Lucretius. The conquering of fear, pain and anxiety; attaining peace of mind; enjoyment of life; and happiness are the elements of grace.

SPINOZA AND THE MODERNS

I have intentionally emphasized above the profound influence of the Greeks on Santayana's thought because they are most foundational to Santayana's philosophy of religion. Again I plead for patience on behalf of the academic reader. The limitations of scope in this book do not permit an extensive analysis of all antecedent influences on Santayana but a brief integrative summary of the influence of Spinoza and selected modern philosophers, especially on Santayana's philosophy of religion, is necessary to provide an adequate basis to move forward. In this regard, Benedict de Spinoza (1632–1677) is of primary importance. His naturalistic philosophical theology both affirmed the lessons of the Greeks for Santayana and extended their scope particularly in a delineation of a naturalistic morality and piety. On the cusp of the Enlightenment and the Moderns' disposition toward psychology and the value of the *a posteriori* , Spinoza affirmed in retrospect for Santayana the validity of his naturalism, as Lucretius's ancient writings seemed to provide a mirror for his soul. In chapter 4 I will introduce a dialectic between Santayana and Spinoza based upon Santayana's essay "Ultimate Religion," given on the occasion of the tricentennial celebration of Spinoza's birth. In this section, I will only briefly touch on some philosophical and religious perspectives influencing Santayana which were generated over two hundred years, beginning with Spinoza's pantheistic monism, and extending through some key aspects of philosophical religious thought in Kant (1724–1804), Hegel (1770–1831) and Schopenhauer (1788–1860). I will take up the influence of William James in chapter 3 in relation to my argument for Santayana's phenomenological method.

Spinoza: The Withdrawal of a Personal God

Spinoza obviated the Cartesian dualism of body and mind and in his definitive pantheism eliminated the dualism between God and the world. God was congruent to nature (*Deus sive Natura*), hence a causality from outside the natural world was not a further consideration. A "personal" anthropomorphic God was lost in the process, but God was not dead, only depersonalized and indifferent to human needs and desires. This unreciprocating God, however, was still worthy of awe and wonder, pious reverence and even an "intellectual" love. As a consequence, good and evil are not external influences or powers, but rather such things that relatively either please and meet the desires of individuals, or not. Although Spinoza accorded humans the power of reason which they may direct at their preservation and happiness, the Cartesian element of "free will" was sacrificed to a deterministic vision in consequence of the human inability to be aware of causality.

Kant: A God of Morality and Humanity Existing Together in a Dream World

As the seminal German idealist subject to Santayana's scathing critique, Kant is more of a "target" than an influential example.[76] As a "particular" target held in a lifelong running dialectic with Santayana, there is value in considering some major contrasts. Kant's idealism, unlike Plato's, has less to complement it in relation to Santayana's philosophy of religion from a metaphysical standpoint; for example, for Kant, the *Ding an sich* (thing-in-itself) was not accessible to human reason, while for Santayana, "faith accumulates sufficient and trustworthy knowledge of things-in-themselves."[77] While Kant on one hand identifies nature as a "phenomenal order," Santayana assigns it to the Realm of Matter and phenomena to the Realm of Essence. Kant's conclusion through "pure reason" that God, freedom and immortality, as postulates of morality, necessarily exist, while he still disclaims a dualism (material and supernatural realms), rests upon his concept that reality, or an object of belief, is conceived of in the mind. From this we can see early on that little can be reconciled with Santayana's materialism and non-theistic naturalism. We will see as we proceed that Kant's divine source of morality and his teleological view is juxtaposed with Santayana's rejection of any knowledge of causality and his attribution of morality to the imagination of humankind. Although both Kant and Santayana deny the logic of the Cartesian *cogito*, Kant's unresolved mind-body duality can be held in contrast to Santayana's *epiphenomenal* construct.

Hegel: The God-Sanctioned Prussian State, and Man, Its Instrument

As in Kant and Spinoza, Hegel's philosophical project is dominated by a non-personal God of power personified in the sanctioned state as the arena for the individual to evolve toward "self-consciousness" of the Spirit, and over history, rising toward God. However, in Hegel, Santayana envisioned the individual as lost in the subgroupings of society and ultimately as a servant of the state, a "puppet" and "vehicle of divine decrees."[78] In spite of the invective substantially evident in his book, *Egotism in German Philosophy*, or in the essay "Apologia Pro Mente Sua," Santayana claimed singular inspiration from Hegel's *Phänomenologie des Geistes* for his *Life of Reason*, taking it as a model of the historical and evolutionary approach and admiring its departure from the quest in Western philosophy for arriving objectively at truth.[79] Despite this inspiration, Santayana felt that Hegel had erred in spoiling a fine subject (i.e., the history of human ideas) through sophistry and myth and regretted not "knitting his doctrine together" at the beginning of his career by writing "a critical thesis, say, on *Logic, Sophistry and Truth in Hegel's Philosophy*.[80] Levinson summarily captures Santayana's basic criticism of Hegel and the other nineteenth-century idealists as trying "to revive the corpse of supernaturalism" thereby "positively imped[ing] reasonable life."[81] For Hegel, this is the *Logos*, revealing itself in history and as both part of ("alienated in") and controlling nature—emerging through history in the cognitive and practical activity of the Spirit.[82] An objective consideration of the *Phänomenologie* raises remarkable similarities of intention with Santayana's *Life of Reason*. After all, Hegel's project is a phenomenology of consciousness from the lowest level through a dialectical progression upward to the ideal of becoming a vehicle of an infinite self-conscious Spirit.[83] Santayana's *Life of Reason* is also a history of consciousness from its incipient awareness of the "immediate" to its essentially moral progression to the harmony of a life of reason, which is ideally a spiritual union with the "Good."[84] Was Santayana's debt to Hegel understated? There is other evidence that bears witness to this possibility but is beyond the scope for discussion here. One example of such evidence, in my view, is the interesting parallel between Hegel's *Das Leben Jesu* (The Life of Jesus) and its depiction of Christ as a moral teacher only claiming to be a messenger from God in order to meet the expectations of his Jewish audience,[85] and Santayana's *The Idea of Christ in the Gospels*—both works humanizing Christ. In both, the theological images of the Christian story (e.g., the Trinity) are reflected in their philosophical depiction of salvation. In Hegel, of course, the German Protestant viewpoint of Christianity was high among the idealist sins for Santayana to anathematize.[86]

Schopenhauer: The Scuttling of Christianity

The line of Protestant Christian belief and attribution of being and existence to a supernatural teleology in German Idealism ended with Schopenhauer's total rejection of any monotheistic model. The "force" of the universe inclusive of all natural drives and interactions he attributed to the "Will," derived by Schopenhauer from the appropriate expression of a familiar anthropomorphic concept (i.e., the will to live or that of human volition).[87] Santayana's attraction to Schopenhauer began in his undergraduate days when his own dim view of the world at the time found company in Schopenhauer's profound pessimism. Schopenhauer's much acclaimed literary style for a philosopher, probably only comparable to the excellence of Santayana's own, also would have provided ample attraction. Schopenhauer considered his philosophy an extension of Kant's project, but held his contemporary Hegel and other German idealists not of his own ilk in considerable contempt for their optimism regarding humanity and the world.[88] He proposes a more pessimistic view that man's only reasonable escape or salvation from a futile life of suffering is to subjugate the Will, inclusive of striving, desire, assertion and conflict for a life of aesthetic contemplation and to become, at least in a transient way, a "disinterested observer."[89] The apex of Santayana's spirituality has a similar "ascetic" character, also contemplative in nature, and at the higher end of his ontology offers also a form of salvation still based upon reason. Of particular interest is a remarkable parallel between Schopenhauer's metaphysics of "presentation" and Santayana's concept of intuited *essences* and *animal faith*. The parallel could also be drawn with the phenomenological method of intuition of *essences* (e.g., in Husserl as discussed in chapter 3) and the descriptive dialectic carried out in the "natural state." This topic, which can be generically termed the illusory nature of experience and related to Schopenhauer's concept of World-as-Representation, cannot be pursued at length here except for a few comments below regarding Schopenhauer's differentiation of the concepts of *intuitive Vorstellungen* (intuitive presentations) and *abstrakte Vorstellungen* (abstract presentations).[90] In this concept, as with Santayana, the subject intuits the "essence," or in Schopenhauer's theory, the representation, and beyond this, arrives at an idea or perception of the intuition or representation. In this process, the subject resorts to reflection or abstract thought in order to describe the symbolic essence presented. This process in Schopenhauer's case is clearly derived from Kant's definition of the phenomenal world as the world of experience, and the unavailability of the *numena* or the *ding an sich*.[91] Although Santayana expresses favorable opinions and admits influence on him by Schopenhauer (certainly not the "representation" aspect of Schopenhauer's project), this relatively obvious similarity, to my knowledge, escapes written acknowledgment in Santayana's work. In consequence of the illusory nature of experience, both philosophers, not unexpectedly, share a view on the epistemic limitations of scientific inquiry. Much more could be said regarding the parallels and similarities between Schopenhauer's and Santayana's project, and they indeed should be given much more attention. Matthew Caleb Flamm in his paper "Santayana and Schopenhauer"[92] provides, with the exception of my above point on the similarities in Santayana's and Schopenhauer's phenomenology, a brief and informative perspective on this subject.

SANTAYANA'S NATURALISTIC PHILOSOPHY

Having set the stage with a view toward to Santayana's philosophical antecedents of influence, I will now examine Santayana's philosophy in terms of two general aspects: (1) the coherence of the logical process and pathway of his thought, and, finally, in a more abbreviated manner (2) the consequent objectives or "attitudes" regarding rational living arrived at and justified through the logical process of his thought. As a framework for understanding his philosophy, I will describe in the process the scope of the ontological field that circumscribes his project. This will be addressed under the form of his ontological categories, the Realms of Being, which are four and consist of *Essence, Matter, Truth* and *Spirit*.[93] The ancient Hellenic materialists—and in Santayana's case, as I commented above, Democritus was of primary importance—viewed mechanism as tantamount to explanation for a natural philosophy.[94] In other words, nature is what is going on. In the process of Santayana's logic, the "mechanism" of nature is apparent but assumed and does not necessitate for Santayana (e.g., as in Plato) a cosmological theory since he leaves to science to determine what it can. As he affirms, "I have been willing to let cosmological problems and technical questions solve themselves as they would or as the authorities agreed for the moment that they should be solved."[95] He further comments on his relegation of cosmology to science.

> But the cosmological problem is one of existence [which Santayana accepts as a "given" of unknown cause], of the source and conditions of all experience: so that if philosophy must leave that question to be solved by specialists, philosophy confesses, as I do, that only physics, not metaphysics and not "experience," must reveal the structure of the world to us, in so far as we can discover it.[96]

Based upon the principles derived from Santayana's project, actions and decisions taken upon different conditions and situations become characteristic of a life-pattern Santayana would call a "life of reason." In Santayana's case, as with his Greek antecedents, consistency is particularly important since he and they lay claims to be thoroughly consistent in life with their stated philosophical principles. Santayana criticizes all but absolute honesty in philosophy consistent with his uncompromising disposition. This is a vision directed at enhancement of individual human life and by deference to society, to life in general in the world. It remains, as Sprigge points out, that Santayana was not a social reformer but presenter of a system of values, relative though they may have been, that reflected the individual "heart's ideal." However, this ideal practiced in balance and harmony in society may consequently be the "highest good in an ideal society."[97] These principles for Santayana then constitute his "personal" dogma, a vision not at all based upon certainty and not imposed upon or even necessarily recommended to others. Similarly, Santayana says of logic that

> like language [it] is partly a free construction and partly a means of harnessing in expression the existing diversities of things; and whilst some languages, given a man's constitution and habits, may seem more beautiful and convenient for him than others, it is a foolish heat in a patriot to insist that only his native language is intelligible or right.[98]

As John Lachs suggests of Santayana, "There are few explicit arguments in his philosophical works," even though they are underlying and can be reconstructed. Nevertheless, "his philosophical system has a remarkable unity and coherence."[99] From this coherence, following a "logical" presentation of the process flow of his philosophical method, we will find that certain objectives can also be derived from his thought. However, consistent with Lachs's observation, since demonstration of truth is considered problematical in any case, the idea of demonstration based upon argument would be considered by Santayana as futile and was of no interest to him.

The two perspectives of "process," on one hand, and "objectives" or attributes on the other, will hopefully put Santayana's basic "technical" philosophy in proper logical perspective in order to move forward to his phenomenology and philosophy of religion. My intent is only to demonstrate particularly those integrative elements of his project that will pertain most obviously to his philosophy of religion. This contrivance is only to minimize any reiteration of previously published in-depth analysis of Santayana's philosophy and historical influences (e.g., in Sprigge, Lachs, Levinson, Woodward, Kerr-Lawson and others) that will not be essential for the reader to appreciate some coherence between his basic "technical" philosophy and his philosophy of religion.[100]

I will follow the sequence of the headings below in relating the logical order of Santayana's philosophical trajectory.

Realism and Materialism and Its Consequences
Scepticism as an Exercise, Not a Life
The Solipsism of the Present Moment and Knowledge of the "Immediate"
Animal Faith: A Path toward Belief and Action
Santayana's Ontological Categories: The Realms of Being
Essence in the Realms of Being: The Grammar of Nature
The Realm of Matter and the Assumption of Substance
The Realms of Truth and Spirit: Spirit Seeking the Eternal
Equality in Being: The Concept of Ontological Parity

Realism and Materialism and Its Consequences

At the very base of Santayana's philosophy is the pervading and governing element of materialism, a subscription to the concept of matter as the sole existent. At the same time, within Santayana's ontology, we find that existence is only one type of reality while reality is *being of any sort*.[101] There is no dualism in existence (as there may seem to be when we deal with his epistemology further on) and there is an explicit denial of spirits, divine beings and the supernatural in general. There is one cosmos extant, and it is nature on the level of matter. There is, however, as indicated above, an ontological distinction between matter and being, and this relates to Santayana's definition of substance. Sprigge suggests that for Santayana, something is substance on the basis of two conditions:

> If, first, it can exist with its own definite character without being thought about by, or revealed to the experience of any sentient being, and if secondly, when it is thought about it is external to the thought of it, in the sense that both object and thought could have had the same intrinsic character without the other existing . . . All belief is belief in substance.[102]

Belief in substance would, by this definition, include belief in matter and its forms, but not in intuitions, ideas, dreams or visions and other nonmaterial, nonexistents of the world. However, in *Realms of Being*, Santayana clearly states in the summary of the chapter "Presumable Properties" in the section "The Realm of Matter" that "the only object posited by animal faith is matter; and that all those images which in human experience may be names or signs for objects of belief are, in their ultimate signification, so many names or signs for matter."[103] However, these are signs given to intuited *essences*. For example, one can believe in gods, ghosts, goblins, trolls or hell, a dream or a vision, but in the end these beliefs revert to matter and the *essences* of troll, hell, and so forth, or *essences* of a "place" or thing believed in or imagined. Santayana affirms that "belief in memory is implicit,"[104] but this is believing in the fact of memory and, necessarily, not in its contents. So it would seem that one then can believe in intuition as well, and indeed Santayana proposes that this function also exists and, in fact, "intuition without memory must be assumed to have existed in the beginning before memory."[105] Hence, Santayana significantly has separated "function" as material, from the *essences*, or content (he disliked this static designation). Professor Lachs equivocates on this issue, suggesting that since intuition does not appear in nature, and is not a physical process, it may not be a subject for direct belief, but rather as "an indirect object of our animal trust."[106] This seems a very technical and non-practical distinction toward a systemic "fit" in an excessively labored interpretation of Santayana's meaning. I would suggest that intuition does exist as a function of the brain, or in Santayana's more integrative depiction, of the psyche, and is a sign for a physical process.

In tandem with the conviction of a one-level non-dualistic natural world is the concept of realism, a theory that the entities of matter in their various forms exist in time and space independent of any mind, consciousness or belief in their reality.[107] At first there seems to be an exception in Santayana's realism since intuitions, for example, exist in time and can be considered historical facts. However, again Santayana clears us of confusion and vulgar perceptions proposing that "they [intuitions] are not substances. Their substance is their organ in its movement and its changing tensions: it is the psyche."[108] This existence independent of mind is contrary to one precept of Idealism, which Santayana's contemporaries, realists, pragmatists and the budding positivists set themselves over against (i.e., that the existence of any object is entirely dependent upon perception by an animal consciousness).[109] Santayana's naturalism is further circumscribed by the concept that events in the world and causation of these events can only result from interactions of matter upon matter (i.e., of existents) occurring in time and space.[110] It is this concept of causality and existence we find to be explicitly derived from Santayana's particular type of *epiphenominalism*, mentioned in the previous section of this chapter. This is a challenging philosophical idea that surprisingly remains somewhat problematic and controversial today.[111] *Epiphenominalism* is the general theory according to which every occurrence of mind (consciousness) has a basis in, and is dependent upon, the neurobiology of the underlying organism. This word was never, to my knowledge, used by Santayana in reference to his own work but rather applied *eiusdem generis* by others. True to form, Santayana does not dally on the subject of causation. In regard to the derivation of human consciousness and the *causa fiendi* of immediate experience from an animal body, he considers it as a brute fact.[112]

Explicit in Santayana's viewpoint then is that only the material world exists independently of human awareness and consequently its reality does not depend in any way upon human existence or existence of any consciousness capable of awareness of the evidence of this world. Containing these principles is the enveloping concept of his brand of naturalism and his *animal faith* that only further extends matter to events involving interactions of matter in space and time but otherwise similarly rejects any entities beyond the scope of science. While we observe the many similarities of the tenets of Santayana's philosophy to that of the Greeks, we must nevertheless temper these parallels and apparent influences with his own caveat regarding the experiential personal origins of his thought:

> My naturalism or materialism is no academic opinion: it is not a survival of the alleged materialism of the nineteenth century, when all the

professors of philosophy were idealists: it is an everyday conviction which came to me, as it came to my father, from experience and observation of the world at large, and especially of my own feelings and passions.[113]

Scepticism as an Exercise, Not a Life

At first there seems to be irony in the perception of Santayana's skepticism since we have come to expect the paradoxical and ironic as a characteristic tone.[114] On one hand, he would claim that philosophy has been too preoccupied with the problems of skepticism and on the other chose to fall back upon a skeptical method in *Scepticism and Animal Faith* to develop his epistemological theory. Santayana was indeed a skeptic in method but not a skeptic in living, which he perceived to be virtually untenable, leaving one incapable of acting on belief alone — an unnatural state resulting in either solipsistic isolation or hypocrisy through violation of the skeptic's dogma. Significantly and fortunately, however, he then paused to consider how or if the thoroughgoing skeptic might live day-to-day in the world, having some access to knowledge and appropriate action. Could one usefully retain a thorough skepticism and yet complement this dogma with another more "common-sense" approach in the world? If not, Santayana would join earlier philosophers who, not being able to see past it, compromised in order to live day-to-day in the world. Santayana proposes,

> The brute necessity of believing something so long as life does not justify any belief in particular; nor does it assure me that not to live would not, for this reason, be far safer and saner. To be dead and have no opinions would certainly not be to discover the truth; but if all opinions are necessarily false, it would at least be not to sin against intellectual honor. Let me then push scepticism as far as I logically can, and endeavor to clear my mind of illusion, even at the price of intellectual suicide.[115]

And "push" it he did in the ultimate rigor of a skeptical process (i.e., where even the most irresistible and convincing belief must be subject to proof). One is led, if one is an "honest" skeptic, to the conclusion that "anything given in intuition is, by definition, an appearance and nothing but an appearance. Of course, if I am a thorough sceptic, I may discredit the existence of anything else, so that this appearance will stand in my philosophy as the only reality."[116] This ultimately leads to the question "Do I know, can I know, anything?"[117] Santayana then responds in what is the final step of the skeptical exercise proposing,

> It will lead me to deny existence in any datum, whatever it may be; and as the datum, by hypothesis [i.e., the sceptic's], is the whole of what solicits my attention at any moment, I shall deny the existence of every-

thing, and abolish the category of thought altogether. If I could not do this, I would be a tyro in scepticism.[118]

Ad extremum then all "change and memory and the reality of all facts," are denied for the thoroughgoing skeptic, and "the last thing he will see is himself."[119] Of particular significance for our consideration next is an instantaneous solipsistic state[120] that Santayana indicates is achieved by the skeptic in this process of epistemological inquiry. This state is the most "immediate" perception of consciousness and is important in Santayana's system as it sets the ground for epistemological limits and is the basis for his theory of *essences*. Further, it is a concept I consider to be foundational to his phenomenology, which I will discuss in chapter 3.

There is little question that this Cartesian modeled exercise has a twofold purpose for Santayana—that is, the anti-foundationalist obviation of the epistemological shortfall of the Cartesian process of skeptical reduction and dualistic model, and the extension of the method to the sole knowable discernment of *essence*.

The Solipsism of the Present Moment and Knowledge of the "Immediate"

The intellectual aspect of Santayana's rigorous skeptical process is validated by virtue of the honesty of the skeptic in arriving at the ultimate inability of apparently affirming no-thing as knowledge. As Santayana suggests above, if no honest opinions can be formed, there is surely no loss of intellectual honor. The next question is whether anything at all of value has been observed in the rigor of Santayana's skeptical methodology that can be brought forward other than a negation of all knowledge in the world. In this regard, the concept of solipsism, a condition of psychic isolation from the world wherein nothing can be known except the content of one's own consciousness, takes on surprising importance in Santayana's logical progression of thought. If through the skeptical process one can ultimately confirm nothing but knowledge of the "self," then one has reached the Cartesian state Santayana calls "romantic solipsism."[121] This condition is considered "logically contemptible" by Santayana but not necessarily self-contradictory "because all the complementary objects which might be requisite to give point and body to the idea of oneself might be only ideas and not facts; and [for example] a solitary deity imagining a world or remembering his own past constitutes a perfectly conceivable universe."[122] Santayana continues by suggesting that only through imagination could this hypothetical deity affirm the memories that would substantiate his belief in his existence. This would be a groundless dogma since although it may be true, the deity would have no basis for belief. The deity would have to confess "that his alleged past [which would confirm his existence] was merely a picture now before him, and that he would have no reason to suppose that this picture had any successive moments or that he had lived through the previous moments at all." [123] Here, Santayana has an anthropomorphic God caught up in the same "Catch-22" that humankind is in, not having access to a demonstrable truth. In the face of this severe critique, not only Descartes's *cogito* falls as it didn't go far enough, but also does any affirmation of awareness of knowledge by Montaigne (knowledge only through faith or revelation) and the extreme skepticism of Hume and any skeptic between the Greeks and Santayana.

Nothing, therefore, can be taken by the thoroughgoing skeptic on the basis of trust or faith. It is, however, in this critique, that a subtle distinction arises between *nihil scitur* (nothing is known) and *sciens nihil scitur* (knowing that nothing is known), the latter being consistent with the Socratic affirmation "All that I know is that I know nothing." [124] Thus Santayana proposes not that nothing can be known, but rather nothing can be known with certainty.

One step beyond the romantic skepticism that Santayana sees as untenable is that most radical step taken by the thoroughly honest skeptic: the position he calls *solipsism* of *the present moment* (*sopm*). [125] It is this difficult step that he suggests "probe[s] this confused and terrible apparition of life to the bottom"; and "since a perfect solipsist, therefore, is hardly found amongst men," this state is essentially ideal, and can possibly be achieved only by "a philosopher trained in abstraction or inclined to ecstasy." [126] This state, facetiously depicted by Santayana, is one that will leave the "tyro" of romantic skepticism behind and become of a significant phenomenological import in chapter 3. [127] In this ultimate state, all certifiable experience begins and ends for Santayana. At the same time, we gain an early insight into a possible association between a state of religious or mystical experience and that state of concentrated objectivity where a perceived object is raised to eminence by "lopping off everything else." Santayana suggests that depending upon the participant in such a state, what remains after such objective isolation may be perceived as Brahma, or Pure Being and Oneness, or the "Idea or Law of the moral world." [128] However, he has no patience for such extensions of experience and proposes that "the mystic must confess that he spends most of his life in the teeming valleys of illusion." [129] The mystic is like the romantic solipsist who "retain[s] his belief in his personal history and destiny . . . and [this] leads the mystic to retain, and fondly to embrace, the feeling of existence." [130] He proposes, then, that such hypostatization of this experience of the "absolute" object is specious, and that in such affirmations the skeptic departs from honesty and falls back upon a hopeful and self-serving "after-image" of uncertainty. [131] From Brentano and Husserl, we recognize the experience of the immediacy of a given moment, entailed in an act directed at an object prior to introspection and reflection upon the act, and grasped instantaneously and intuitively. [132] This then for Santayana is the only absolute presentation to animal-kind as he describes it as follows:

> Anything given in intuition is, by definition, an appearance and noth-
> ing but an appearance. Of course, if I am a thoroughgoing sceptic, I
> may discredit the existence of anything else, so that this appearance
> will stand in my philosophy as the only reality. But then I must not
> enlarge nor interpret nor hypostatize it: I must keep it as the mere
> picture it is, and revert to the solipsism of the present moment. [133]

We may recall here Lucretius's caution in not slipping into the "abyss of
scepticism" as we note the isolation of Santayana's certainty of *only* the
immediate. Santayana, in referring to the inexplicability of experience
itself, that extension or extrapolation beyond the *sopm*, suggests that "my
hold on existence is not so firm that nonexistence does not seem always at
hand . . . and more natural than existence." [134] In any case, we seem to
have reached an endpoint in Santayana's skeptical, reductive method. If
the only absolute knowledge is both of the moment and in the moment,
then past cannot rely absolutely on memory and the future can only be
guessed at; therefore, we can have no reliable certainty of change. He
reflects on his intuition of the fading and lapsing on either side of the
"instant," the *sopm* (we could say, in the time interval of a series of neuro-
synapses!) allowing the vastness of "these opposite abysses, the past and
the future," [135] that great reservoir of unknowness, only fully realized by
the thoroughgoing skeptic. For Santayana there can only be what he calls
"the spark itself as a point of departure": that is, that instantaneous experience of *sopm* and, after this, reflection and descriptive dialectic through
the imagination. [136] However, "to urge, therefore, that a self or ego is
presupposed in experience, or even must have created experience by its
absolute fiat, is curiously to fail in critical thinking, and to renounce the
transcendental method." [137] How then in such a predicament can the
skeptic live and operate in the world and achieve fulfillment and happiness having driven the exercise to the limit of the *sopm* with prospects for
only uncertainty and denial even of the self? Has the bottom line been
reached for the skeptic in a total state of *disillusion*? Yes, for in fact Santayana concludes that inclusive even of the *sopm*, "nothing given exists" for
the subject, and since the object of the *sopm*, that instantaneous intuition,
is *essence* and therefore does not exist, the derivative of the *sopm* (i.e.,
experience) is an illusion. [138]

Animal Faith: A Path toward Belief and Action

The bleak prospect of a practicing skepticism is life with everything
taken away and no path to belief. Lachs cleverly suggests that if skepticism has destroyed beliefs, then Santayana intends *animal faith* to "restore
them little by little." [139] If such thoroughgoing skepticism driven to the
ultimate of the *sopm* is essentially "honest" and irrefutable as Santayana
proclaims, then it cannot readily be cast aside and a new beginning made.
In the *epoché* of skepticism, "all of his [the skeptic's] heroic efforts are

concentrated on not asserting and not implying anything, but simply noticing what he finds." [140] Santayana's speculation that *sopm* may be the "experience" of many animals [141] is helpful in gaining an understanding of the concept, since one can readily appreciate that most lower mammals or animals in general other than humans are likely not to be consciously capable of reflection or anticipation or true memory beyond reflex or instinct and therefore truly respond to the *immediate*. In skeptics, as in lower animals that act only on instinct, there are no conscious doubts since nothing is believed! At this level of immediate intuition, there seems to be an uncanny common ground among all conscious life. It seems then, for the skeptic, all that can be expressed is personal "feeling" because "anything given in intuition is, by definition, an appearance," and only this appearance is the reality. [142] Santayana especially focuses his logic and skeptical method upon the impossibility of ascertaining "change" despite the "feeling of movement on which you so trustfully rely." [143] As we follow his thought to this point, we can readily appreciate that he is justified in proposing that "there is no avenue to the past or future, there is no room or breath for progressive life, except through faith in the intellect and in the reality of things unseen." [144] Impressions occur as instantaneous "still shots," and the sense of "flux" and then change can only be intuited and remains always illusory. [145] From this we might anticipate Santayana preparing for a contradictory transcendental "leap of faith" from the dead-ended intellect in the manner of Kierkegaard, or resorting to the transcendental investigations of William James into the world of the "unseen." Rather, for Santayana, it is the reality of the natural world only attained through perception of sign and symbol that is truly "unseen," but the desire for a "progressive life" necessitates that we interpret these perceptions as reflecting, at least in part, real objects in the world. It is at this juncture that Santayana moves from the solipsism of the skeptic into a practical and productive life through attainment of faith and belief as a basis for action. This vehicle of consciousness to the world then, is what Santayana calls *animal faith*.

> The object of this faith is the substantial and energetic thing encountered in action, whatever this thing may be in itself; by moving, devouring, or transforming this thing, I assure myself of its existence; and at the same time my respect for it becomes enlightened and proportionate to its definite powers. [146]

In the final chapter of *Scepticism and Animal Faith*, Santayana scolds Hume and Kant, "skeptics in their day," at great length along many lines regarding their deconstructionist projects which "made no attempt to build on the foundations so laid bare." Especially Hume had dug himself into the vacuum of skepticism, an untenable life, and left it there out of touch with natural objects and experience in the world. This "limping skepticism" for both Hume and Kant left any access to knowledge impossible and entailed a bipartite life between their skeptical convictions and their normal intercourse with the world. The bleak outlook of liberal Protestantism again takes the blame for Kant and Hume's "retrenchment" into an unlivable philosophy. For Santayana, the skepticism of both Hume and Kant stands arrested in this deconstructed epistemological dead-end and "never touched bottom."

Animal Faith concerns itself with the existence of things as does skepticism but the skeptic has no recourse to this realm since he has come to doubt or deny it.[147] The concept of "animal" has deeper connotations than may be obvious and suggests, in itself, action and seeking. There is a conscious intent in animality to seek out knowledge and opportunity in the existing world. Santayana is deliberate in defining "existence" as only "those facts or events believed to occur in nature," and further, that these, in addition to physical things and events, are inclusive of "intuitions themselves, or instances of consciousness, like pains and pleasures, and all remembered experiences and mental discourse."[148] We are left, however, without "direct" access to existing objects and events, and only with "indirect" perceptions in the form of symbols (*essences*), or as Hodges and Lachs remind us, of Santayana's conclusion that "nothing given [as the perception] exists, and nothing existent is ever given."[149] Belief or faith, then, attained through perceptions of signs and symbols of the world, is the only manner in which we can approach knowledge of real objects. If skepticism is rejected as untenable, but the truth of the *sopm* remains, then Santayana must reject absolute certainty as a standard of cognition. In the manner of an empirical approach, if we are honest in a life of reason, we come to belief only through an enactment or "testing" of our perceptions through action and finding them to be implicated in our life, that is, as more or less true, in the manner we perceived them. The example is given by Hodges and Lachs, that "when we jump out of the way of a car speeding toward us, we testify to our true belief that independently existing things enjoy causal powers."[150] In this "shrewd orthodoxy which the sentiment and practice of laymen maintain everywhere,"[151] we sense the Pragmatic Peircean notion of habit formation and belief as the precursor to action and the path to degrees of knowledge.[152] The point of separation between Santayana and the Pragmatists, however, relates to the "more or less hazardous views about truth" where "an idea is true so long as it is believed to be true," or if it has value.[153] Truth for Santayana, just as for Aristotle, is beyond opinion or utility, and "therefore, is as irrelevant to dialectic as to merely aesthetic intuition."[154]

Animal Faith is our only avenue to science, art and our sociopolitical environment, and the apparently repeating pattern characterizing events in nature which Santayana termed *tropes*, that cause us first expectation and then transition to belief or "laws," are our best approximation of truth.[155] Surely it is possible to "know" the truth of a thing, but there is no way to ascertain it. Truth is real, but nonexistent, while also, "truth is dateless and eternal, but not timeless, because, being descriptive of existence, it is a picture of change. It is therefore frozen in history."[156] Moreover,

> possession of Absolute Truth is not merely by accident beyond the range of particular minds; it is incompatible with being alive, because it excludes any particular station, organ, interest, or date of survey: the absolute truth is undiscoverable just because it is not a perspective. Perspectives are essential to animal apprehension.[157]

SANTAYANA'S ONTOLOGICAL CATEGORIES: THE REALMS OF BEING

One can hardly better and more concisely explain Santayana's concept of his categorical ontological framework than the philosopher himself.

> My system . . . is no system of the universe. The Realms of Being . . . are not parts of a cosmos, nor one great cosmos together; they are only kinds or categories of things which I find conspicuously different and worth distinguishing, at least in my own thoughts. I do not know how many things in the universe at large may fall under each of these classes, nor what other Realms of Being may not exist, to which I have no approach or which I have not happened to distinguish in my personal observation of the world.[158]

In this short paragraph we can surmise much of his philosophical perspective. He is no scientific cosmologist and only makes claims for his own perspective, his personal vision of Being, depicted in the four ontological realms of *Essence, Matter, Truth* and *Spirit,* leaving others to find more or different ontological categories if they can. The stage was set for the *Realms of Being* in *Scepticism and Animal Faith* (1923) with the derivation of *Essence* which is that infinite realm of character defining qualities applying to all the other Realms of Being. Hence, at the outset, there is a certain foundational or primary character to *essences* which in fact define character itself. There is an epistemological modesty, clearly derived from Santayana's claims we have discussed above, regarding our inability as humans to ascertain truth in the world. At the same time our destiny for self-fulfillment is to respond with faith and courage to the idea that we can attain through *animal faith,* at least to some extent, the truth of the world but simply can't ascertain it. Santayana does not profess to know what matter is in itself, and waits for science to determine this. However, he bridges the unknowable by an operating *common sense* applied to the natural world. Although he cannot have immediate access to the nature of matter, he responds in confidence to the accessible symbolic environment of *essences,* and "call[s] it matter boldly, as I call my acquaintances Smith and Jones without knowing their secrets: whatever it may be, it must present the aspects and undergo the motions of the gross objects that fill the world." He modestly suggests that if this is metaphysics, "then the kitchen-maid is a metaphysician whenever she peels a potato."[159] It is then, acting in common sense, that all humans reach out for knowledge of the world in the universal heuristic mode of *animal faith*, a natural seeking for the nature of reality.

Essence in the Realms of Being: The Grammar of Nature

If the object is not directly given to perception, and *animal faith* is the conscious mode of operating in the world, what then do we perceive as "given to us" so we can interact with our environment? Santayana's mature epistemological writings are addressed, within the existing theme of his naturalistic philosophy, to an elaboration of "the analysis of perception, of belief, and of ideas in general."[160] As early as in *The Life of Reason*, Santayana designated "concretions in discourse and in existence" as "the first objects discriminated in attention and projected against the background of consciousness."[161] The association of the early term "concretion" as a progenitive term for *essences* has been made by Sprigge and others.[162] Eighteen years after *The Life of Reason*, as indicated earlier, Santayana derived his concept of *essence* in *Scepticism and Animal Faith*. In 1927 he published the first volume of four, *The Realm of Essence*, a realm solely consisting of the eternal elements of pure Being.[163] In this first volume Santayana rigorously extended his theory of *essences*, the essential grammatical vehicles for his naturalistic-ontological project and proclaimed that the objective in this later elaboration was to "reduce evidence to the actually evident, and to relegate all the rest to hypothesis, presumption, and animal faith."[164] I find this particular statement a remarkably concise format of his epistemological project and objective. (In chapter 3, we will see the close parallel of Santayana's objective to reduce "evidence" to the "evident" with Husserl's phenomenological method.) The realms are the manifestation of this objective, and are identified by Santayana as summary categories of logical process through which only the "evidence" is considered in reflection.[165] Santayana's *essences*, he indicates, are those myriad and eternal "ghosts," as he referred to them, which ironically "are the only realities we ever actually can find."[166] These "ghosts" then are the datum of reality. To return to the concept of a life of reason, Santayana would undoubtedly claim that such a life could be led through an understanding of the realms, and the logical process therein.

In the process of arriving at the theory of *essences*, he proposed that there are three ways in which a skeptic can dispel the fear in illusion. First, in death all illusion would vanish forever. A second option is to find a substitute belief for skepticism, but having arrived at it honestly, one cannot honestly reject it so easily without resorting to a new unsubstantiated dogma. And then, finally, a third option:

> The third way . . . is to entertain the *illusion* without succumbing to it, accepting it openly as an *illusion*, and then forbidding it to claim any sort of being but that which it obviously has; and then, whether it profits me or not, it will not deceive me. *What will remain of this deceptive illusion will then be a truth,* and a truth the being of which requires no explanation, since it is utterly impossible that it should have been otherwise.[167]

We can note that this element of illusion (i.e., what is given to us and what we perceive) has been attributed to both being and truth by the philosopher. However, paradoxically, *essences*, although true and real as beings, do not exist. Santayana's doctrine of *essences* is critical to an integrated understanding of his project. Further, it is the language of the Realm of the Spirit, and the "key" to his phenomenology and philosophy of religion. One perspective relating *essence* intuited to an event in space and time is given early in Santayana's preface to *Realms of Being*.

> Different observers may be addressed to different regions of nature, or sensitive to different elements in the same region . . . each responding to a different constituent of the total event [e.g., an eclipse] and not simultaneously. So an eclipse may be known in various entirely different terms. *All these indications are entirely inadequate to the facts they reveal in the realm of matter, and qualitatively unlike these facts; they are a set of variegated symbols by which sensitive animals may designate them.*[168]

We see here the qualitative nature of *essences* revealing imperfectly to us the Realm of Matter, in the above case, an event. We also note the symbolic nature of *essences*, and since they are symbols of communication of the natural world to the animal mind, *essences* are therefore, as indicated above, the grammar of a universal language.[169] We can also deduce from this, although Santayana states it clearly many times, that no two symbols are alike, therefore no two essences are either. "Determination, individuality, variety infinitely precise and indelible (degrees of articulation being themselves all equally distinct) is the very being of essence."[170] We can emphasize here that "indelible" means not transmutable, therefore an *essence* may supplant another one in qualifying an intuition, but no *essence* will turn into another one. Any slightest degree of difference entails an altogether different *essence*.

> The terms in which they [observers] describe things, unlike the things they meant to describe, *are purely specious, arbitrary and ideal; whether visual, tactile, auditory or conceptual their terms are essentially "words"* . . . All possible terms in mental discourse are *essences existing nowhere.*[171]

Here Santayana characterizes the ideal nature of *essences* and their various sensuous or cognitive forms that they do not exist. The paradoxical aspect of this notion is that *essences* as symbols representing facts, are neither fact nor true! Only the fact of their reality is true.

> Such diversity in animal experience taken in itself exhibits sundry forms of being, a part of the infinite multitude of distinguishable ideal terms which (*whether revealed to anybody or not*) I call the *"Realm of Essence."* Pure intuition, in its poetic ecstasy, would simply drink in such of these essences as happened to present themselves; but for a wakeful animal they are signals [or symbols]. They report to his [the subject's] spirit, in very summary and uncertain images, the material events which surround him and which concern his welfare. *They may accordingly become terms in knowledge if interpreted judiciously, and if interpreted injudiciously they may become illusions.*[172]

Finally, Santayana indicates above that the *essences*, infinite in number (and therefore since they don't exist, they are eternal, i.e., beyond time), are the constituent symbols of the Realm of Being, and are subject to interpretation by the observer. Further, as eternal and beyond time, they exist as possibilities, even if not manifested yet in space and time, to someone attempting to gain an impression of an object. In all cases it is the observer's intuition that captures *essences* as they present themselves. Sprigge emphasizes the eternal character of *essence* by using the example of a rose and its inevitable destruction compared with its scent, an olfactory *essence*, which might be absorbed in its identical quality by a consciousness millions of years hence.[173] It also becomes clear that *essences*, as ideals or universals, may be given to multiple consciousnesses, simultaneously.

We recall that "existence" for Santayana pertains only to facts or events believed to occur in nature which do include, besides matter, intuitions. It is through intuition, however, that we attain the nonexistent *essences* as qualities (e.g., red, tall, round), but the *essences* are gathered as part of the total existing organic complex called the intuition. In any existent, *essence* cannot be individuated as existing apart from the intuition which it qualifies (i.e., if it were separable it would not exist). This is a technical point and even somewhat obscure, made here only to clarify that *essences* do not "exist" in intuitions but are part and parcel to the intuition itself just as they are to any object or event in the Realm of Matter or of Spirit. Santayana proposes that in the case of Substance (see below) "it lends existence to certain eternal *essences*, and enables them to figure in the flux of events."[174]

The Realm of Matter and the Assumption of Substance

Santayana's metaphysics underlying the definition of matter and substance can be, in my view, an obscure differentiation. For that reason, I will take the space to deal with this topic particularly because it bears substantially, and even foundationally, on his philosophy of religion.[175] I am in accord with Lachs in the opinion that Santayana, by his sometimes apparently synonymous use of the designations "substance and matter" in *Realms of Being*, and earlier in *Scepticism and Animal Faith*, is the major cause of the confusion.[176] On the other hand, there are blatant clues, even direct defining statements, that obviate any sense of identity between the two terms. I will return to this important topic further on. It is interesting that in the context of his treatment of Matter and Substance, Santayana broaches the concept of a personal cosmology for what is the first and last time in *Realms of Being*. If nonexistent *essences*, as Santayana's grammar of being, are to provide our presumed (not certain) vehicle of interface with the natural world, this interface is presumed to be with the Realm of Matter. Therefore, communication with the existing world can only be with that aspect of it that can have, if you will, in Aristotle's definition, form and substance. In Santayana's scheme, this is "essence and matter," or that which only in the existing world can "give essence" to the observer. Here it may be useful to note that when Santayana suggests that "no thing is given," he means no existent, but rather, in its stead a non-thing, an *essence*, and it is given as a symbol. In our response to these symbols, why would we presume that there is anything "out there" to symbolize? It is in response to this question that we arrive at the concept of *substance* which we will discover is the basis for Santayana's materialism as well as the basis for *animal faith*. The category of Substance for Santayana relative to Matter seems at first a subtle distinction, and one, surprisingly enough, that turns out to be possibly closer to the *naive* concept of Matter than Santayana's concept of Matter itself. Lachs provides us a cogent differentiation between Substance and Matter: All Substance is material and is, for both Santayana and Aristotle, made up of form or *essence* that is exemplified in matter, while matter is an ontological category and a "necessary ingredient in the fully developed notion of substance."[177] This suggests, as I imply above, that Matter is a *condition* for Substance as well as being a condition for other existents. Santayana puts us further on track by indicating that "the postulate of substance—the assumption that there are things and events prior to discovery of them and independent of this discovery—underlies all natural knowledge."[178] Substance, then, is what we would normally think of as the material world, external to the thought which posits it, and it has "parts" and exists in time and space. Therefore, since Substance would include "all out there," even beyond our experience, Santayana puts it in the category of "*a relative cosmos*" and further, proposes that "substance is posited, and not given in intuition, as *essences* may be given," and again, "*substance is external to the thought which posits it.*"[179] In other words, Substance is *posited*, but not known, to be included in the Realm of Matter (which one must claim according to Santayana, is also posited) and is posited as subject to the conditions of Matter. The nature of Matter cannot be "known" and Santayana, in *Realms of Being* suggests that it is a "metaphor" in its symbolic representation of an unknown. Indeed, it is in the field of action in nature—and it is indeed, as Substance, made up of elements in the Periodic Table and falls, as Santayana suggests, in the province of physics.[180] Substance has parts and constitutes a physical place, and Substance is in flux and exists in physical time.[181] Professor Lachs summarizes the concept nicely: "Substances are existing things, and substance is the sum of all existents."[182] It is this position that constitutes Santayana's materialism (belief in nature, independent of a subject's mind) and without such an assumption (belief) "an intelligent creature cannot honestly act or think."[183] "Then, the mind engaged in action may begin to live by faith in the outlying conditions of life, and by an instinctive tension towards obscure events."[184] It is on this basis that *animal faith* can be exercised with confidence in establishing justifiable beliefs of the real world.

Returning to the subject of Matter, it is helpful to take careful note of Santayana's statement in the preface to *The Realm of Matter* that "matter . . . is the principle of existence: it is all things in their potentiality and therefore the condition of all their excellence or possible perfection."[185] That is to say, if all *essences*, as possibilities, were to be realized into existence, this would be the condition of their perfection (there is an uncanny resemblance of this perfection in existence to Anselm's logic in his ontological proof of God). Also, if as Santayana proposes, "the Realm of Matter is the matrix and source of everything," then "matter" must include not only material things of the world such as rocks, minerals, tables, but also intuitions and cognitive manifestations or "acts of synthesis" that are not composed of atoms in the Periodic Table but are historical facts and occur in time.[186] In any case, "the realm of matter, then, from the point of view of our discovery of it, is the field of action: it is essentially dynamic and not pictorial . . . [it] is the matrix and the source of everything."[187] Then follows an important inclusion that "in reality, the realm of matter contains more than half of that which from the dawn of life has been the object of human religion: it contains "the gods or the veritable influences represented by their names and conciliated by the worship of them" (e.g., hell and heaven).[188] Here, one may interpret Santayana to mean that these images or symbols have arisen from those natural things in the world (e.g., mysterious storms, deaths of animals and people, eclipses of the moon) and are manifestations of these natural phenomena. An alternative interpretation may be that all of these religious images were *attributed* existence and therefore hypothetically existed in the realm of Matter where they were worshipped as such. I would lean toward the latter interpretation or both together, wherein the real event originated the myth and the aspects of the myth were attributed existence.

I am indebted to Lachs for his rigorous treatment of that aspect of Matter that clearly differentiates it from Substance and delineates the "conditional" aspect of Matter that seemed apparent to me in the preface to *The Realm of Matter*. It is sufficient for our purposes here to fall back on Lachs's summary definition which I concur with.

> Matter adds nothing to the essence it embodies except this embodiment itself. It is a featureless, faceless force; having no qualities or nature, it is a sheer status of existence . . . It is simply a necessary condition of there being any existents at all, where the other necessary condition is the realm of essence.[189]

The Realms of Truth and Spirit: Spirit Seeking the Eternal

The Realm of Truth and the Realm of Essence share both eternal being (i.e., a reality, and nonexistence). The Realm of Spirit, however, which consists of intuitions (not the function of intuition but the intuition itself) or conscious imaginative acts, is an existent but immaterial Realm.

> Let us admit that something called spirit exists, and exists invisibly, in a manner of its own, by virtue of an intrinsic moral intensity. Its essence lies in willing, suffering, looking, being pleased, absorbed or offended . . . It remains spirit throughout, not only in its specific character of witness and living light, but in its capacity for recollecting and prefiguring its experience.[190]

However, consistent with Santayana's epiphenomenal theory, Spirit is a first derivative or, in Aristotle's terminology, an entelechy of the biological organism. The Realms of Matter and Spirit thus are existential Realms, and the Realm of Truth and the Realm of Essence are realms of qualitative and characterizing realities manifested as symbols. The Realm of Spirit is essentially mind (not Santayana's preferred term since "the notion of mind has become confused and treacherous!") or consciousness or, metaphorically, "that light of actuality or attention which floods all life as men actually live it on earth."[191] It is, therefore, a manifestation, or better, a creation of the organism. Santayana takes particular pains in *Realms of Being* to define precisely what he means by his unconventional usage of psyche (i.e., as that "self-maintaining and reproducing pattern or structure of an organism, conceived as a power").[192] Therefore, the psyche is physical and constitutes the total functional and reproductive "dynamic" of an organism, that movement or power driving those tropes, or repeating process patterns, that sustain the existence of the organism. Of particular importance is the fact that each psyche is very individualistic and definitive, "a specific form of animal life"[193] reflecting the organism's hereditary and acquired capabilities and individual nature. Although Spirit is the neurological manifestation of the organism, there is still no dualism here unless it relates to efficacy of body and essential non-efficacy of Spirit. The Spirit is no ghostly transcendence from the material world, but is still not in the Realm of Matter where all interactions occur and where power is manifested in events. Lachs suggests that Spirit "yearns for efficacy and suffers the pain of its vulnerable state."[194] It is in the yearning for efficacy that we arrive at a point of considerable scholarly controversy. Since all power and efficacy in Santayana's natural world must arise from the Realm of Matter (i.e., from existents), then spirit is not capable of effect. It has no power to move the world of natural objects. Does Santayana mean by this that "ideas" have no power to impact the world; that ideas are not where great inventions, movements, wars or social schemes arise? Evidently he does and this is implicit in his *epiphenominalism*, which honors the biological source of the human function of the *psyche*, and the unexplainable power of material substance behind it. The arguments pro and con (i.e., that of "mind" as a causative agent versus the notion of epiphenominalism) are again particularly well explored by Lachs.[195] Thorough exploration of this topic is beyond the scope of this book, although to briefly state Santayana's rationale for his position is helpful.

I have indicated that as a materialist with an epiphenomenal viewpoint, Santayana affirms that action in nature can only occur through the natural force inherent in material objects. The intentional force behind animal or human action, the volition or will to do something would seem by many to come from the idea itself (i.e., the motivation). However, Santayana would insist that the force or volition derives from the underlying physical organ of the brain and neurological system as a response to the environment, and the act itself is implemented through the body (i.e., hands for writing, drawing or striking, voice for verbal communication, and so forth). If mind is dependent upon body, and not vice versa, then the logic behind the epiphenomenal claim is consistent with his theory. Santayana's materialistic theorem is simply that spirit is an entelechy of the underlying substance, or a "perfection of function realized" or in parody of Aristotle, "If a candle were a living being, wax would be its substance and the light its spirit."[196] This notion, as in Heidegger's projected biological lifespan for *Dasein*, apparently circumscribes our opportunities to this natural world. The Realm of Spirit may reach for the ideal and eternal, but the vehicle by which the Realm is attained is mortal, existing in time and space as the material organism.

The immediate objects of the spirit, either in the natural rhythm of daily life or in the more disciplined state of contemplation, are the eternal *essences*, realized in intuitions. As we have noted, the Realm of the Spirit is a realm of intuitions. However, the reality which is sought, that which the intentional effort is directed at—is the *truth*. We do not seek out untruth or lies unless they be the *truth* of the fact of the untruth we seek. *Truth* is a quality of the world which is characteristic of that condition in which an *essence* (or *essences*) is totally in congruence with the fact of an existing object in the world. If we have awareness of this truth, it is called knowledge. In Santayana's ontological scheme, *truth* is an *essence*, a quality of a fact, descriptive of those events or objects in historical space and time,[197] and therefore it is eternal but nonexistent. However, because of the special nature of *truth* as *essence*, Santayana categorizes it for attention in a Realm of Truth rather than in the Realm of Essence.

For Santayana, *truth* is used in the sense "which the word bears in ordinary conversation; and such refinements as I may be led to suggest are not calculated to subvert the plain signification of the word."[198] Santayana's brief but provocative definition of *truth* in the terms of his system (i.e., "Truth is the complete ideal description of existence") suggests the apparent identical character of truth and *essence*.[199] As idealism waned in the late nineteenth century, the assumption of supernatural teleological powers diminished, and in the fray was left the residue of two millenniums of Christian thought as fodder for a new language of naturalism. Santayana begins *The Realm of Truth* with an emphatic rejection of Idealism's various "necessary truths." He bases this upon his principle of the infinite possibilities offered for actualization in the world by the variety of *essences*, and the statistical consequence of total contingency.

> So that truth being descriptive of existence and existence being contingent, truth will be contingent also"[200] . . . Are there no truths obviously necessary to common sense? If I have mislaid my keys, *mustn't* they be somewhere? . . . The necessity asserted foolishly parades the helplessness of the mind to imagine anything different. Yet this helplessness on which dogmatism rests, is shameful, and is secretly felt to be shameful. Spirit was born precisely to escape such limitations, to see the contingency and finitude of every fact in its true setting. Truth is groped after, not imposed by presumptions of the intellect.[201]

This then is an uncompromising logical proposition that underlies Santayana's naturalism and philosophy of religion in the light of his grammar of *essences*. If the Realm of Truth provides no necessary truths, then, in fact, Santayana has disclaimed any justification for the traditional quest for metaphysical disclosure.[202] By the *truth*, Santayana means a complete ideal description of existence, eternal, and given in the language of *essences*, infinite, omnimodal and totally enveloping. Since *truth* then is contingent, one cannot be certain of it, consistent with my earlier discussion of the residuum of Santayana's reductive exercise in *Scepticism and Animal faith*. Ultimately, then, *truth*, in Santayana's epistemological philosophy, is an identity between knowledge and object, or "the identity of a fact asserted and the fact existing."[203] Consequently, the Realm of Truth has great significance, as we will find in Santayana's philosophy of religion, in that it is a total repository or inventory of all *essences* that have been or ever will be instantiated by matter. In the case of humans, attainment of *truth* can only be rough, approximate, short of complete—and one then can act only on these approximations through the "leap" of animal faith. Ultimately, Santayana suggests, "our knowledge is but faith moving in the dark."[204]

We briefly contrasted earlier the value-based *caveat* regarding truth of James, Peirce and the Pragmatic school with the uncompromising ideal of absolute truth identified with the Platonic school and Santayana. Moreover, the concept of Absolute Truth, consistent with Santayana's position, "is not merely by accident beyond the range of particular minds."

> It is incompatible with being alive, because it excludes any particular station, organ, interest, or date of survey: the absolute truth is undiscoverable just because it is not a perspective. Perspectives are essential to animal apprehension.[205]

Santayana is uncompromising in upholding his epistemological limits as one is guided by his admonition that "we are in the region of free intuition and construction, as in music, with no claims to propounding a revealed or revealing truth."[206] For Santayana, not inconsistent with the Pragmatist line, for example, Rorty, James, and the later Wittgenstein, where there is no obsession with a single criteria of truth, the element of subjectivity is introduced in the form of belief.[207] Animal faith, implying action based on faith, must ride on the heels of the act of believing. Peirce asserts that the scientific method (which Santayana believed in but left to the scientists) represents a "self-corrective," rather than a building-block model, of knowledge. Outside of science, and the partial truths or theoretical knowledge derived from the method, the pragmatic residue of an individual's experience bridges the gap through "common sense" knowledge. The inaccessibility of absolute truth in the general course of pragmatic thought is reflected in Santayana's assertion that "mind was not created for the purpose of discovering the absolute truth."[208]

Equality in Being: The Concept of Ontological Parity

In the logical spheres of Santayana's Realms of Being, the scope of being and existence is spread before us. Three of the four Realms are nonmaterial (i.e., those of Essence, Truth and Spirit); and two of the Realms, Essence and Truth, are nonexistential.[209] However, since all Realms represent an entire ontology, all forms of being are represented with no presumed "overlap." In Santayana's ontology, neither existence nor materiality influence the "degree" of being; therefore none are privileged and the concept of ontological parity prevails. Given Santayana's poetic disposition, it is interesting that Buchler suggests that "the poet's attitude is an acceptance of ontological parity" (i.e., poetic query insists that any trait discriminated is as real as any other).[210] This is consistent with Santayana's theory of *essences*, in which it is given that pure Being "appears alone to the human intellect in its ultimate reaches; and even when not realized separately in intuition, it can be discerned both analytically and intuitively in every *essence* whatsoever."[211] If all things, then, and all their external relations, are reduced to their internal being (i.e., their *essences*), they are transported into a realm of being which is necessarily eternal. The existent (matter) then becomes continuous with the nonexistent (*essence*) and "neither [is] more or less real than any other eternal essence."[212] Ultimately then, we can conclude that ontological parity is clearly and logically present in Santayana's project:

> Pure Being excludes particular determinations within its own bosom, but it does not annul them in the world, because it is not on the plane of existence at all[213] . . . It is perfectly possible for anyone who will consider the realms of being together, to honor each in its place and to disregard the scorn which those who have eyes for one only must needs pour upon the others."[214]

This concept of ontological parity connotes a respect for freedom and all aspects of being, and has probable spiritual and moral consequences for Santayana's attitude toward not privileging one particular individual's position or ideal over another. Therefore, it has important bearing on his view of religious claims for the absolute, the singular truth of dogmas, persecution or damnation of "non-believers" and other consequences of the exclusivity of theological claims.

SOME CONCLUSIONS

We have then, a conception of Santayana's logically conceived "technical" philosophy and can conclude this chapter with a brief summary consideration of some resultants of his materialistic vision that bear upon his philosophy of religion. As we take leave of his technical metaphysics it is helpful to be reminded of his claim, "My philosophy is like that of the ancients, a discipline of the mind and heart, a lay religion."[215]

In summary, products of consciousness, that is, intuitions of *essences*, perceptions and concepts, are powerless as movers in the material world. Any adage regarding "the power of the human mind" can only pertain for Santayana to that world of imagination that arises from the organic psyche, and serves the individual's transcendent world. There is no concession to contemplating cosmological issues in Santayana's thought. Yes, there are cosmological "truths" and even absolute "truths," but they are, given Santayana's rigorous materialism, *ipso facto*, beyond the reach of humans' certain understanding. Santayana's Realms of Being are ontological categories which seem to him as "conspicuously different," but *"no system of the universe."*[216] Given that Santayana's naturalism characteristically affirms the materialistic realm as the only "field of action," the only vehicle for human transcendence and spiritual life remains consciousness, and that consciousness is an *epiphenomenon*, whose sentient tenure is terminated by the death of the organism. Epistemological limitations govern the limitations on certified knowledge and consequently the ascertainment of universal or simple absolutes. The equality of all that is being *qua* being in Santayana's Realms is evident and each is honored in its place. This viewpoint of ontological parity extends even to Santayana's moral philosophy—for example, in the admonition against "scorn which those who have eyes for one only must needs pour upon the others."[217]

If there is only one world that is the natural world and "only one truth about it," then a spiritual life is contained within it and "looks not at another world but to the beauty and perfection that this world suggests, approaches and misses."[218] Spiritual life is therefore directed at the "ideal," and Santayana's scheme of the *Realms of Being*, involved in the totality of nature, contains both the possibilities of the ideal in *essences* and their ultimate realization in Matter to form the Substance of the world. In the path of history, and the striving to obtain knowledge of the world, certain beliefs have been brought to bear in experience, generating a certain orthodoxy of belief and practice, traditions and a commonsense approach to a fulfilling life. Appropriate symbols of human experience and ideals have been utilized linguistically in the analogical use by Santayana of Christian theology to unfold his naturalistic ontology.[219] Given the uncertainty of all knowledge in general, this common sense, arrived at over time through experience, must be respected. In all of this "unknownness" must be one's acceptance of a stark and bereft material world seemingly in a flux of contingency. In this predicament, courage rather than melancholy and despair is possible through a spiritual life which is an explicit aspect of and "concomitant" with a life of reason.

> The good, as I conceive it, is happiness, happiness for each man after his own heart, and for each hour according to its inspiration. I should dread to transplant my happiness into other people; it may die in that soil; and my critics are the first to tell me that my sort of happiness is a poor thing in their estimation. Well and good. I congratulate them on their true loves . . . [for] No man can set up an ideal for another.[220]

NOTES

1. Timothy Sprigge suggests that "one can seldom find a single place where all the essential features of his treatment of some single issue are gathered together. His best remarks on a topic are often found in a chapter, or in a book dealing, on the face of it, with some quite other matter." Timothy Sprigge, *Santayana: An Examination of His Philosophy* (London: Routledge & Kegan Paul, 1974), 3.

2. Justus Buchler, "One Santayana or Two?" *Journal of Philosophy* 51 (January 1954): 52–54. Buchler draws parallels between Santayana's early and later works (e.g., between *Reason and Common Sense* and *Scepticism and Animal Faith*), proposing that "even the manner and terms of the later book are to be found in the earlier (54).

3. Santayana, *Persons and Places*, 167.

4. William Ray Dennes, "Santayana's Materialism," in *The Philosophy of George Santayana*, ed. Paul Arthur Schilpp (LaSalle, IL: Open Court Publishing, 1971), 423. At

the time of Dennes's essay (1931), the fourth book of *Realms of Being, Realm of the Spirit* was not yet published. Any shift in Santayana's philosophical tone (e.g., a "softening") would be more evident in this fourth volume. There seems to me, however, to be no shift in his essential realistic-naturalism in this last volume of his ontology.

5. John P. Anton, "Santayana and Greek Philosophy," *Overheard in Seville* 11 (Fall 1993): 15–29.

6. John Lachs, *George Santayana* (Boston, MA: Twayne Publishers, 1988), 20–21.

7. Irwin Edman, ed., *The Philosophy of George Santayana*, viii.

8. J. H. Faurot, "Santayana's Philosophy of Religion," *Hibbert Journal* 58 (1960): 262. Also see chapter 3, "Normal Madness," in Santayana's *Dialogues in Limbo* (New York: Charles Scribner's Sons, 1928), 36–57.

9. Woodward, *Living in the Eternal*, 49–50.

10. Ibid., 35.

11. Ibid.

12. Santayana, *Persons and Places*, 167.

13. Ibid., 36–38.

14. Frederick Copleston, SJ, *A History of Philosophy*, vol. 1, "Greece and Rome" (New York: Doubleday, 1993), 11.

15. Frederick Copleston, SJ, *A History of Philosophy*, vol. 1, "Greece and Rome" (New York: Doubleday, 1993), 11.

16. George Santayana, "Bishop Berkeley," in *Animal Faith and Spiritual Life*, ed. John Lachs (New York: Appleton-Century Crofts, 1967), 103.

17. Richard C. Lyon, in the introduction to the critical edition of *Persons and Places* by George Santayana, depicts the dilemma. "Among the philosophers whose thought most influenced his own [Santayana's] one might name Plato and Aristotle, Democritus and Lucretius . . . I cite these figures in particular for the reason that various critics at various times have suggested that Santayana's own philosophy may be found entire in one or more of them." Lyon goes on to suggest that if Santayana's genius is to be recognized in our time, "it is a recognition of his power to assimilate and appropriate for his reflection the work of these and many other thinkers" (xvii).

18. Buchler, "One Santayana or Two?" 54. Buchler comments on the "seeds of irony" possible in Santayana's lapses in attribution. On the other hand, he notes Santayana's ready admission (e.g., in a letter to Buchler, October 15, 1937) that Peirce's theory was in fact useful to him.

19. Santayana read Husserl and commented on his phenomenology in the postscript to *The Realm of Essence* (*Realms of Being*, 172–74.) I will address this in chapter 3.

20. Bruce Wilshire, *William James and Phenomenology: A Study of "The Principles of Psychology,"* (Bloomington: Indiana University Press, 1968) addresses the phenomenological character of *The Principles* and James's unacknowledged characterization of his method as such. Wilshire also makes clear the enthusiastic acknowledgment by Edmund Husserl of James's phenomenology and the debt he owed to James in moving away in his own methodology from psychologisms. One can't help but wonder about the extent to which James's unacknowledged phenomenology influenced Santayana's own approach.

21. Sprigge, *Santayana*, 9–11. Timothy Sprigge has addressed this issue effectively and thoroughly, pointing out observations from different interpreters; for example, "But really, most of what Santayana is saying is just Locke refurbished," or "Well, really most of Santayana is just Aristotle presented in a modern guise." Sprigge counters by proposing that "if Santayana's philosophy were somehow the systems of Plato, Aristotle, Locke, Leibniz and Hume rolled into one consistent whole [and I agree with Sprigge that it seems indeed a consistent whole] that would surely make it something rather remarkable."

22. Santayana, *Scepticism and Animal Faith*, v.

23. Santayana, "A Brief History of My Opinions," Edman, 12.

24. Santayana, "A General Confession," Schilpp, 13. He further comments that it was not until ten years later (1896–1897) that he felt "collected or mature enough to pursue the matter" (e.g., in *The Life of Reason*, published 1905–1906).

25. Edman, *The Philosophy of George Santayana*, xi.

26. Santayana, "A General Confession," Schilpp, 10.

27. Santayana, "A General Confession," Schilpp, 10.

28. Santayana, "A General Confession," Schilpp, 12.

29. George Santayana, "Ultimate Religion," in *Obiter Scripta*, ed. Justus Buchler and Benjamin Schwartz (New York: Charles Scribner's Sons, 1936), 289.

30. Howgate, *George Santayana*, 138.

31. An interesting parallel in Santayana's own experience exists here. His mother, who like his father was officially a Catholic, was essentially a Deist who believed that "God was too great to take special thought for man." His father was of a similar view (Santayana, "A Brief History of My Opinions," Edman, 5).

32. *Penguin Dictionary of Philosophy*, 1996, s.v. "Heraclitus."

33. Copleston, *A History of Philosophy*, vol. 1, 39.

34. John P. Anton, "Santayana and Greek Philosophy," *Overheard in Seville*, 10 (Fall 1992): 15–29.

35. Ibid., 40.

36. Santayana, *Realms of Being*, 186.

37. Anton, "Santayana and Greek Philosophy,"15–29.

38. Celestine J. Sullivan, "Philosophical Inheritance," Schilpp, 82.

39. Santayana, *Realms of Being*, 845.

40. Copleston, *A History of Philosophy*, vol. 1, 125.

41. *Penguin Dictionary of Philosophy*, s.v. "Democritus."

42. Copleston, *A History of Philosophy*, vol. 1, 125–26.

43. Santayana, *Realms of Being*, 802.

44. I will not attempt here in any way to differentiate Socrates's vs. Plato's ideas except to generally accept the theory that the early dialogues more likely represented Socrates's thought and the middle and later dialogues Plato's. The theory of the Forms are worked out in the middle and later dialogues (see *Penguin Dictionary of Philosophy*, s.v. "Plato").

45. Copleston, *A History of Philosophy*, vol. 1, 177.

46. Ibid., 176.

47. Ibid., 166–169.

48. *Penguin Dictionary of Philosophy*, s.v. "Plato."

49. Jaegwon Kim and Ernest Sosa, eds., A *Companion to Metaphysics* (Cambridge, MA: Blackwell, 1995), 395.

50. Ibid., 398.

51. The limit of causality as applied to *spirit* or consciousness in Santayana's philosophy is implicitly related to his *epiphenomenalism* and has been substantially dealt with by John Lachs, *Mind and Philosophers* (Nashville, TN: Vanderbilt University Press, 1987), 29–34; Sprigge, *Santayana*, 110–14; Angus Kerr-Lawson, "Santayana's Epiphenominalism," *Transactions of the Charles S. Peirce Society* 21 (Spring 1985): 200–221, and other authors.

52. Santayana, *The Life of Reason*, 463.

53. Copleston, *A History of Philosophy*, vol. 1, 163–206.

54. Kim and Sosa, *A Companion to Metaphysics*, 399.

55. In the first chapter, I commented on Santayana's reluctance to compromise across a broad front. Santayana's realism was sustained throughout in its "harshness," and the methodological "tool" of skepticism, ultimately transcended by *animal faith*, was not only committed to doubt and "unknowing," but also to truth wherever it lay. Santayana's periodic comments regarding his negative perception of the relativity of truth in pragmatism are telling; for example, "pragmatism seems to involve a confusion between the truth and the meaning of truth" (letter to Fuller, Avila, October 5, 1905; McCormick, *George Santayana*, 186).

56. Louis Harap, "A Note on Moralities in the Philosophy of Santayana," in *Animal Faith and Spiritual Life*, ed. John Lachs (New York: Appleton-Century-Crofts, 1967), 361.

57. Lachs, *George Santayana*, 44.

58. *The Encyclopedia of Philosophy*, vol. 7, 1967, s.v. "Skepticism," Richard H. Popkin.

59. Santayana, *Realms of Being*, 530.

60. George Santayana, "Comparison of Other Views of the Spirit," in *Animal Faith and Spiritual Life*, ed. John Lachs, 279–80.

61. Lachs, *George Santayana*, 12.

62. Santayana, "A General Confession," Schilpp, 25–26.

63. Marvin Perry, *An Intellectual History of Modern Europe* (Boston: Houghton Mifflin, 1992), 18–22.

64. Anton, "Santayana and Greek Philosophy," 7.

65. Lachs illustrates well Aristotle's idea of "functional" [My word. Lachs uses "activity"] optimization as leading to happiness through the spiritual life of reason by using the example of the functional optimization of an organ, i.e., the eye. "Our eyes . . . yield pleasure when they are used to observe beautiful things. This suggests the idea . . . that perfectly executed complex organic processes, although physical, are normally accompanied by intrinsically delightful moments of consciousness" (Lachs, *George Santayana*, 114). Such a parallel, reduced to physiological or organic function and use, illustrates the *epiphenomenal* foundation of both Santayana's and Aristotle's life of reason.

66. *The Penguin Dictionary of Philosophy*, s.v. "Aristotle."

67. Copleston, *A History of Philosophy*, vol. 1, 314–19.

68. Santayana, *Persons and Places*, 538.

69. *The Internet Encyclopedia of Philosophy*, s.v. "Lucretius," David Simpson, www.iep.edu/.

70. Ibid.

71. Ibid.

72. Lucretius, *The Nature of Things* (Book III), trans. Frank O. Copley (New York: W. W. Norton, 1977), 75.

73. Santayana provides a concise description of the materialist's philosophy in *Three Philosophical Poets*, 32–33. "The materialist is primarily an observer, etc." Also revealing is his view that "the moral hue of materialism in a formative age, or in an aggressive mind, would be aristocratic and imaginative; but in a decadent age, or in a soul that is renouncing everything, it would be as in Epicurus, humanitarian and timidly sensual" (34).

74. Lucretius, *The Nature of Things*, 29.

75. Santayana, *Three Philosophical Poets*, 32.

76. Santayana's *Egotism in German Philosophy* (New York: Charles Scribner's Sons, 1915) explores the "egotism and selfishness" of German philosophy from Kant to Nietzsche. Edward L. Schaub, "Santayana's Contentions Respecting German Philosophy," Schilpp, 401–15, renders a severe critique of Santayana's treatment of the Germans, pointing out many perceived contradictions (e.g., in regard to Schopenhauer, whom Santayana generally admired).

77. Santayana, "Apologia Pro Mente Sua," Schilpp, 512.

78. George Santayana, "Hegel and the Egotism of Ideas," in *Egotism in German Philosophy, George Santayana: Selected Critical Writings*, ed. Norman Henfrey (Cambridge: Cambridge University Press, 1968), 179–80.

79. McCormick, *George Santayana*, 145–46. Santayana indicated in his critique of Hegel's *Phänomenologie des Geistes* in the preface to the 1922 Triton edition of *The Life of Reason* (published in 1936) that his writing *The Life of Reason* was inspired by the work.

80. Henry Samuel Levinson, *Santayana, Pragmatism and the Spiritual Life* (Chapel Hill: University of North Carolina Press, 1992), 122.

81. Ibid., 125.

82. *Penguin Dictionary of Philosophy*, s.v. "Hegel."

83. Copleston, *A History of Philosophy: Modern Philosophy*, vol. 7 (New York: Doubleday, 1994), 185–86.

84. Santayana, *Realms of Being*, 769–70.

85. Copleston, *A History of Philosophy*, vol. 7, 163.

86. Santayana, "Hegel and the Egotism of Ideas," Henfrey, 183.

87. Copleston, *A History of Philosophy*, vol. 7, 273.

88. Ibid., 275.

89. Ibid., 277.

90. Ibid., 265.

91. Ibid., 263–64.

92. Matthew Caleb Flamm, "Santayana and Schopenhauer," *Transactions of the Charles S. Peirce Society* 38, no. 3 (Summer 2002): 413–31. Flamm concentrates on the kinships in Schopenhauer and Santayana as primarily (1) the limits of scientific understanding, (2) the illusory character of human experience and (3) the cognitive account of aesthetic contemplation.

93. Santayana, *Realms of Being*. *Realms* was initially published in four volumes: *The Realm of Essence*, 1927; *The Realm of Matter*, 1930; *The Realm of Truth*, 1938; and *The Realm of Spirit*, 1940. These volumes were preceded by what can be considered an introduction to *Realms*, i.e., *Scepticism and Animal Faith*, 1927. These works incorporate the mature systematic metaphysics of Santayana's philosophy.

94. Dennis, "Santayana's Materialism," Schilpp, 422–23.

95. Santayana, "A Brief History of My Opinions," Edman, 11.

96. Santayana, "Apologia Pro Mente Sua," Schilpp, 522.

97. Sprigge, *Santayana*, 19.

98. Santayana, *Scepticism and Animal Faith*, vi.

99. Lachs, *George Santayana*, 7.

100. Comprehensive analyses of Santayana's philosophy that I have found particularly helpful are in Timothy Sprigge's *Santayana* and Henry Samuel Levinson's *Santayana, Pragmatism and the Spiritual Life*. More abbreviated but still insightful perspectives include Anthony Woodward's *Living in the Eternal*, and John Lachs's *George Santayana*. Particularly attuned to the Roman Catholic influences on Santayana and with a more literary perspective are George W. Howgate's *George Santayana*, and Mossie M. Kirkwood's *Santayana: Saint of the Imagination*.

101. Santayana, *Scepticism and Animal Faith*, 33.

102. Sprigge, *Santayana*, 54. In *Realms of Being* (202), Santayana outlines the five "indispensable Properties" of Substance. Sprigge's definition captures these well summarily, although his conclusion on the exclusivity of belief to substance I hold in question (e.g., Why can't one believe in *any* reality?).

103. Santayana, *Realms of Being*, 234–35.

104. Santayana, *Scepticism and Animal Faith*, 150.

105. Ibid.

106. Lachs, *George Santayana*, 58–59.

107. *The Penguin Dictionary of Philosophy*, s.v. "Materialism," and "Realism."

108. Santayana, *Realms of Being*, 205. On this sometimes confusing point, Santayana seems quite clear. Also see *Scepticism and Animal Faith*: "I therefore propose to use the word existence . . . to designate not data of intuition but facts or events believed to occur in nature" (47).

109. Plato's hypostatization of the Forms as the only reality, or George Berkeley's (1685–1753) *esse est percipi*, are more obvious examples of idealistic dualisms. Santayana's attack on German Idealism—for example, "Egotism in German Philosophy," in *George Santayana, Selected Critical Writings*, ed. Norman Henfrey, vol. 2 (Cambridge: Cambridge University Press, 1968), 172–86—reveals his incredulous view of its legacy from "Protestantism [and] its earnestness and pious intention." Implicit in Santayana's response to German Idealism is all that he stands against in the "metaphysical preoccupations" of transcendentalism. The idealistic machinations initiated through experiencing nature and corrupted by egotistical thought are comically depicted in Santaya-

na's comments on Emerson's Transcendentalism. "For the transcendentalist is precious because it is his own work, a mirror in which he looks at himself and says, 'What a genius I am! Who would have thought there was such stuff in me'" (George Santayana, "The Genteel Tradition in American Philosophy," Henfrey, 95).

110. Santayana, *Realms of Being*, 189. "From the point of view of origins, therefore, the realm of matter is the matrix and source of everything, etc."

111. The concept of, and issues relating to epiphenominalism and the notion of cause have been extensively considered by John Lachs in *Mind and Philosophers*, and also perceptively treated by Timothy Sprigge in *Santayana*, and Angus-Kerr Lawson in "Santayana's Epiphenomenalism." Benjamin Allen has also provided a broad comparative study of Santayana's epiphenomenalism in "Epiphenomenalism in the Moral Philosophy of George Santayana Particularly as It Affects Free Will" (PhD diss., Drew University, 1953). Angus Kerr-Lawson draws interesting parallels pertinent to epiphenominalism and human feelings between Santayana, the brain-scientist Antonio Damasio and their common inspiration in Benedict de Spinoza. Kerr-Lawson, "Two Philosophical Psychologists," *Overheard in Seville* 21 (Fall 2003): 31–42. Also see Damasio's *Looking for Spinoza: Joy, Sorrow and the Feeling Brain* (Orlando, FL: Harcourt, 2003). The mind-body relationship is an important consideration in modern behavioral psychology and brain-science (e.g., the behaviorist B. K. Skinner is an epiphenomenologist). I will address this subject further in chapter 5.

112. Santayana, "A General Confession," Schilpp, 17–18.

113. George Santayana, "A Brief History of My Opinions," Edman, 11. (Originally published in *Contemporary American Philosophy: Personal Statements*, ed. George P. Adams and William Montaque, vol. 2 [New York, Macmillan, 1930], 239–57).

114. Santayana, *Scepticism and Animal Faith*, 69. "But scepticism is an exercise, not a life; it is a discipline to purify the mind of prejudice and render it all the more apt, when the time comes, to believe and to act wisely."

115. Santayana, *Scepticism and Animal Faith*, 10.

116. Ibid., 25.

117. Ibid., 21.

118. Ibid., 35.

119. Ibid., 40–41.

120. Solipsism is a theory holding that the human mind has no basis for believing in anything but itself. Santayana's concept of solipsism seems to be closest to a "metaphysical solipsism," or one that has the consequences of drawing the *reductio ad absurdum* that there is also no certain basis for even believing in the "self" (in part from Reese, *Dictionary of Philosophy and Religion*, s.v. "Solipsism").

121. Santayana, *Scepticism and Animal Faith*, 13.

122. Ibid.

123. Ibid., 14.

124. Paul Edwards, ed., *Encyclopedia of Philosophy*, vol. 7 (New York: Macmillan/Free Press, 1967), s.v. "Skepticism," Richard H. Popkin.

125. Sprigge, *Santayana*, 34.

126. Santayana, *Scepticism and Animal Faith*, 14–16.

127. John Lachs suggests that *solipsism of the present moment* is an inappropriate designation for the state Santayana describes. He bases this observation on the definition of solipsism referring to "oneself as the only real existent," and that Santayana rather refers to "impersonal objects given in consciousness," and additionally does not affirm the existence of the *self*. "Since *ipse* means 'self' and *datum* means 'given' in Latin," Lachs proposes "sol-datism of the present moment" as a more appropriate terminology (Lachs, *George Santayana*, 36).

128. Santayana, *Scepticism and Animal Faith*, 18.

129. Ibid., 31.

130. Ibid., 33.

131. Ibid., 19.

132. Dermot Moran, *Introduction to Phenomenology* (London: Routledge, 2000), 8.

133. Santayana, *Scepticism and Animal Faith*, 24–25.
134. Ibid., 24.
135. Ibid., 15.
136. Ibid., 23.
137. Ibid.
138. Ibid., 52.
139. Lachs, *George Santayana*, 43.
140. Santayana, *Scepticism and Animal Faith*, 16.
141. Ibid., 17.
142. Ibid., 24–25.
143. Ibid., 29.
144. Ibid.
145. Ibid., 28–29.
146. Santayana, "A General Confession," Schilpp, 19.
147. Santayana, *Scepticism and Animal Faith*, 42.
148. Ibid., 47.
149. Michael P. Hodges, *Thinking in the Ruins: Wittgenstein and Santayana on Contingency* (Nashville, TN: Vanderbilt University Press, 2000), 30.
150. Ibid., 34.
151. Santayana, *Scepticism and Animal Faith*, v.
152. The consideration of the Pragmatic character of Santayana's philosophy, particularly his epistemology, could be considered a controversial issue. Despite Santayana's dissociation of himself from the Pragmatic school, the notions of value, relativity of morality, freedom, and so forth, characteristics of a Pragmatic naturalism are evident. There are also major departures—for example, Santayana's attitude toward truth, religion and his categories of *Essences*, the latter having some relation, however, to Peirce's ontological category of "Firstness." For one extensive treatment affirming Santayana's pragmatic naturalism, see Levinson's *Santayana, Pragmatism and the Spiritual Life*. A more abbreviated negation of the relationship is represented in Angus Kerr-Lawson, "Pragmatism and Santayana's Realms," *Overheard in Seville* 12 (Fall 1994): 17–22.
153. George Santayana, *Character and Opinion in the United States* (New York: Charles Scribner's Sons, 1921), 159.
154. Santayana, *Scepticism and Animal Faith*, 262.
155. Santayana deals with tropes in a brief chapter in *Realms of Being*, 293–309. He characterizes a trope as an *Essence* of an event, i.e., that universal form of the event that may manifest itself in another event, hence a pattern may be recognized—for example, patterns of regeneration in organisms and deterioration of tissues in old age. Tropes, then, are eternal, repeatable forms like other *Essences*, but characterize the complex sequences in events. See also Lachs, *George Santayana*, 70–71, for a concise treatment of tropes.
156. Santayana, *Realms of Being*, 271.
157. Santayana, *Realms of Being*, xiii.
158. Santayana, *Scepticism and Animal Faith*, vi.
159. Ibid., viii.
160. Santayana, "A General Confession," Schilpp, 28.
161. George Santayana, *The Life of Reason: Introduction to Reason and Common Sense* (New York: Charles Scribner's Sons, 1920), 163. Santayana considerably revised this text in collaboration with Daniel Cory for the one-volume revised edition (Scribner's, 1952) which I am using as the primary reference in this discussion. In any case, the association of *essence* and "concretion" is even more clearly made in the revised edition.
162. Sprigge, *Santayana*, 125–26.
163. Santayana, *Realms of Being*, 1–168.
164. Santayana, "A General Confession," Schilpp, 28.
165. Santayana, *Realms of Being*, 831.

166. Ibid., 29.

167. Santayana, *Scepticism and Animal Faith*, 72–73; italics mine.

168. Santayana, *Realms of Being*, vii; italics mine.

169. Phenomenology, while insistent on the role of intuition, generally tends to deny the importance of empirical experience and language. In the next chapter I will deal with this apparent contradiction in considering *essences*, the grammar of a language of intuition.

170. Santayana, *Realms of Being*, 27.

171. Ibid., viii; italics mine except where indicated by quotation marks.

172. Ibid; italics mine except where indicated by quotation marks.

173. Sprigge, *Santayana*, 66. In my view, Sprigge's extensive treatment of *essence* and other elements of Santayana's philosophy would be difficult to surpass in its thoroughness and clarity. His treatment has been invaluable to me in identifying elements in Santayana's philosophy that give evidence of a phenomenological character and in clarifying more technical aspects of the philosopher's project.

174. Santayana, *Realms of Being*, 218.

175. Santayana, for example, addresses issues regarding cosmological claims, teleology, immortality and gnosticism in relation to his theory of Substance throughout "The Realm of Matter" (*Realms of Being*, 183–398).

176. John Lachs, "Matter and Substance in the Philosophy of George Santayana," *Modern Schoolman* 44 (1966): 1–12. Lachs notes a number of scholars (e.g., Dennis, Munitz and Arnett) who seem to have equated Substance and Matter as a result of Santayana's ambiguous presentation.

177. Lachs, *George Santayana*, 73.

178. Santayana, *Realms of Being*, 186.

179. Ibid., 201–3.

180. Ibid., 202. Also see Santayana, *Scepticism and Animal Faith*, 287, where Santayana emphasizes that Spirit is neither Substance nor Matter.

181. Ibid.

182. Lachs, "Matter and Substance," 10.

183. Santayana, *Realms of Being*, 200.

184. Ibid., 204.

185. Ibid., 183.

186. Ibid., 205.

187. Ibid., 189.

188. Ibid., 191.

189. Lachs, "Matter and Substance," 9.

190. Santayana, *Realms of Being*, 573.

191. Ibid., 549.

192. Ibid., 569.

193. Ibid., 331.

194. Lachs, *George Santayana*, 78.

195. Lachs, *Mind and Philosophers*.

196. Santayana, *Scepticism and Animal Faith*, 217.

197. Santayana, *Realms of Being*, 826.

198. Ibid., 401.

199. Ibid., 420.

200. Ibid., 408.

201. Ibid., 417.

202. Levinson, *Santayana, Pragmatism and the Spiritual Life*, 234.

203. Ibid., 185. From Santayana, *Character and Opinion in the United States*, 156.

204. Santayana, *Realms of Being*, 823.

205. Ibid., xiii.

206. Ibid., 424.

207. Woodward, *Living in the Eternal*, 30.

208. Santayana, *Realms of Being*, xiii.

209. Ibid., 828.

210. Robert Corrington, Carl Hausman, and Thomas M. Seebohm, eds., *Pragmatism Considers Phenomenology* (Washington, DC: Center for Advanced Research in Phenomenology, University Press of America, 1987), 24. Justus Buchler, *The Main of Light* (New York: Oxford University Press, 1974), 126.

211. Santayana, *Realms of Being*, 45.

212. Ibid., 49.

213. Ibid., 52.

214. Ibid., 63.

215. Ibid., 827.

216. Santayana, *Scepticism and Animal Faith*, vi.

217. Santayana, *Realms of Being*, 63.

218. Ibid., 833.

219. Ibid., 853.

220. George Santayana, *Soliloquies in England and Later Soliloquies* (Ann Arbor: University of Michigan Press, 1967), 258–59.

THREE

The Phenomenological Character of Santayana's Philosophy of the Spirit

> It is not misleading to say that these various works by Santayana comprise a rather complete and sympathetic phenomenology of prayer rare in American philosophy.
>
> Daniel T. Pedarske, SDS, "Santayana on Laughter and Prayer"

The objective of this chapter is to establish that Santayana's philosophical project is characterized by aspects of a phenomenological approach. In comparing Santayana's approach with that of other philosophers characterized by a phenomenological method, I will not offer any in-depth description or critique of their methods but only address their methodology in an abbreviated manner for comparative purposes. When Santayana indicates in the preface to *The Realm of Spirit* that it is "descriptive" study, having made the same claim in the introduction to *The Life of Reason*, we attain a glimpse of an approach that suggests an aspect of phenomenology. Critical for my argument here is that the phenomenological approach and mindset of Santayana are substantially operative and advantageous in his philosophy of religion. I believe a more extensive scholarly effort is required (and invited) to rigorously define the nature of Santayana's phenomenological bent, and this chapter will hopefully "scratch the surface" and provide a beginning.

When one seeks out the evidence of possible phenomenological aspects in Santayana's project, a number of subtle but abbreviated suggestions by various authors infer that it is there—somewhere. The epigraph to this chapter by Pedarske regarding Santayana's phenomenological approach to prayer, referring particularly to Santayana's descriptive approach in *Reason in Religion* and *The Realm of the Spirit*, may be one of the most direct claims.[1] I will not yet begin to stake my own claims on Santayana's falling clearly within any phenomenological tradition or even that he can be considered consistently throughout his works as a phenomenologist of religion, in the sense that Geraardus van der Leeuw, Mircea Eliade or Rudolf Otto might be categorized. However, I will argue that his method is characterized by some very clear elements of a phenomenological approach in his intuition of *essences,* his preliminary radical skeptical method and, intermittently, in his descriptive approach. If we can define other characteristics of a phenomenological approach—for example, description of phenomena as they are given to consciousness and avoidance of all previous impositions on consciousness from encrusted traditions or foundational axioms, we may develop a profile of Santayana that supports the argument. An in-depth analysis of Santayana's phenomenological approach vs. that of other phenomenologists is beyond the scope of this chapter and must be dealt with separately. I will provide only enough comparison to these figures in order to give evidence that Santayana may be considered in their company. I will begin where most critiques and expositions of phenomenology do—that is, in the foundational methodological paradigm of Edmund Husserl (1859–1938), the acknowledged modern originator of the formal phenomenological method. By relating elements of Santayana's approach in his philosophy of *essences* to Husserl and other selected philosophers utilizing a phenomenological method of one variety or another (e.g., Heidegger, Alfred North Whitehead, William James and Charles Sanders Peirce), I hope to establish more clearly than has been done in prior scholarly work that Santayana's philosophy is at least in part characterized by a phenomenological approach. My intent is simply to bring forward some evidence of a phenomenology in Santayana's project and move forward to his philosophy of religion.

It is important to note that Santayana, consistent with his avoidance of any claims for "system" and even method in his philosophy, never claimed a phenomenological approach for his project or, to my knowledge, except in his postscript to *The Realm of Essence* dealing with some comparisons of his own work and Husserl's, even rarely mentioned the term.[2] I will return at some length later in the chapter to this particularly important commentary on Husserl. Santayana's colleague and mentor William James (1842–1910) in his own *Principles of Psychology* has been only relatively recently acknowledged as practicing a phenomenological method—that is, in the case of his psychology, a "phenomenological psychology," but, possibly due to James's late exposure to Edmund Husserl's work, James never made an assertive claim for himself in this regard. However, Husserl notably found some common ground with James's radical empiricism.[3] James's *Varieties of Religious Experience* is, in my opinion, a remarkable phenomenological work, an opinion I can find singular support for from James M. Edie in his book *William James and Phenomenology.* Edie proposes that James represents a Husserlian approach in his phenomenology of religious experience more so than Van

Der Leeuw, Eliade, Merleau-Ponty or others who claim some association with Husserl's phenomenology. Further, he claims that James was the *"first* to attempt a phenomenology of religion in an experiential sense . . . [and] has had almost no successor in this endeavor up to the present time [1987]."[4] The claims for James as a phenomenologist are significant for my argument in two respects. First, James was a mentor, however much resisted, for Santayana during his student days at Harvard and had significant influence on him. Primarily, Santayana credited James, among other both positive and negative influences, for giving him a sensitivity for "the immediate; for the unadulterated, unexplained, instant fact of experience."[5] This immediate vision, free of prior judgments, presuppositions and opinions, provides in Santayana's approach the opportunity for intuiting *essence*, and is the "platform" for phenomenological description. I will certainly not contend here that James was the root cause of Santayana's phenomenological bent by any means, but that his influence in relation to the sense of "immediacy" is important.

In a process of comparison and elimination of phenomenological approaches that will reveal Santayana's own approach more clearly, one encounters major differences in trajectory that can arguably be used to eliminate Santayana's philosophical project from rigorously meeting the criteria for a phenomenology. One such major "screening" criterion may be the "Existential" approach; for example, in Heidegger, where, in his case, a hermeneutical phenomenological description of our own (human) self-encounter is the focus (*Dasein*) vs. the *eidetic* or transcendental and "psychological" approach of Husserl focused on "essential being."[6] This is not to suggest that more study couldn't find much common ground in Heidegger and Santayana in a less "orthodox" phenomenological model leaning more toward life in the world and away from transcendental limitations. Sartre and Heidegger may in a general sense be said to be Existential in that they begin with existent man and move toward ontology (existence before essence) whereas Santayana, in a general sense, would be seen to begin with ontology and move only tentatively toward existence through his concept of *animal faith* (essence before existence). Husserl's method is essentially ontological, intensely epistemological with causality and existence bracketed and eliminated from the field of description. Another criterion may relate to the foundations or origins of one phenomenological method (e.g., Husserlian) vs. another, such as the variant phenomenology of the Americans William James and Charles Sanders Peirce and the limiting perspective that there cannot be a naturalistic (vs. idealistic) phenomenology.[7]

EVIDENCE OF A PHENOMENOLOGICAL APPROACH

In order to support early in this chapter that that there is indeed some clear, but granted thin, content in the secondary literature suggesting Santayana's possible phenomenological approach, I will begin by citing some observations from a few scholars and follow this with other evidence from Santayana's writings and the phenomenological literature. Of significance in regard to the former, there are Anthony Woodward's observations as he attempts to characterize Santayana's philosophy.

> Fully focused mental attention rises toward the Realm of the Spirit; its local status is in the Realm of Matter. The mechanism of interaction remains obscure, though plentifully adorned with elevated imagery that prevents him from appearing to be a crude materialist. That imagery, and the contradictions into which it appears to lead him, has the possibly salutary effect of leaving the reader poised over a mystery that no amount of analysis is ever going to dissolve. On a strict view, however . . . his terminology suggests flirtation with a substantial spiritual transcendence his materialistic outlook does not warrant.[8]

In Santayana's characteristic manner, he leaves Woodward responding to the paradox of Santayana's contradictory "colors," as Santayana the materialist seems to resort to a "spiritual transcendence" more characteristic of idealism than naturalism. Ultimately, Woodward suggests that "perhaps it is best to nudge Santayana's reflections in the direction of phenomenology, which helpfully brackets such ontological dilemmas and asks us simply to attend to the qualities of awareness."[9] Woodward perceives Santayana as "leaving behind the distracted ego," and passing into a state of depersonalized awareness. He goes further to note Santayana's comments in the postscript to *The Realm of Essence* and Santayana's recognition of the similarities between his *essences* and the "pure ideas" of Husserl. He makes reference to the following quotation from the aforementioned postscript where the approaches of Santayana and Husserl are similar:

> [For Husserl,] objects, in order to meet the realm of this phenomenology, must be thoroughly *purified*. This purification consists in reducing the object to its intrinsic and evident character, disregarding all question of its existence or non-existence, or of its locus in nature; or in my language, it consists in suspending animal faith, and living instead contemplatively, in the full intuition of some essence . . . Nothing is therefore removed from experience by purifying it, except its distraction; and an essence, far from being an abstraction from a thing, is the whole of that thing as it ever can be directly given, or spiritually possessed.[10]

Here we can unreservedly acknowledge that, with the major exception of Husserl's idealistic bent toward attaining absolute or necessary truth (apodicticity) in his investigations, there is more than a hint of a path leading to a remarkable similarity between Husserl's phenomenology and the approach that Woodward suggests, and that I also will claim for Santayana.

Timothy Sprigge in his rigorous analysis and critique of Santayana's philosophy submits that the philosopher's intention is "to contrast our usual envisagement of temporal facts with their actual character" (i.e., in the *essences*). Sprigge proposes that the complexity of perception of the "immense difference between past and future [and] the sharply contrasting sort of reality they seem to have for us" is receptive to a literary language like Santayana's as opposed to a "cut and dried formula." He concludes that such a style, one that Santayana calls "literary psychology," *"is what phenomenology at least ought to be about."* [11] It is indeed apparent in reading Santayana that his language is broadly descriptive, and one is often left at the end of a paragraph or sentence with a broad and in-depth image of the thought that the philosopher has invoked. His descriptive language is poetic, metaphoric and non-technical and resorts to everyday usage. His descriptive goals cannot be accomplished within a codified or structured approach as in the style of analytic philosophy, hence the criticism of his style by more "technical" philosophers. However, despite the poetic and literary style, the discipline of striving for a true perception of an experience, event or concept is evident, and Santayana's accurate reflection to us of the intuited *essences* or *complex* essence of the object from a field of complexity is the intent. [12] Typical of what seems to be an intuitive sensitivity to this intent, Sidney Feshbach, in a paper published in the phenomenological journal *Analecta Husserliana* on the subject of Santayana's student friend at Harvard, the poet Wallace Stevens, refers to the "idiosyncratic pragmatic phenomenology of Santayana." [13] Also typical of such observations, unfortunately, no further justification or explanation is offered by Feshbach for Santayana's presumed phenomenology. However, Feshbach's rather broadly accommodating expression of an "idiosyncratic pragmatic phenomenology" may ultimately best suit Santayana's approach as it may for a number of purported phenomenologists who did not adhere to Husserl's orthodox approach.

John McCormick is sensitive to the similarities of Santayana's theory of *essence* to those of phenomenologists, but he falls short of suggesting Santayana practices phenomenology. McCormick depicts Santayana as eagerly seeking "cousinship" in his doctrine of *essences*, and in 1934 Santayana seemed to have found it in Whitehead, Husserl and René Guénon. Further, Santayana expressed his joy in finding "the theory of essence so beautifully expounded in Proust's second volume of *Le Temps Retrouvé*." [14] Proust, a novelist long associated with a phenomenological approach (e.g. phenomenology of memory), could also bear elsewhere some scholarly comparison to Santayana's approach. Santayana was somewhat contemptuous of the phenomenological Existentialism of the

French—for example, that of Sartre depicted in *The Imagination* (1936) and *Being and Nothingness* (1943)—but claimed to have extensively read Husserl, particularly in the earlier form of his Pure Phenomenology, and also Heidegger.[15] I will return to these "cousins" of Santayana in regard to the theory of *essence* and with comments on the phenomenological character of their methods in relation to Santayana's project.

Herbert Spiegelberg, in his comprehensive history of the phenomenological movement, draws a comparison between "Santayana's ultimate skepticism" and Husserl's phenomenological reduction. The relationship of Santayana's radically skeptical method to arrive at the untenability of skepticism and the resolution to live in *animal faith* and Husserl's phenomenological reduction certainly demonstrates Spiegelberg's "instructive parallel."[16] In doing so, however, no claims are made by Spiegelberg that Santayana is a phenomenologist *per se*, either intentionally or inadvertently by nature of his independent approach. If Spiegelberg's intention was to reflect the full range of parallels in phenomenological characteristics between the two philosophers only based upon Santayana's skeptical method to discern *essence* in *Scepticism and Animal Faith*, he would fall far short, in my opinion, of bringing forward all the evidence that Santayana, indeed, practiced and encouraged a form of phenomenology. It is significant, however, that Santayana would finally be cited at length in an important historical work on phenomenology and that Spiegelberg perceives at least some phenomenological aspects in his project. I believe that Spiegelberg's inclination to draw parallels between Husserlian phenomenology and Santayana's skeptical methodology and the related observations of Woodward are clearly warranted, if only based upon the following passage from the chapter "The Discovery of Essence" in *Scepticism and Animal Faith*:

> Retrenchment [think "bracketing"] has its rewards. When by a difficult suspension of judgment I have deprived a given image of all adventitious significance, when it is taken neither for the manifestation of a substance nor for an idea in a mind nor for an event in a world, but simply if a colour for that colour and if music for that music, and if a face for that face, then an immense cognitive certitude comes to compensate me for so much cognitive abstention. My skepticism has touched bottom, and my doubt has found honorable rest in the absolutely indubitable. Whatever essence I find and note, that essence and no other is established before me. I cannot be mistaken about it, since I now have no object of intent other than the object of intuition.[17]

Here, at the limits of radical skepticism, in what is the *sopm*, Santayana finds his path to capturing *essence* in a process that is "the clearing ground for debris," in a form of Cartesian-like phenomenological bracketing or *epoché*.[18] Up to the point where Santayana takes the "leap" of *animal faith* to the world of matter, he sustains his field of consciousness to the *a priori* as does Husserl throughout his method. The analogical correlates of both Santayana's and Husserl's thought on essences are apparent in Platonic metaphysics and the Greek Skeptic's suspension of prejudiced sources of experience.[19] As we move forward to chapter 4, we will further associate Santayana's intuition of *essences* with spiritual and even soteriological aspects which are aspects of Santayana's debt to Platonic spiritualism.

> Thus a mind enlightened by skepticism and cured of noisy dogma, a mind discounting all reports, and free from all tormenting anxiety about its own fortunes or existence, finds in the wilderness of essence a very sweet and marvelous solitude.[20]

Any soteriological solution for the skeptic finding "in the wilderness of essence a very sweet and marvelous solitude" is juxtaposed by practical life in the world in *animal faith*, a state wherein the symbols derived from the *essence*s may be assigned and interpreted as potentially associated with matter. However, in Santayana's mature philosophy there is a balance between *animal faith*, as the *sine qua non* of a human life in the world, and spiritual contemplation—that is, a temporary return to the Realm of Essence with the suspension of reflective thought, as the intermittent solitary restorative with which this life may be lived with happiness and virtue. I will address this subject in relation to *spirituality* in chapter 4. At the same time, as discussed in the last chapter, the radical skeptic, Santayana proposes, "may leap at one bound over the whole tangle of beliefs and dogmatic claims" in intuiting the eternal *essence* and, at this extreme, leave himself stranded in solipsistic isolation.

> To this mirage of the non-existent [here recall that essences have no existence], or intuition of essence, the pure skeptic is confined; and confined is hardly the word; because without faith and risk he can never leave that thin and bodiless plane of being, this plane in its tenuity is infinite; and there is nothing possible elsewhere that, as a shadow and a pattern is not prefigured here.[21]

Consequently, since Santayana arrives at a kind of intellectual "dead-end" in his skeptical reduction, and envisions nothing but isolation in solipsism, he moves on to *animal faith* as a tenable approach to life. As Spiegelberg suggests, "So after showing, as a supreme feat, the omnipotence of skepticism, he [Santayana] could return to the realms of animal faith in full freedom without feeling any longer the crushing burden of its tyranny."[22] This condition or mode of *animal faith* is analogous to that mode in which Husserl would find the subject in a non-phenomenological attitude, or the *natural attitude*, where there is a direct association (not an identity) between phenomena and the material world. Santayana proposes that "animal faith" posits substances and locates their locus in the field of action of which the animal occupies the center."[23] However, un-

like the *natural attitude* of Husserl, *animal faith* allows promise for approaching knowledge of the "real" world, however tenuous, and relies
upon an inductive approach to affirmation of material relationships. That
is, the symbolic "description" of *essence* or phenomenon may be anticipat-
ed to possibly reflect some level of truth in nature. Therefore, the phenomenological attitude and *epoché* of Husserl, the "turn" from the *natural
attitude*, would all occur in the mode of *animal faith* for Santayana, and for
both philosophers, an escape from skepticism would be accomplished on
opposite sides of the dialectical divide. For Husserl, this escape is in the
ideal where existence has been put aside in the *epoché*, and for Santayana
in a "leap of faith" toward the Realm of Matter. This will not make for
Santayana any confident association with *essences* given to consciousness
and the nature of the substantial world, but living in faith, "as-if" such an
association is possible, allows a tentative relief from the straightjacket of
solipsism. It is a leap over the sense images to the assertion that the
intuited *essence*, contingent on experience and testing, is helpfully related
to the *essence* of an existence encountered.[24] In this manner, one eludes, at
least in part, "normal madness."

Although *animal faith* provides for a "common sense" transition natural to the consciousness of the human psyche upon which the realm of
spirit emanates, it poses the problem of a major divergence of Santayana's approach from that of Husserl. Recall, however, that Santayana's
skepticism is never abandoned but remains foundational, only to be diminished in the "reconstruction" of a relationship of trust, through pragmatic testing of symbolic *essences* and objects of the world. At the same
time, Husserl was engaged in a "battle" with skepticism as *a way of life*,
just as Santayana was. The problem is simply that Husserl, while abandoning skepticism, never escapes from the epistemological confines to
formally seek out, as Santayana does, an approach to an imperfect but
pragmatic knowledge of nature in *animal faith*.[25] This very foundational
and problematical departure of Santayana's naturalistic philosophy from
Husserl's idealistic method will remain problematic for those who adhere
to the criteria of orthodox phenomenology.

A PROTEST AGAINST REDUCTIONISM: THE SIGNIFICANCE OF A
PHENOMENOLOGICAL BEARING IN THE PHILOSOPHY OF
RELIGION

One could reasonably ask why a major departure into the question of a
phenomenological approach is important in considering Santayana's philosophy of religion. Since it has not been a significant question addressed
in prior scholarship, why should I claim it to be now? It is not enough for
my purposes here to merely suggest that there is a phenomenological
approach unless it has pertinence to Santayana's philosophy of religion

which I will explore in chapter 4. Therefore, I offer the following rationale for why, beyond the interesting question of whether Santayana, indeed, practices a form of phenomenological inquiry, a consideration of the question is further justified.[26]

William James (1842–1910), in his Gifford Lectures in Edinburgh in 1901–1902, published as *The Varieties of Religious Experience*, can be minimally considered to have set the cornerstone for the scientific study of religion.[27] It is significant that the approach he used was a descriptive and phenomenological one, as I indicate above, unclaimed for himself, but nevertheless evident in retrospect as phenomenological philosophy has developed. James presented case-study descriptions of religious experiences, and in at least one case, a melancholic panic attack of a religious character, purportedly of his own but one he attributed to an anonymous "sufferer."[28] James advocated to his audience and readers a suspension of existential judgment and preconceived notions enabling "a true record of the inner experience.[29] The religious experience as described by the believer may be startling, incredible and unbelievable—or even morbid, or apparently psychotic, inviting judgment and rejection—but ultimately must be recognized and studied as a phenomenon that is given to us independent of any predisposition to rationalizing causality. The nature of religious experience itself can be a unifying orientation toward the immediate experience of the divine for the consciousness that experiences it. As Spiegelberg suggests, "The first objective of the phenomenological approach is enlarging and deepening the range of our immediate experience."[30] In this approach, there is an empathetic and open willingness to accept and describe the religious phenomenon as it is given. Other than the "given," any notion toward *querandum verum* departs from the essential phenomenological paradigm and the experience *per se*. In illustration, Edward J. Jurji suggests the following:

> There are scholars, of course, who act as though they considered the history of religion a history of gradual dissolution and disappearance of religion. Behind their investigations and discoveries is an attempt to reduce religion to psychological and sociological factors. Religion defies reduction, however, to non-religious categories and formulations. That religions are alive today may be partly due to their doctrinal tenets validated in meaningful experience.[31]

One could assert that the phenomenological method sustains the sacred and in opposition to reductive analysis, this attitude is precisely what James reflects in addressing his scientific-materialist audience at Edinburgh. In the sense of going behind the phenomena for causative aspects or presumptuous systematic scientific rationale, phenomenology is essentially non-reductionist. Such "reduction" of course is independent of the inherent reduction of presuppositions and prejudgments in phenomenology and, in the case of Husserl, of the bracketing of existence. We will see evidence of Santayana's non-reductive approach as we progress. Phenomenology as a method, or even as an attitude (i.e., bracketing of presuppositions and taking the experience as it is given), yields a different outcome than other, more analytically reductive approaches to religion, sciences or the arts. It responds, if you will, to the phenomenon or *essence* that is given without going beyond description to reductive analysis. It is therefore critical to understand, in our case of Santayana or any philosopher, what philosophical approach lies beneath his or her own perspective on religion.[32]

In chapter 1 of *The Idea of Christ in the Gospels*, Santayana presents two extreme viewpoints that might be taken in writing a "Life of Jesus" that are illustrative in considering the resultant of polar views, one of a believer, and the other of a critic or one with a reductionist approach.

For a believer, if he were greatly inspired, such an undertaking [i.e., writing a "Life of Jesus"] might be legitimate; yet it would hardly be required, since the narratives [Gospels] though independent, fall together of themselves, in the pious mind, into a total and impressive picture. But this presupposes an innocent state of mind that accepts every detail, no matter how miraculous . . . and is ready sympathetically to piece out the blanks in the story.[33]

On the other hand,

> If, however, the would-be biographer of Jesus is a cool critic, with no religious assumptions, his labors will be entirely wasted, because he has mistaken the character of his texts. The gospels are not historical works but products of inspiration. They are summonses and prophecies.[34]

The above is not so much illustrative of a phenomenological method in Santayana, but rather an indication that he recognizes the importance of language and method when considering the inspirational aspects of the religious response to Holy Scriptures vs. that of the critical historian. We find that Santayana's approach honors the meaning of the symbols manifested and the spiritual response elicited rather than the presumption of a scientific or psychological analysis. Michael Weinstein makes a valuable contrast in regard to this issue when he proposes that "speech fails from one side when it becomes a mere instrument for, to use Santayana's phrase, 'recording acts.' Speech fails from the other side, when it becomes a private language . . . the language which is constituted by Santayana's pathetic fallacy."[35] I will address the importance of the *pathetic fallacy* and its significance in a later section of this chapter. Also, in *The Idea of Christ in the Gospels*, it is pertinent to a phenomenological perspective in regard to the aspect of "recording acts" that Santayana gives evidence of his sensitivity to lack of "attention" to the object (i.e., the "idea of Christ") when he nearly wanders into the particulars of the mystery of salvation. In this divergence, he recognizes that "this is an ulterior mystery that must not distract us here from the task of simple inspection [description]."[36] The sense of Santayana, in clear accordance with other phenomenologists of religion, is that the point is missed if all myths are reduced to explanations or to literal science, and indeed, the "earnestness of the fact-seeker" ultimately results in "death to the spirit."[37] As a corollary to this view, Santayana expresses the same critical attitude as James (or Jurji above) and others of a phenomenological disposition toward psychological or logical reduction of religious doctrine and faith that would allow prior judgment to obscure the realization of the experience of those with religious belief and the value and power of religious symbols.[38]

I discussed in chapter 1 the importance of religious symbols, doctrine and the *kultur* of the Roman Catholic Church to Santayana. I particularly emphasized the paradox of his apologetic for both the teachings of the Catholic Church and Christianity in general and the value of their preservation in lieu of a modernistic, positivistic and scientific-materialistic-driven culture. Granted, his personal view was one of unbelief in the divine source and literal truth of foundational myths and doctrines in Christianity (or, for that matter, any religion), but he claimed rather that they were symbolic of ideals that ultimately had important moral value to the individual and society. Such sensitivity to the value of religion to society is analogous to that of John Dewey, but in Dewey, the value to society is privileged over the value to the individual. In this manner Santayana, just as James does, flies in the face of analytic philosophy and scientific materialism in the study of religion, despite his own *disillusion* in regard to the supernatural. Hence, we understand better his contempt for the liberal Protestant reduction of myths and symbols in the spirit of science and modernistic compliance. Consistent with his disposition for "no compromise," one must take the myth and its traditional trappings as given. I will return to this at length in chapter 4. In Santayana's project, there is a wholesome and rigorously deliberate and objective characteristic of a phenomenological approach—that is, a suspension of presuppositions of causative factors, prior impressions, preconceived notions, presumption to unfounded prior knowledge and any inclinations to be judgmental. For example, a phenomenological approach may "bracket" or suspend any metaphysical questions of the real presence of the divine but sustain the importance of the symbolic and poetic power of such a notion. Foundational, of course, to his view is the profound limitation of human consciousness in attaining knowledge and truth. There is then, from an individual perspective, an implicit "fairness" in the perception of a phenomenon. This honesty and fairness can result in a more authentic representative view of the phenomenon (e.g., expressions of religious belief).

As I consider Santayana's philosophical "consequences" discussed in chapter 2 and the balanced and integrated life of reason involving an aesthetic and spiritual integration and harmonization, a "holistic" character in a process toward self-development and happiness is evident. A similar sense may be gained from Anna-Teresa Tymieniecka, editor of *Analecta Husserliana* and a widely published phenomenologist, whose view on the function of phenomenology is summarized by Marlies E. Kronegger as follows:

> Her view [is] that the most vital function of phenomenology is to foster the unfolding of the individual's integrity in accord with himself (the microcosm), his culture (the mesocosm) and the universe (the macrocosm), and with the ultimate mystery both beyond and within himself and in all things, in life and death, in inward sacredness and transcendence. [39]

Within such a profile we can readily find a place for Santayana even with only a tentative commitment to any phenomenology in his project. We also see in Santayana, just as we do in Friedrich Schleiermacher and Rudolf Otto, the differentiation of the spiritual transcendence in religion and the experience of the spirit in the realm of ethics and morals. In Otto, as a phenomenologist seeking the essence of the religious experience, such a discrimination only resulted from his phenomenological method of attention to the feeling or experience aspects of religion. In Santayana's phenomenological discernment of *essence* (i.e., through the radical skeptical method), value considerations, which are the work of the imagination, are absent. [40] These separate determinations of the independence of the religious experience and morals in Otto, and of spiritual life and morals in Santayana, are tantamount to the useful separation of practice and feeling in religion. I suggest, based on the above, that the significance of a phenomenological approach, in our case toward religion, even in major variation from the classical methodology of Edmund Husserl, can make a significant difference relative to other methods in developing a philosophy of religion. Since there are strong indications that elements of such an approach are evident in Santayana, as I have demonstrated above, it is important to demonstrate some of these elements as we move forward.

THE HUSSERLIAN "HERESIES" AND SOME THEORIES OF ESSENCE

For the purposes of my argument regarding Santayana's philosophical method incorporating elements of phenomenology, we can accept the commonly held premise that Edmund Husserl (1859–1938) is the founder of the formal method of phenomenology in modern philosophy. In an analogous manner to the departures or "heresies" from Freud's psychoanalysis as time passed and the founder's theory was tested in individual practice, there were departures from Husserl's formal methodology, some of these quite evident in the treatment of philosophy of religion. Husserl conceived phenomenology to be an objective and rigorous science, free of "unexamined assumptions" including existence (bracketed in the *epoché*) and ultimately the "universal foundation" of all natural sciences and the arts. It is the rigor of Husserl's radical claim for phenomenology as a "vigorous science" and modeled upon the idealistic Cartesian model of reduction that has encountered much resistance and been significantly responsible for divergences in method from his orthodoxy.[41] The noteworthy observation of the French philosopher Paul Ricoeur was that "phenomenology is the story of deviations from Husserl; the history of phenomenology is the history of Husserlian heresies."[42] This is important in considering Santayana in the sense that a phenomenological approach outside of the rigorous idealist Husserlian transcendental method can still be characterized by phenomenological aspects (e.g., the contra-Cartesian existential phenomenology of Heidegger or the naturalistic phenomenology of Peirce). As I emphasized earlier, Santayana's theory of *essence* is the *Grund* of his ontology and epistemology. It is the "grammar" of the interface between the speculated world and the consciousness or Spirit. Husserl also utilizes a concept of *essence* in that same presumed interface between percept, concept, *essence* and consciousness, wherein we are "grasping" an object as phenomenon and then its *essence*, through the process of intuition. Santayana recognized the importance of Husserl's theory of *essence* (and the earlier mentioned "cousinship" between them) in the postscript to the *Realm of Essence* (hereafter referred to as Postscript), and devoted a chapter, "Comparison of Kindred Doctrines," in acknowledgment that "the type of being which I call essence has long been familiar to philosophers."[43] *Essence*, then, is an appropriate platform to continue our discussion on the possible phenomenological aspects of Santayana's approach.

Since Santayana's theory of *essences*, in light of Husserl's similar theory, is an early clue to a phenomenological orientation, I will first consider some important philosophical models of *essence*. These models play a role in the phenomenological methods of Husserl, as well as for those of Alfred North Whitehead, Martin Heidegger and Charles Sanders Peirce. A theory of *essence* is foundational, not only to Husserl and Santayana, but in modern philosophy is also related to the thought process of Alfred North Whitehead (1861–1947.) All three of these philosophers are predated by Charles Sanders Peirce (1839–1914), who, John Passmore claims, was instrumental in Santayana's theory of *essence* by teaching him Peirce's theory of indices.[44] Santayana, however, claims in a letter to Justus Buchler that his idea for *essence* came from Plato, and otherwise "from Russell and Moore in their early phase."[45] In the case of Peirce, his philosophical analytic method required analysis of an initial phenomenon he coined as the *phaneron*, for the most part, another name for an *essence*. Peirce, then, is also important for our comparative exercise, given his founding position in American Pragmatism, Santayana's limited exposure to him in the Harvard environment and his self-defined phenomenological or *phaneroscopic* method.

There is a commonality in most concepts of *essence* that might be commented on at the outset. Of foremost importance is that essence is a "quality" or "form" that is characteristic of any specific existent, is universal in its being and, in the Aristotelian model, is actualized in space and time in an association with substance. We can first gather a clear notion of *essence* in the epistemology of Plato and Aristotle. As we discussed in chapter 2, for Plato, *essences* were tantamount to Forms (*eide*) or Ideas (*edea*), except hypostatized to a higher, even supernatural level of reality of which existing objects were imperfect replicates. These Forms become available to us as *a priori* notions, a process which will be of particular importance as we further differentiate aspects of phenomenology.[46] Aristotle naturalized Plato's concept of fixed and eternal Forms that are universally associated with matter, allowing our perception of an object, while Aquinas associated causative qualities to essences (*esse*) that, in the process of creation, were conferred upon substance, giving it existence. In modern phenomenology the notion of *essence* as fixed possibility (i.e., eternal), and only dialectically differentiated from an existent—matter without form, not objective and not perceivable—was inherited from this tradition. Heidegger and Santayana both traced the notion of essence beyond Kant to the Greeks. The question for us here is how these modern concepts of *essence* are the same or different, recognizing that they are all foundational to variants of a phenomenological theory.[47] Thanks to the objective view available to us in Santayana's Postscript we can arrive at some important similarities in the views on essence of Husserl, Whitehead and Santayana with some relative ease.

Husserl and Santayana

Santayana, quoting his own translation from Husserl's *Ideen zu einer reinen Phänomenologie* and *phänomenologishen Philosophie*, elaborates on the characteristics of Husserl's concept of *essence*.

> Pure or transcendental phenomenology [Husserl's designation for his phenomenology] is not a science of fact but a science of essences and forms. The phenomena of transcendental phenomenology are in their nature non-existent (*characterisiert als irreal*). All immediate data (*Erlebnisse*) transcendentally purified are non-existent, and are situated out of all local relation (*Einordnung*) to the "real world." *As the datum of personal experimental perception is a particular thing, so the datum of intuition is pure essence.* [Santayana continues to translate.] Immediate vision, not necessarily sensual observation of things, but awareness yielding any original datum, no matter of what quality, is the ultimate source of validity for all rational assurance. All that I believe to exist in the world of things has, in principle, only a presumptive existence.[48]

Here, then in Husserl's own words, approvingly translated by Santayana, is Husserl's eternal *essence*, the only source of all "rational assurance" of what we might believe, given by intuition and situated independently of any relation to the existing world; and for Santayana, *essence* is the phenomenon that is in any way presented to consciousness that we intuit, in immediacy, as the only recognizable *Evidenz*, in a Husserlian sense.[49] At the same time this means making a decision not to rely on any beliefs which involve the world or make any impositions on the experience before the phenomenon is understood by an unprejudiced description. For Husserl, it seems that the reflective process of *ideation* transforms the awareness we have of the *phenomenon* into an awareness of the *essence*.[50] In the most general sense, however, Santayana's *essence* as well as Husserl's incorporates the notion of *essence* and *phenomenon* defined as anything given as *being* in consciousness. In this definition we can note a departure from Kant's theory which differentiates phenomena as accessed through the senses and noumena as objects of thought. In any case, for both philosophers, *the datum of intuition is essence.*[51]

There is in Santayana an interesting indication of a process similar to Husserl's in the description of what Santayana calls *complex essences*.[52] These are such *essences* that exhibit complexity typically in their incorporativeness—for example, the *essences* of "the system of the world," "the realm of essence itself" and "Euclidian space," or an *essence* that one seeks to appreciate that was intuited by a person long dead (e.g., Socrates). Santayana, for example, provides the following approach toward seeking out an "ulterior" *essence* experienced once by, say, an ancient philosopher.[53] One is trying here to describe an *essence* in the manner which it was intuited and described by the ancient.

> The most interesting essences, like the thoughts of ancient philosophers, may be at some remove; how should they be known in their absence except by description? The imaginative inquirer is reduced to retailing the circumstances or to specifying sundry qualities in which the intended object [the essence] presumably differs from those within his own ken, until he catches or thinks he catches a glimpse of the essence sought.[54]

In this manner, the *essence*, is being "sought out" through reflection of earlier *essences* related to experience and associations rather than being instantaneously intuited followed by an effort to describe it. Such an exercise with a purpose, it seems, to enter another person's mind and intuit his or her thoughts has been termed *literary psychology* by Santayana and indeed could be considered a *phenomenological psychology*. This characteristic of empathy and intersubjectivity in phenomenology refers to the experience of another human body as another, and I will return to this in more detail as we progress. We can, upon considering Santayana's concept of *essence* as described in chapter 2, appreciate what appears to be a nearly identical concept to that of Husserl.[55] Bear in mind that this comparison relates to the definition of *essence, qua essence*, for we will expect to see other important differences in practice as we progress. I will discuss these differences in the treatment and description of *essences* in more detail later in this chapter.

Whitehead and Santayana

Alfred North Whitehead's concept of *essence* is also addressed by Santayana in the Postscript, and in relation to Whitehead, just as to Husserl, Santayana proclaims that it is "true, my doctrine [of essence] was neither new nor extinct."[56] As indicated earlier, he is gratified to have found these "cousins" and happily observes that "I am not dreaming alone," and "in the most various quarters, the same intuition is returning to the world."[57] He refers to Whitehead's eternal objects as *essences* and not existing elements. Santayana quotes from Whitehead's *Science in the Modern World*:

> "Each eternal object," he tells us, "is an individual, which in its own peculiar fashion, is what it is." "Each eternal object is just itself in whatever mode of realization that it is involved. There can be no distortion of the individual essence without thereby producing a different eternal object." "Thus actualization is a selection among possibilities." Each "is systematically and by necessity of its nature related to every other eternal object." "The realm of eternal objects is properly described as a 'realm' because each eternal object has its status in this general systematic complex of mutual relatedness."[58]

Although Santayana finds fault with "the entanglements" of Whitehead's approach to the theory of *essence* in regard to "refraction in the thicker atmosphere in which he approaches it," he strongly affirms its acceptability as follows: "The nature of essence could hardly be recognized more frankly: it is eternal, compacted of internal relations, indifferently simple or complex, and at every level individual. It composes an infinite pure being."[59]

Based on the above, I suggest that the definitions of *essence* among the three philosophers, Husserl, Whitehead and Santayana, are close enough to be judged congruent for purposes of discussion here. This conclusion is substantially based upon Santayana's own apparent concurrence as he recognizes these theories as very closely related in the Postscript. In chapter 5 I will return to some important differences between Santayana's concept of *essence* and that of Whitehead and process thought.

Peirce and Santayana

Here we move away from Santayana's commentary in the Postscript to a concept of phenomenology (i.e., Peirce's *phaneroscopy*) that was never commented on by Santayana, and arguably never read by him.[60] With Peirce and Santayana we have two naturalists and realists whom Husserlians would consider outside the frame of his idealistic science of phenomenology. Peirce proclaims, "The business of phenomenology is to draw up a catalogue of categories and prove its sufficiency and freedom from redundancies, to make out the characteristics of each category, and to show the relations of each to the others."[61] More consideration should be given elsewhere as to whether we can consider Santayana's categories of reality (i.e., *Realms of Being*) to be phenomenologically derived since they certainly appear to meet Peirce's criteria in the manner he derived the categories of *Firstness*, *Secondness* and *Thirdness*. Not unlike James's phenomenological approach, the importance of Peirce's phenomenology has only more recently been acknowledged, and as Hauser proposes, the phenomenological derivation of his categories of *Firstness*, *Secondness* and *Thirdness* could have important implications for philosophy.[62] Although space does not allow for a thorough consideration of the comparison of the respective categories of Peirce and Santayana, I will briefly point out where they closely coincide in relation to some phenomenological aspects.

Peirce defines *phaneron* "as a proper name to denote the total content of any one consciousness, the sum of all we have in mind in any way whatever regardless of its cognitive value."[63] This definition, on first consideration, is not obviously associated with the earlier definitions above of *essence*, and in fact, Peirce leaves the definition rather vague. However, can one be conscious of one or many impressions or intuitions in immediacy? Such a question brings the two concepts closer to congruency. Peirce's notion becomes clearer in its relation to *essence* as he provides a phenomenological example of the simplest form of awareness.

> Imagine, if you please, a consciousness in which there is no comparison, no relation, no recognized multiplicity (since parts would be other than the whole), no change, no imagination of any modification of what is positively there, no reflexion—nothing but a simple positive character. Such a consciousness might be just an odor, . . or it might be one infinite dead ache; it might be the hearing of a piercing eternal whistle. In short, any simple and positive quality of feeling would be something which our description fits that it is such as it is quite regardless of anything else.[64]

This state of "no comparison" would reflect the state of phenomena before association with a previously experienced *essence*. It is a helpful notion that we could classify an *essence* or *phaneron* as falling within Peirce's category of *Firstness* and in Husserl's "realm of possibilities." Robert Corrington draws our attention to the "immediacy" of this simplest, precognitive, pre-perceptive experience that I would claim is tantamount to Santayana's intuition of *essence*. These phenomena (i.e., odors and sounds) are examples of the appearances and/or experience of *phanerons*. Further characterizing the *phaneron*, Peirce proposes that "phaneroscopy has nothing at all to do with the question of how far the phanerons it studies correspond to any realities [existents]."[65] *Phanerons*, therefore, have that "ghostly" character, as in Husserl's and Santayana's essences, of being given to consciousness through intuition independent of reality and the empirical mode. Recall that for Santayana, this immediate intuition of an *essence* is the totality of verifiable experience, limited by the *sopm*. The ultimate perception of that *essence* (e.g., that "dead ache" that Peirce refers to above) requires that all those faculties referred to in the above Peirce quote be missing in the simplest awareness. The *phaneron*, like the *essence* of Santayana, is "pre-semiotic," or "signless" (but still potentially symbolic) and in its immediacy has yet to signify anything. It is a sensual "feeling" upon which one begins the semiotic process of forming a perception and describing the experience.[66]

Further pertinent considerations of Peirce's phenomenology bring us to the concepts of the *percipuum* and the *percept*. If the *phaneron* is closely associated with the concept of *essence*, the *percept* can be considered a more singular or "selected" aspect of the *phaneron* and itself can also be considered an *essence* since as Corrington indicates, "the percept does not have any representative status . . . [and] is not about anything other than itself."[67] Both concepts seem to be a grammar of phenomena distinguishable wherein the *percept* becomes distinguishable from the conscious field of the *phaneron* by "looking" (i.e., an *essence* from a field of *essences*). Further, Peirce recognizes the automaticity of the reflexive swing from *percept* (pre-semiotic and non-representational) to the semiotic stage of *perceptual judgment* and perceives it as a "combined reality," an indistinguishable separation that he terms the *percipuum*.[68] In Peirce's categorical terms, it seems that intuition transitions instantaneously from immediacy, or Firstness into Secondness, and in resolution of meaning is already moving toward Thirdness. In Santayana's phenomenological flow, one can choose to be sustained or suspended in immediacy through contemplation, whereas in Peirce such a state seems more ephemeral.

From this brief comparative exercise we can surmise minimally a similarity in Peirce's intuited *phaneron* and *percept* to Santayana's intuited *essence*. Moreover, Peirce's *phaneron*, Santayana's *essence*, and, indeed, the other generally congruent concepts of essence I mentioned earlier, can find a relationship to Peirce's ontological categories of Firstness, Secondness and Thirdness as a transition past the pre-symbolic stage to individually attributed signs in the development of a concept.[69] Corrington relates the "immediate sense certainty" of Hegel's phenomenology to Peirce's consciousness of the immediate and its relation to "firstness . . . given over to the mind in its simple positive character."[70] As indicated earlier, the relationship to the "possibilities" inherent in "firstness" and Santayana's realm of unrealized *essences* as possibilities arising from an eternal reservoir of such possibilities is evident. A rigorous comparison of Peirce and Santayana in regard to their respective phenomenological approaches and derivation of their categorical scheme of reality would provide a rich subject for scholarship whereas space here only allows for the above brief treatment.

James and Santayana

In the case of William James, despite Edie's claim that his phenomenological method, as evidenced in *The Varieties of Religious Experience*, is substantially Husserlian, a specific enough definition of an *essence*-like term is not directly evident in his writings. However, James's definition of the "object of thought" may be seen to have some important relationship to an *essence*, and further to the modern phenomenological notion of the phenomenon.[71] Peirce indicated that James's concept of "pure experience" was "very near" to his idea of phenomenon although James's concept takes place independent of time.[72] Indeed, James's "pure experience" does take place in the continuum or "flux" of the *immediate* prior to any symbolic derivation of the "experience," and "objects" of this experience are not objects of the world.[73]

Heidegger and Santayana

Martin Heidegger, an early protegé of Husserl, following a successive series of departures from Husserl's formal phenomenology, ultimately arrived at a hybrid stance of a "hermeneutic phenomenology" that rejected Husserl's notion of the pure or transcendental ego.[74] Existence moved out of the brackets, and in that sense, a presumption of existential presence of the substantial world was tantamount to the extension into the world by Santayana in *animal faith*. In addition to the shift toward an existential phenomenology seeking man's experience of Being in the world, the Husserlian doctrine of *essence* seems to become obscured or lost with Heidegger's negation of Husserl's notion of intentionality in a transcendental attitude (i.e., in *epoché*). Heidegger's focus is on the fact of being, whereas Husserl's is on consciousness. In Heidegger's etymological derivation of phenomena, he arrives at "that which shows itself," but this must be taken as meaning that which shows itself in any ontological sense (e.g., being in the world). On the other hand, for Husserl, the entire approach is epistemological and substantially devoid of ontological concerns.[75] Heidegger and Santayana, both ontologically oriented, anti-Cartesian, anti-rationalist and highly influenced by their Greek antecedents and Roman Catholicism, are more proximal to pragmatism and offer a scholarly opportunity for a comparison of their phenomenological approach. However, my choice of a comparison of Santayana with the more "orthodox" Husserl allows, I believe, a more compatible model for comparison (and contrasts) given their concept in common of the intuition of essences. I briefly comment further on the possible parallels between Heidegger's and Santayana's phenomenology.

THE PHENOMENOLOGICAL ASPECTS OF HUSSERL AND SANTAYANA

We have established some significant degrees of similarity in theories of *essence* with Whitehead, Peirce, Heidegger and James. Nevertheless, Santayana's comments in the Postscript constitute a negative-leaning critique of the rigorous, step-wise, *eidetic* methodology of Husserl, and would also reject, as Heidegger does, any characterization of phenomenology as an academic discipline and certainly, as a science, even if that science is, as Husserl claims, "a science of essences or forms."[76] There are then, obviously, some important differences in Husserl's and Santayana's ideas as to what this intuitive access to essence should bring to bear. As differences go, Santayana's critique of Husserl's phenomenology in the Postscript, in one way or another, is consistent with other departures from Husserl's doctrine. Additionally, it is important to consider Husserl's "transcendental idealism"[77] vs. Santayana's realism, naturalism and materialism. Santayana's *animal faith* projects his characterization or assignment of *essences* as having possibilities of some congruence with matter and the world, while Husserl "brackets" out any notion of association of essence with existence and remains in the *Lebenswelt*, the world of consciousness (i.e., Santayana's *animal faith* is not a way out for Husserl). Santayana acknowledges in the Postscript the analytical-psychological character of Husserl's project, and in *Scepticism and Animal Faith*, he acknowledges his own disposition toward *literary psychology*.[78] I will leave for the moment Husserl's claim that phenomenology is an "apodictic" science vs. any view on apodicticity that Santayana might have, and discuss it below in relation to the "object" of the phenomenological experience.

THE INTENTIONAL "OBJECT" FOR HUSSERL AND SANTAYANA

Husserl

Husserl proposes that each science is characterized by its own object-province of investigation."[79] Phenomenology is a reflective investigation of phenomena which the phenomenologist considers as objects. These objects, in Husserlian terms, are *essences*, and the subject's experiential access to them in consciousness through intuition must be only and precisely as they are given to him or her. We have seen to this juncture the obvious parallel with the intuitive access to *essences* in Santayana's methodology discussed earlier. When Husserl pronounces "the clarion cry of phenomenology, 'back to the things themselves'" (*zu den Sachen selbst*), he refers to only that which is given in immediate intuition (i.e., *essences*) as the only "things" legitimate as sources of cognition in phenomenology.[80]

Therefore, the only legitimate objects for Husserl, in the transcendental state or phenomenological attitude, are essences.

Santayana

In chapter 2, I quoted Santayana's comment from *The Life of Reason* on "concretions," the earliest progenitive references to *essences* as "the first objects discriminated in attention and projected against the background of consciousness."[81] Indeed, *essence* is then that first "object" that for Santayana is explicitly the first object that comes to us in consciousness. In *Scepticism and Animal Faith* he expresses concern about the manner in which "object" is commonly used—for example, the expression "independent object," which he suggests is often used by "modern philosophers." I omit here his argument against such usage but quote him on his preferential use of the term "object."

> If abuses of language were not inevitable, I should be tempted to urge philosophers to revert to the etymological and scholastic sense of the words object and objective, *making them refer to whatever is placed before the mind, as a target to be aimed at by attention.* Objective would mean then present to the imagination; and things would become objects of thought in the same way in which they become objects of desire."[82]

For Santayana, we can say that first objects in all cases are, and can only be, *essences*. I believe we can also say, in the full rigor of his doctrine of *essences*, that these are the *only* realities (beings) that can be directly attained as objects. Santayana, as Husserl, "sees" *only* intuited *essences*. However, it is only Santayana who figuratively departs from the "brackets" against existence by looking to the world (i.e., to the *a posteriori* through animal faith) for evidence of a pragmatic congruence between intuition, perception and matter. This difference, relative to Husserl, characterizes Santayana's Naturalism as opposed to Husserl's Idealism.

Given the above very brief summary of Husserl's and Santayana's similar ideas of a phenomenological "object," we can now proceed step by step and compare other important aspects of Santayana's philosophy to that of Husserl's method. In order to accomplish this, I will discuss the comparison under the following broad aspects of Husserl's method: (1) phenomenology as a "science," (2) the natural attitude, (3) bracketing and the phenomenological attitude, (4) empathy and intersubjectivity, and (5) reflection upon and description of essence. As I proceed, I will point out some further differences and similarities between the orthodoxy of Husserl and the question of a "naturalistic" phenomenology in Santayana.

APODICTICITY, EVIDENCE AND TRUTH AS THEY PERTAIN TO
PHENOMENOLOGY AS A "SCIENCE"

Husserl

In summary then, Husserl proclaimed that his phenomenological method is a "science of essences" which are intuitively experienced (*Wesensschau*) in an intentional conscious act of focus on that immediate appearance of the *essence*, and then, in a meticulous and rigorous exercise, the intuition of the *essence* is reflected upon and described. He believed that access can be gained to *essences* given in acts of consciousness even if they (the *essences*) are not actualized in the world (i.e., if they remain only possibilities for actualization), and that the truths revealed are solely of an *a priori* nature.[83] Phenomenology, therefore, is an *a priori* science for Husserl. The designation "pure science" is based upon the "stripping" of all empirical content in the phenomenological reduction. Husserl's concept of this science (*Wissenschaft*) is removed from the empirical scientific disciplines of physics or other experimental sciences and rather associated with the *a priori* sciences of mathematics and logic.[84] Since one does not make judgments, form theories or arrive at conclusions regarding the experience of the phenomenon, Husserl's "science" is purely descriptive and carried out in a transcendental state, or phenomenological attitude. Its object-field of science is the realm of *essence* and is removed from the realm of *fact*. The juxtaposed state of mind in life Husserl calls the natural attitude (*die natürliche Einstellung*), which I will discuss in more detail further on, and in this day-to-day attitude, the natural attitude takes a representational and empirical approach toward objects in the material world. This, then, is how we all move about our business from day to day and is in fact the state in which empirical sciences are practiced. We will later associate this "leap" of judgment and belief in direct access to the material world with what Santayana terms the *pathetic fallacy*. However, Husserl, in order to truly "grasp" or capture the experience of the phenomena or *essence*, prescribes a change of attitude (*die gänderung Einstellung*) by which this can be accomplished in the disciplined, focused state of the phenomenological attitude.[85]

Michael Hammond, Jane Howarth and Russell Keat helpfully summarize Husserl's concept of his science, as any science, entailing "*judgements*, which rest ultimately upon *evidential* foundations that are both *apodictic* (indubitable) and *first in themselves* (dependent on nothing else)."[86] The *caveat* that Husserl imposes is that "what has been grasped from an intuitive point of view can be understood and verified only from an intuitive point of view."[87] Therefore, one does not reason to evidence or apodicticity but rather "grasps" it as "something that is and is thus." An example of this evident intuition is simply a sense perception of a "non-imagined" bodily object such as a tree or a sound perceived as guitar music. The grasping of the idea that the three angles of a triangle are equal to two right angles is another example of evidence as well as apodicticity.[88] Of primary importance is that Husserl accepts Descartes' *ergo sum* or *sum cogitans* as apodictic, on one hand, but still suspends what he calls the "empirical ego" on the other,[89] while Santayana evades the *cogito* through *animal* faith. This is that state or perspective in which one would recognize empirical evidence, as opposed to the "transcendental ego" in which one would not. Evidence is then, to Husserl, an *immediate* validation of an experience of "truth." What is "given" then is also the *only* source of knowledge.[90] An adequate demonstration of arriving at *apodictic evidence* involves the intuition of an essence while in the phenomenological attitude and reflecting on the possibility of whether what was presented can be other than what it was that was presented. If one cannot imagine this, the evidence is *apodictic*; if one can, then the evidence is non-apodictic. For Husserl, evidence, in any case as indicated above, is "self-evidence," based upon intuition and without resort to any "existent" evidence. Santayana quotes from Husserl's *Ideas* in the Postscript:

> Between immediacy and existence yawns a veritable abyss in the quality of being (*Sinn*). Existence is posited in perspectives, never given absolutely as it is, and has an accidental and relative status: whereas being in the immediate is certain and unconditioned, and by its very nature not subject to perspective or given in an external view."[91]

Santayana

For Santayana we can note substantial departures in regard to evidence, certainty and truth from Husserl. As we discussed in chapter 2, Santayana removes knowledge from a position of the ideal and sustains certainty only in the *sopm*. Therefore, theoretically, to seek evidence beyond the *sopm* is one thing, but to be certain of arriving at it is a risky extrapolation into a fact. As I have indicated, *for Santayana as for Husserl, "nothing given exists," but Santayana sustains a rigor that, unlike Husserl, never presumes certainty or apodicticity beyond immediacies and only approaches knowledge in animal faith, as Husserl cannot under the strictures of the transcendental attitude.* However, as for Husserl, the evidence that does exist lies in the *a priori*, in the "self-evident," until, in *animal faith*, where it is tested in the faith-supported world of matter. Santayana suggests that the existent "is cognitively and from my point of view, less than apparent." He proposes, "I shall prove no sceptic if I do not immediately transfer all my trust from existence reported to the appearance [*essence*] reporting it." *But through animal faith in the world one still seeks to confirm evidence by arriving at a belief that* a priori *intuitions are verified with* a posteriori *"testing." In regard to truth, unlike Husserl who finds it in the apodictic quality of discerned essences, Santayana can never be certain of attaining it, but affirms that it has being as a representation of fact in the world (all that exists or has existed).*

Santayana, in a radical departure from Husserl, claims no "science" in anything except empirical science where, in practice, phenomena are generally associated with events rather than appearances.[92] On the other hand, like Husserl, Santayana is intuiting idealities or *essences* that have reality but no existence, but ironically, Santayana still claims, as Husserl does, that these *essences*, in an imagined relationship, even if unrealized in existence, can constitute an "exact science." The imagined chess game (described below) in *Realms of Being* seems to agree with Husserl's claims as to the irrefutable "being" of what has been imagined in consciousness as an event. For Santayana, despite the implication below, any attainment of knowledge can only be ascertained by extension and testing of the game in space and time in *animal faith*.

> If chess were not a well-established game and if material chess-boards and chess-men had never existed, a day-dream in which particular imaginary matches were traced out, could hardly be called knowledge: but every possibility and every consequence involved at each juncture would be equally definite, and the science of chess—even if chess never had existed in the world—*would be an exact science*. Evidently an exact science is not without an object, ideal as this object may be [i.e., an *essence*]: indeed the ideal definition of that object, the absence of all ambiguity as to what it is, renders exact science of it possible. Such definable non-existent objects of exact science have being in an eminent degree; *their nature and their intrinsic relations to other comparable natures are perfectly determinate. They are what they are.*[93]

Given the above, we can claim that *both Husserl and Santayana distinguish between two kinds of science—that is, (1) that arising in the* a priori *in the intuition of essences (eidetic) and the validity and essential being of mental constructs, and (2) that arising from the inductive or the* a posteriori *mode.* For both philosophers, the idea that science can arrive at certainty of physical facts (matter) is, of course, doubtful.[94]

THE NATURAL ATTITUDE AND THE PATHETIC FALLACY

I defined the *natural attitude* earlier in summarizing Husserl's phenomenological method as a normative state of day-to-day living. In an everyday experience of seeing a child run or a house on a street, in the natural attitude, one assumes that what is seen and perceived exists as such in the world independent of our perceptual experience of it. This is life on an empirical level where we assume that our perceptions of the world represent fact. Hammond, Howarth and Keat quote Husserl in an echo of a Cartesian axiom regarding the potential error of such an assumption.

> Not only can a particular experienced thing suffer devaluation in an
> illusion of the senses; the whole unitarily surveyable nexus, experi-
> enced throughout a period of time, can prove to be an illusion, a coher-
> ent dream.[95]

Husserl is not concluding that in fact the world does not exist independently of our perception (here recall Santayana's realism concluding with
a belief through faith that it does exist), but that we cannot know this (i.e.,
we cannot guarantee the truth of such a conclusion). He is therefore
concluding that the perspective of a "naive realism" results in distortion
of the real world.

Santayana rests his entire epistemology on the basis of a similar conclusion regarding the unreliability of confidently drawing conclusions
regarding our conscious perceptions and the state of objects or events in
the world. The ontological and existential consequences of such a presumption bear upon the very *Grund* of both Santayana and Husserl's
philosophies. We have noted that "nothing given exists," in the case of
Santayana, and for Husserl, in my view, there is only a slightly less tenuous grip on existence based upon what he calls "evident verification."[96]
Santayana emphasizes that "the animal mind treats its data as facts, or as
signs of facts, but the animal mind is full of the rashest presumptions."[97]
Daniel Moreno postulates that this issue "is the bond underlying Santayana's work as a whole."[98] Let us consider a remarkably compatible reflection by Santayana in relation to Husserl's claims quoted above and what
Santayana terms the *pathetic fallacy.*

> We are condemned to live dramatically in a world that is not dramatic.
> Even our direct perceptions make units of objects that are not units; we
> see creation and destruction where there is only continuity. Memory
> and reflection repeat this *pathetic fallacy*, taking experience for their
> object, where in fact everything is sketchy, evanescent and ambiguous.
> Memory and reflection select, recompose, complete and transform the
> past in the act of repainting it, interpolating miracles and insinuating
> motives that were never in the original experience but that seem now
> to clarify and explain it.[99]

And further,

> An object of faith—and knowledge is one species of faith—can never,
> even in the most direct perception, come within the circle of intuition.
> Intuition of things [as opposed to phenomena or essences] is a contra-
> diction in terms. If philosophers wish to abstain from faith, and reduce
> themselves to intuition of the obvious, they are free to do so, but they
> will thereby renounce all knowledge, and live on passive illusions.[100]

*These conclusions of both Husserl and Santayana provide the basis for an alter-
native "corrective" approach which for both philosophers necessitates a disillusionment in regard to what seems to be true while in the state that Husserl terms
the natural attitude, and synonymously in Santayana, the attitude or philosophy*

of the common man. The *pathetic fallacy* is of particular importance regarding Santayana's philosophy of religion in that religious myths originating from imaginative symbolic representations of man's experience in the world are accorded actual existence by the faithful. A corollary to the *pathetic fallacy* is the idea of *normal madness*, or the human inclination to relate "things as they exist in nature, and things as they appear in opinion."[101] I will discuss this human trait in chapter 4 in relation to religion.

BRACKETING AND THE PHENOMENOLOGICAL ATTITUDE

Husserl

In summary, phenomenology seeks to recover that relationship between what Husserl would call *evidence* (*Evidenz*) and claims for truth, which are unattainable in the "naive" natural attitude. Husserl seeks to accomplish this through a systematic process, a methodology for attainment of the transcendental or phenomenological attitude. For Husserl, attainment of this relationship is intended to establish the apodicticity of essences as they are presented to consciousness (i.e., that which is lacking in the confirmation of any existence of the world and its variety of existents). To reiterate, the first step in his phenomenological method is one undertaken to enable a "seeing" of a certain kind that is only attainable in transcendence from the natural attitude. It is from this platform or through the vehicle of this phenomenological attitude of "seeing" that Husserl claims to be positioned to intuit the *essences* in a disciplined or focused pre-reflective experience, and through a subsequent description, analysis and reflection, to establish a universal and rigorous science free from all "unexamined assumptions."[102]

In order to achieve the phenomenological attitude and consequently gain access to essences, the process of *bracketing* is critical to Husserl's methodology. Here all theories and assumptions from life and the natural attitude (*Einstellung*) are put aside in order to focus unobstructed on the phenomenon or *essence* which is the *intended object*. Science of the world based on the causative factors underlying phenomena (e.g., scientific psychology) are left behind (i.e., bracketed). Through this first step, one thereby reaches a presuppositionless "pure" state of the phenomenological attitude, the transcendental ego, or a "suspension of judgment" in the *epoché*. In the sense that the cognitive field has been for all purposes cleared for a presuppositionless experience, this exercise is known as the *phenomenological reduction.*[103] Where in this or a similar process can we discern a phenomenological approach by Santayana?

Santayana

It is helpful, to begin with, to draw a relationship between Santayana's skeptical method to discern *essence*, which I discussed earlier, and a phenomenological approach. It is apparent, as I indicated earlier, that Santayana in his extreme exercise of the skeptical method both transcends the natural attitude and in a mode of "suspension of judgment" finds "that essence and no other is established before me" [and] I cannot be mistaken about it, since I now have no object of intent other than the object of intuition." [104] There are two of the phenomenological characteristics that we are considering which are implicitly and affirmatively addressed in this description Santayana gives of his method to discern *essence*. The first of these is that in Santayana's "suspension" of what he calls a few pages later in *Scepticism and Animal Faith* "noisy dogma"; [105] he is transcending the *animal* or *normative attitude* and establishing a non-presuppositional attitude, a *phenomenological attitude*, generally meeting the criteria for a Husserlian *epoché*. Further, in affirming that *essence* about which "I cannot be mistaken," he establishes the apodicticity of the intuited event (i.e., the absolute fact of it as an experience). Spiegelberg's commentary on the "remarkable and instructive parallel" of Santayana's approach in radical skepticism to Husserl's phenomenological reduction tends, in my view, to adumbrate Santayana's radical skepticism in Santayana's move toward *animal faith* as if it were to be erased and forgotten. True, for Santayana, radical skepticism is an unacceptably limited approach to life, and unlike Husserl, he moves on to the more tenable mode of *animal faith*. However, what Spiegelberg seems to overlook is that skepticism and its discernment of *essence* never goes away for Santayana. It could be considered a one-time "revelation" if you will, and its shadow remains over Santayana's philosophical attitude, his realism and his attitude toward religion and morality. Skeptic he remains as a result of this phenomenological discovery, but day to day he approaches the world in *animal faith* and pragmatic reconciliation of perception and interaction with the material world. [106]

If we have, in Santayana's skeptical method, a one-time exercise in discovering *essence*, where else then, as he moves forward in a life based upon *animal faith*, can we find his phenomenology? Where else, importantly, can we find a method of "bracketing" or *epoché* in a *phenomenological attitude*? If we consider Santayana's overall project and intention in *Realms of Being*, we need to recall the importance of the nature of his claims for his approach:

> After having cleared my mind as much as possible of traditional sophistry, I have endeavored to recover the natural and inevitable beliefs of a human being living untutored in this world and having a reflective soul. [107]

An implicit "bracketing" and phenomenological attitude is evident here. At one extreme, given this introduction to his approach, it could be suggested that since Santayana has demonstrated to his satisfaction that the *only* basis of human experience is through the intuition of *essences*—which through reflection and imagination are elevated to perceptions which then may be described and reflected upon—then he is exercising an important preliminary phenomenological requisite. Consistent with Husserl is the uncertainty of the existent world, wherein we might say that the certainty of the world of matter is "bracketed" and then through *animal faith* treated "as if" it existed. For Santayana, we are precluded from certainty by the biological limit: "Mind was not created for the sake of discovering the absolute truth."[108] In the following comparison of Santayana's *literary psychology* and Husserl's method of "intersubjectivity," we will note further evidence of bracketing or intentionally reducing the field of examination.

SANTAYANA'S "LITERARY PSYCHOLOGY" AND HUSSERL'S INTERSUBJECTIVITY AND EXPERIENCE OF THE OTHER

Santayana provides a helpful comparison of *literary psychology* and "scientific psychology" in chapter 24 of *Scepticism and Animal Faith*. He notes that they may be practiced in tandem but that they are inherently dealing with different fields. Scientific psychology deals with what are perceived to be observed facts in nature (i.e., the psyche), and it provides a record of how animals act. Santayana's *literary psychology* in the broadest sense is the art of imagining how animals act and think. Since imagination is in the realm of the spirit, in consciousness, it can, unlike a scientific approach, gather a sense of attitudes, feelings or responses of the emotions by "imitative sympathy."[109] Therefore, as Santayana claims, "literary psychology however far scientific psychology may push it back, always remains in possession of the moral field,"[110] and indeed, Santayana would describe himself as a moralist pursuing value in human experience. There is a dimension available to *literary psychology* which is not in the field of interest of science nor does science have the ability to attain it. It is this dimension that Santayana's philosophical project explores and mines and indeed is that in which Husserl, ultimately, as well as Heidegger concern themselves (i.e., the non-scientific realm). Santayana uses the following observation to make a point that is of phenomenological importance.

> Whereas scientific psychology is addressed to the bodies and material events composing the animate world, literary psychology restores the *essences* intervening in the perception of these material events, and re-echoes the intuitions aroused in these bodies. This visionary stratum is

the true immediate as well as the imagined ultimate. Even in the simplest perceptions on which scientific psychology, or any natural science, can be based, there is an *essence* present which only poetry can describe or sympathy conceive.[111]

In this observation, Santayana is presenting a method that is more poetic and more sympathetic but also provides a more effective descriptive language where scientific description or causative perspectives do not apply. The scientific view is indeed "bracketed" for Santayana in the exercise of *literary psychology* since the phenomenon is not receptive to scientific description. In such a method, one can experience the *essences* and not obscure their evidence by the pursuit of facts. Here, we can recall the observation I quoted earlier from Sprigge that "literary psychology is what phenomenology at least ought to be about."[112] In order to further develop his idea, Santayana provides a pertinent example of how *literary psychology* differs from scientific observation.

> Schoolroom experiments in optics, for instance, are initially a play of intuitions, and exciting in that capacity; I see, and am confident and pleased that others see with me, the colour of an after-image, this straight stick bent at the surface of the water, the spokes of this wheel vanishing as it turns. For science, these given essences are only stepping stones to the conditions under which they arise, and their proper aesthetic nature, which is trivial in itself, is forgotten in the curious knowledge.[113]

Instead of intuited *essences* being just a sign of material facts for the scientist (i.e., a reductive approach), the literary psychologist perceives the *essences* as the immediate experience with no effort to analyze beyond the response of the imagination to the essences described in the classroom event. The scientific view, on the other hand, is an *intentional* one that has gone beyond the immediate to one of perception and interpretation of signs wherein knowledge is sought based on the phenomenon (i.e., aspects of causation in the experiment).[114] The poet, as an example of the former case, in a sensitivity to the immediate, may be thought of as the paradigm of a literary psychologist and as a kind of phenomenologist as well, and Santayana is a self-proclaimed poet before a philosopher. He suggests that

> the poet feels the rush of emotion on the other side of the deployed events; he wraps them in an atmosphere of immediacy, luminous or thunderous; and his spirit, that piped so thin a treble in its solitude, begins to sing in chorus. Literary psychology pierces to the light, to the shimmer of passion and fancy, beyond the body of nature.[115]

The phenomenologist is concerned with the realm of appearances, the phenomena, the *essence*, and not, as the scientist is, with that reality which lies "behind" or "beyond."[116] When one is attuned, it is the experience of that which is given to consciousness which is of interest. The poet in

Santayana, we can conclude, captures the immediate, the *essence* of a discriminate experience, and upon reflection and arriving at perception of the phenomena, represents the vision in symbolic description.[117] The phenomenological character implicit in Santayana's concept of a *literary psychology*, it seems to me, cannot be mistaken. The experience of the immediate is dominant; there is an intentional discrimination of an experience of *essence* or of a complex of *essences*; there is no intent to go "beyond" or "behind" the phenomena as judgment and causality are ruled out. Finally, there is reflection and description in symbolic terms.

In chapter 18 of *Scepticism and Animal Faith*, "Knowledge Is Faith Mediated in Symbols," there is what I would call a "dense" phenomenological description. Santayana's description is one of a "proverbial child" crying for the moon and a sympathetic observer discerning the *object* of the child's attention and desire.

> The attitude of the child's body also *identifies the object for him, in his own subsequent discourse*. He is not likely to forget a moon that he cried for. When in stretching his hand towards it he found he could not touch it, he learned that this bright good was not within his grasp, and he made a beginning in the experience of life. He also made a beginning in science, since he then added the absolutely true predicate "out of reach" to the rather questionable predicates "bright" and "good" (and perhaps edible) with which his first glimpse had supplied him. That active and mysterious thing coordinate with himself, since it lay in the same world with his body . . . the thing that attracted his hand was evidently the same very thing that eluded it.[118]

Here Santayana's *literary psychology*, although it has obvious phenomenological features (i.e., intuition of *essences*, reflection and description), carries with it some presumption. This presumption is that which is characterized by the attribution based upon intuition and memory of the signification and recognition of earlier phenomenological experiences. The observed object (e.g., the "proverbial child") will respond to objects as Santayana might respond to the same object in the same situation. He indicates, "I must appeal to my faith in nature . . . that this child and I are animals of the same species, in the same habitat." The anticipation of behavior, in this particular case and others similar to it, is based upon a belief predicated on the memory of earlier experiences, or recalled *essences* experienced and semiotically assigned, and the belief that other conscious subjects will see things as the observer sees.[119] It is a recognition of a complex of *essences* that has presented itself before and is retained in memory. Through knowledge (belief) of a particular pattern earlier discerned, for example, signs of attention in animals to an object such as physical attitude or behavior, one then can discern when an animal (e.g., the child) has discriminated an object for attention. Further, Santayana proposes that such "knowledge of discourse in other people or of myself at other times [he refers to *literary psychology*] . . . is, or may be . . . the most literal or adequate sort of knowledge of which a mind is capable."[120] It is in this approach of empathy and intersubjectivity that we will see marked similarities to an important aspect of Husserl's method.

Husserl

In phenomenology, empathy is the expectation that the experience of your own subjectivity may be projected to another. Clearly, in such a projection there is the possibility or even a likelihood of an unreasonable imposition of this subjectivity where little or no congruence is present and one is then in the danger zone of Santayana's *pathetic fallacy* or Husserl's natural attitude. Intersubjectivity is the expectation that as a subject among subjects, one might behave as others do in a similar situation. One may therefore recognize and interpret intentions, emotions or behavior in others. Both Santayana and Husserl, particularly in his later work, utilize aspects of this approach. Dermot Moran captures Husserl's perspective from the *Cartesian Meditations*.

> Our natural life is a life in community, living in a world of shared objects, shared environment, shared language, shared meanings. Moreover, there is something I can read off the world at first glance. I see a tree in the garden and know it is a publicly accessible object, a tree others can also see . . . precisely as a tree. In other words, my perception of the tree already indicates to me that it is a tree for *others*.[121]

Husserl's ideas on empathy evolved somewhat in his later work, but for my purposes here, they seemed to sustain the same character, essentially that "when I experience another person, I *apperceive* them as having the kind of experiences I would have if I was over there."[122] There is an analogical association in responding to the *essences* in the "other" and relating them to those established in the subject's own memory from past experience. For Husserl, the "other" was grasped "within my ownness," resulting in the other being a "phenomenological modification of myself."[123] However, Santayana reflects the same concept of analogical association as Husserl but with the specific requirement for "scientific" preparation (i.e., falling back on tested correspondence of rational thinking to the realm of matter).

> If literary psychology is to interpret the universe at large, it can be only very cautiously, after I have explored nature scientifically as far as I can, and am able to specify the degree of analogy and the process of concretion that connect my particular life with the universal flux.[124]

Here Santayana's *animal faith* allows for the validity of pragmatic foreknowledge to support the analogies drawn. Otherwise, it seems to me

that this aspect of Santayana's and Husserl's approach having the characteristics of empathy and subjectivity is nearly identical.

It may be that further study of Santayana's *literary psychology* will find
some common ground with phenomenological psychology. Santayana
related the practice of psychoanalysis to that of *literary psychology*. Heidegger's existential phenomenology moved closer to a compatibility with
psychoanalysis as he moved away from the strictures of the Husserlian
epoché. My sense is that an understanding of its scope is obscured by
Santayana's simple and preliminary definition in *Scepticism and Animal
Faith* that "literary psychology is the art of imagining how they [animals]
feel and think."

REFLECTION UPON AND DESCRIPTION OF PHENOMENA

Husserl's Method

Basically there are two broad aspects differentiated by Husserl in
what he calls the *intentional analysis*. These are (1) the *noetic* description
which describes the *acts* of consciousness (e.g., remembering, believing,
loving), and (2) the *noematic* description which describes the *objects* or
cognitive content of consciousness.[125] We can safely equate the *noema*, for
our intents and purposes, with the *eidos* or essence and as that which
would be "given" to all persons who have the same act of consciousness,
while the *noesis* may vary from person to person and for the same person.
Husserl goes on to describe in meticulous procedural detail in the *Cartesian Meditations* the method of *eidetic* description. A rigorous consideration of this detail is of no purpose for my argument, but a brief summary
of three broad phases of the "descriptive" process will prove helpful as
we proceed.

First, in the *noematic* phase the structure or constitution of the "object"
experienced by consciousness through consideration of the phenomenal
object *in cogito* from different angles, distances or perspectives is arrived
at in an intuitive sense of the "unity" of these perspectives. This step is
one of synthesis and the unified structure arrived at is the "synthetic
structure." The subject is here describing the experience more or less in a
scientific manner. Following this step is a switch to the *noetic* phase
where attention is turned to the subject (consciousness itself) and the
"experiencing" nature of what was seen. This is a turn from "what" to
"how" and entails the description of how seen, in what temporal frame,
close up or from a distance and so forth. Beyond this, "horizons" of
possible appearances are described which are visualized in the imagination and beyond actual experiences and involve associations that seem to
either detract or verify the developing notion of the perception of the
object. These perspectives, then, of *noematic* and *noetic* description are

"unified" to provide a perception of the object that is to some degree "verified." I have abbreviated here Husserl's process as presented in his *Cartesian Meditations* to a minimalistic extreme but what I have provided should lend itself to some comparison with Santayana's project.[126]

Santayana and the Limits of Phenomenological Description

It should be noted that for Santayana the idea of a "description" of an *essence* is in one sense a redundancy since this is tantamount to a "description of a description." He points out the absurdity of considering *essence* as something that can be described since "essences do not need description, since they are descriptions already."[127] This claim may at first seem an antinomy, but it is thoroughly consistent with Santayana's axioms that we have earlier put forth: that is, that (1) *essences* are the only elements that might give a sense of the world through consciousness, and (2) there is no certainty and description followed by any association with the realm of matter is an exercise in *animal faith*. Any direct comparison of Santayana's approach to description of the vision of the *essence* in Husserlian terms of *noesis* and *noema* is problematical. However, we can much more readily associate *noesis*, as Santayana's effort at description of what is given (i.e., *essence*), with the method of Husserl. One can attach signs and symbolic meaning to the immediate experience of the *essence* to form perceptions, and this can be a worthwhile, even a necessary exercise for life in the world. Consequently Santayana proposes that "nevertheless the attempt to describe certain essences instead of simply inspecting them has some justification and meets with some success."[128] Santayana provides us the excellent example of such an attempt in the description of a melodic *essence*: "So written music is a means of reviving melodies; the phonograph is another and even verbal descriptions and similes may not be useless in suggesting musical essences and distinguishing them clearly in their own category."[129] One therefore "attempts" to describe through signification in order to retain some useful association (i.e., translating the intuition of the *essence* to a perception).

ANIMAL FAITH, MEMORY AND THE PHENOMENOLOGICAL APPROACH

In chapter 18 of *Scepticism and Animal Faith* Santayana describes a methodological approach which is somewhat uncanny in its parallel character to Husserl's phenomenological method. I will attempt to briefly characterize the steps in Santayana's approach with a description beginning with his own words.

> Since intuition of essence is not knowledge, knowledge can never lie in
> an overt comparison of one datum with another datum given at the

same time; even in pure dialectic, the comparison is with a datum *believed* to have been given formerly. If both terms were simply given [both data or *essences*] they would compose a complex essence without the least signification. Only when one of the terms is indicated by intent, without being given exhaustively, can the other term serve to define the first more fully, or be linked with it in an assertion which is not mere tautology. [130]

We can see the correlation between Santayana's idea here of the importance of earlier intuitions and the anticipation involved in the quotation given in the last section describing the child's experience with the moon and its relation to *literary psychology*. The comparison of two "unknowns," he suggests, does not move one toward knowledge. The comparison must be of a previously intuited *essence* upon which reflection has developed into a perception of an object or event which is held in memory. This is not unlike the aspect of Husserlian reflection or intentional analysis wherein one compares the object (phenomenon or essence) with other images in an "is-it-like-this" process, which refines the "meaning" of the object. [131] As Spiegelberg indicates in relation to eidetic intuitioning, "There is no adequate intuiting of essences without the antecedent or simultaneous intuiting of "exemplifying particulars." [132] Such particulars may be given either in perception or imagination, a combination of both or drawn from memory. When Santayana indicates that the *essence* is "without the least signification," he is illuminating a point that is sometimes missed in the understanding of *essence* (i.e., that it is devoid of any indication of what it is in the immediacy of the intuition). It is only through subsequent description, association and reflection that one arrives at a *perception* to allow an imaginative progression toward an intuited grasp, for example, of another human's feelings or behavior, or any event or phenomenon. As we know, this relationship between the intuition of *essence*, the need to build through reflection and *animal faith* to a perception and the pragmatic association of this perception, through experience in the world (i.e., *action*), is that exercise by which one arrives at what Santayana concludes is *knowledge*, or the closest approximation of it. The limitations of such an exercise draw their importance, again, from Santayana's idea of the *pathetic fallacy*.

Finally, a major departure in Santayana from Husserl must be emphasized when we arrive at the notion of *animal faith* in relation to the "description" of *essences*. When Santayana responds to *essences*, describes them or relates them to other *essences*, he is responding to them in consciousness as Husserl would. It is only in his projection of those *essences* to a potential relation with matter that *animal faith* carries him tentatively into the natural world where *animal faith* allows him to consider the *a posteriori* relationships to his intuitions.

In chapter 1 of *Realms of Being*, "Various Approaches to Essence," Santayana proposes four "avenues of approach" to *essence*. These approaches are *skepticism, dialectic, contemplation* and *spiritual discipline*, all of which, he claims, lead to the discrimination or intuition of *essence*.[133] We have adequately addressed his important skeptical method earlier. In all of these approaches, Santayana imposes one general requirement or "single avenue" (i.e., "attention," without which *essence* cannot be intuitively attained). This seems, in Husserlian terms, to approximate the elimination of distractedness in the phenomenological attitude or consciousness directed at the "object" (i.e., the "inexistent" phenomenon or essence).[134]

In describing the *dialectical* approach to *essence*, Santayana clearly depicts its limitations. Indeed, the transcendental state of Husserlian phenomenology would obviously be considered as limited within dialectic and thereby not a possible contributor to what Santayana would consider knowledge. The encounter with *essence* in dialectic "does not destroy its native competence to describe essences; in its purity it will be free from error because free from any pretence to ultimate existence (refer to the chess-game example given earlier).[135] In dialectic, he asserts consciousness builds imaginary structures but not ulterior existences and "churns" in essences, building and contriving "logical" structures and arriving fallaciously at "certainty."[136] Santayana suggests that "only when dialectic passes its own frontiers and, fortified by a passport countersigned by experience . . . has dialectic itself any claim to truth or any relevance to the facts."[137] Here recall the earlier quotation in the last section where the approach to knowledge in the exercise of *literary psychology* depends upon the prerequisite of exploring nature as far as possible. *Essence* has indeed been irrefutably intuited, but the dialectician in his or her solipsism is stuck in the imagination and, for Santayana, limited to a "dead and eternal" realm.[138]

The *contemplative* approach to *essence* is a relative spiritual "leap" from the *dialectical* approach in respect to the intention of the exercise and in respect to its "arrested" nature in regard to holding back from description or any effort through *animal faith* to associate the object with external facts. Of the four approaches, Santayana "retains" this one and that of *spiritual discipline* as serving a role in *spirituality* which he indicates in a letter to Justus Buchler in 1936 is "concomitant" to a life of reason.[139]

Spiegelberg observes that Santayana's approach in contemplation is "something like a liberation of the human spirit," while Husserl's methodology "is one of deadly seriousness, a matter of scientific conscience and uncompromising radicalism.[140] It may be excusable to consider, as Spiegelberg does, that Santayana's objectives, relative to Husserl's, are "much less pretentious and less solemn than Husserl's."[141] This should not however, in my view, be allowed in any way to devalue the moral seriousness and virtuous intent of Santayana's contemplative approach toward achieving "the whole happiness possible to man."[142] Santayana's ontological purpose, relative to Husserl's epistemological one, is evident.

> Awaken attention, intensify it, purify it into a white flame, and the
> actual and unsubstantial object of intuition will stand before you in all
> its living immediacy and innocent nakedness. But notice: this attention,
> discovering nothing but essence, is itself an animal faculty: it is called
> forth by material stress, or by passion . . . and it is only a passionate
> soul who can be contemplative.[143]

It is Santayana's prerequisite for "passionate contemplation" as this initial step in the immediacy of the experience of intuiting *essence* that is of
particular interest to us here. It is of interest both in regard to its phenomenological character short of description or reflection as well as to its
bearing upon religion and particularly upon the limited phenomenological character of mysticism. At the core of Santayana's idea of transcendence to a spiritual attitude is the dominance and intensity of the attention of consciousness. I will address this aspect of contemplation in more
detail in chapter 4.

SOME CONCLUSIONS

In this chapter I have tried in limited space to associate certain elements
of phenomenology with Santayana's philosophy in order to depict and
justify his unbiased and open view toward religion in the face of his own
disillusionment. I recognize that there are gaps in the argument which
can only be filled with further study and characterization of his overall
approach. The common ground in Husserl's and Santayana's projects of
the importance of essence as the first object of awareness in consciousness
was the most obvious point of comparison for me to begin the discussion
on my claims for Santayana's phenomenology. We may ultimately discover in Heidegger's rejection of Husserl's transcendental attitude and
his Idealism that there is closer alignment in his more "unstructured"
notion of phenomenology to that of Santayana. Heidegger's idea that
phenomenology is more a general attitude toward thinking and "seeing"
than an exclusive method is an appealing notion as well as his idea that
"there is no such thing as one phenomenology." Such notions may leave
the door open to further consider Santayana's approach outside the category of orthodox phenomenology. Certainly the characteristic phenomenological aspects in the philosophies of William James and Charles
Sanders Peirce have opened the door to the possibilities for a naturalistic
phenomenology.

   At this juncture, my view is that Santayana's entire mature philosophical project may be considered an unstructured phenomenology, and
more specifically, a phenomenology of the spirit. If we consider *Realms of
Being* to be, at its core, not a descriptive psychology, but a description of
the conflict in the human spirit between fact and illusion, intuition and

absolute apprehension and the work of the imagination vs. the truth of nature then such a broad categorical term may be appropriate.

NOTES

1. Daniel T. Pedarske, "Santayana on Laughter and Prayer," *American Journal of Philosophy* 11, no. 2 (May 1990): 144. Pedarske refers particularly to Santayana's treatment of prayer in *The Life of Reason* (*Reason in Religion*) and *Realms of Being* (*Realm of the Spirit*). I will address Santayana's treatment of prayer in chapter 4. Pedarske's brief observation seems to derive from a sense of a characteristic generic quality of description and certainly a sensitivity by Santayana dealing with the phenomenon of prayer, rather than to a rigorous interpretation of his phenomenological approach in regard to "bracketing" or *epoché*, intentionality of consciousness or other "technical" aspects of the method.

2. Santayana, *Realms of Being*, 172–74.

3. A comprehensive treatment of the phenomenological method in relation to James's *Principles of Psychology* is found in Bruce Wilshire, *William James and Phenomenology: A Study of "The Principles of Psychology"* (Bloomington: Indiana University Press, 1968). Additional references on James's phenomenology are Charles Haddock Siegfried, "William James's Phenomenological Methodology," *Journal of the British Society for Phenomenology* 20, no. 1 (January 1989): 62–76; and Ash Gobar, "The Phenomenology of William James," *Proceedings of the American Philosophical Society* 114, no. 4 (August 1970): 294–308.

4. James M. Edie, *William James and Phenomenology* (Bloomington: Indiana University Press, 1987), 52. Edie's claims are indeed singular to my knowledge, and of particular interest in regard to his association of James's phenomenological approach with Husserl. James, categorically considered an American Pragmatist, has been perceived as having more in common with Merleau-Ponty, Heidegger or Schutz rather than Husserl by Robert Corrington and others. See Robert Corrington, Carl Hausman, and Thomas Seebohm, eds., *Pragmatism Considers Phenomenology* (London: Center for Advanced Research in Phenomenology and University Press of America, 1987), 217.

5. Santayana, "A General Confession," Schilpp, 15.

6. Heidegger rejects Husserl's concept of "pure" transcendental ego, *epoché* or *bracketing* in all its stages, and, in a very general sense, Heidegger's style of philosophizing begins from man rather than nature. See Antonio Barbosa da Silva, *The Phenomenology of the Sacred as a Philosophical Problem* (Sweden: CWK Gleerup, 1982), 53–63. The reference to Husserl's phenomenological method as "psychological" refers to its focus on consciousness and cognition through the intuition of *essences* (as opposed to facts). This point is made to avoid confusion with Husserl's decision to purge his early references (e.g., his psychologistic treatment of arithmetic) to "psychologisms," or the identity of empirical psychological generalizations with non-empirical logical statements. See Paul Edwards, ed., *The Encyclopedia of Philosophy*, 1967, s.v. "Phenomenology," Richard Schmitt.

7. Charles Sanders Peirce, independently of Husserl by virtue of predating him, did claim a phenomenological method *per se* to ascertain and study "the kinds of elements universally present in phenomenon; meaning by phenomenon, whatever is present at any time to the mind in any way." William L. Rosensohn, "The Phenomenology of Charles Sanders Peirce: From the Doctrine of Categories to Phaneroscopy," *Philosophical Currents* 10 (1974): 2. From Charles Hartshorne and Paul Weiss, eds., *The Collected Papers of Charles Sanders Peirce*, vol. 1 (Cambridge, MA: Harvard University Press, 1931), paragraph 280. In regard to the argument for and against a naturalistic phenomenology, see Scott F. Aiken, "Pragmatism, Materialism and Phenomenology," *Human Studies* 29, no. 3 (September 2006), 317–40.

8. Woodward, *Living in the Eternal*, 85.

9. Ibid.

10. Ibid. Taken from Santayana, *Realms of Being*, 173.

11. Sprigge, *Santayana*, 182. Notably, Sprigge, in his excellent exposition of Santayana's theory of *essence*, doesn't anywhere else in his book draw similarities or parallels to phenomenology. Sprigge sharply differentiates phenomenology from realism. See Timothy Sprigge, "Whitehead and Santayana," *Process Studies* 28, nos. 1–2 (1999): 44.

12. Santayana emphatically claims "that *complex essences* are not compounded"— that is, a complex essence is "evoked in sense [and] is single and novel" (*Realms of Being*, 140–41.) An *essence* that is evoked, either single or complex, is evoked as *one* symbol. A *complex essence* with all its internal and external relationships is not subject to division into "parts" or primary *essences*. It is evoked as one impression and if attention is drawn to a detail of the complex, this is evoking or intuiting an entirely different *essence*. Sprigge reminds us that for Santayana, "all essences are equally primary." Foundational to this paradoxical concept is Santayana's doctrine that "essences have no origin [they are eternal], and in that sense, not constituents" (*Realms of Being*, 89.) See Sprigge's comprehensive exegesis of the doctrine of complex essences in Sprigge, *Santayana*, 74–78.

13. Sidney Feshbach, "An Orchestration of the Arts in Wallace Stevens's 'Peter Quince at the Clavier,'" *Analecta Husserliana: The Yearbook of Phenomenological Research* 63 (2000): 188.

14. McCormick, *George Santayana*, 278. See also Van Meter Ames, *Proust and Santayana: The Aesthetic Way of Life* (New York: Russell & Russell, 1964); and George Santayana, "Proust on Essences," in *Obiter Scripta*, ed. Justus Buchler and Benjamin Schwartz (New York: Charles Scribner's Sons, 1936), 273–79.

15. Santayana to Arthur M. Cohen, February 9, 1948, from the *Partisan Review* 25 (1958): 632–37. This in response to Cohen's inquiry of Santayana regarding Santayana's reactions to Kierkegaard and the existential emphasis on subjective cognition. Santayana's disparagement of the Existentialist concept of *angst* is very evident in the letter.

16. Herbert Spiegelberg, *The Phenomenological Movement* (The Hague: Martinus Nijhoff, 1982), 123–24. Spiegelberg's only citation in his comparison is from Santayana's postscript to *The Realm of Essence*.

17. Santayana, *Scepticism and Animal Faith*, 74.

18. Ibid., 69.

19. This is an obvious analogy with the Platonic method but it remains that Santayana draws his similarity to Platonism primarily from its essential contemplativeness rather than with other imperatives of this school. The relationship of skepticism to phenomenology is helpfully addressed in Brice R. Wachterhauser, ed., *Phenomenology and Scepticism: Essays in Honor of James M. Edie* (Evanston, Illinois: Northwestern University Press, 1996).

20. Santayana, *Scepticism and Animal Faith*, 76.

21. Ibid., 75.

22. Spiegelberg, *The Phenomenological Movement*, 123.

23. Santayana, *Scepticism and Animal Faith*, 214.

24. Thomas N. Munson, SJ, *The Essential Wisdom of George Santayana* (New York: Columbia University Press, 1962), 43.

25. Ibid., 124. Also see Joseph J. Kockelman's essay "Association in Husserl's Phenomenology," in *Phenomenology and Scepticism*, ed. Wachterhauser, 63.

26. A consideration of phenomenological aspects of Santayana's philosophy independent of any relationship to his philosophy of religion may shed even more light on the validity of claims supporting the presence of these aspects.

27. William James, *The Varieties of Religious Experience* (New York: Modern Library, 1957). Most of the scholarly assessments of the phenomenological character of James's project are based upon critiques of his *The Principles of Psychology*, and all of these focus on a comparative analyses vs. Husserl. There is not space here to deal with this issue except to say that Bruce Wilshire, in his book *William James and Phenomenology: A*

Study of the Principles of Psychology, has made broad and convincing claims for James as a phenomenologist and as the earliest major contributor to phenomenological psychology as a method. A rebuttal to this claim, based substantially on James "not passing over the threshold of Husserl's program into phenomenological psychology," is represented in a reply by Stuart F. Spicker in *Journal of the British Society for Phenomenology* 2 (October 1971): 69–74.

28. Ibid., 156–57.

29. Ibid., 6–8.

30. Spiegelberg, *The Phenomenological Movement*, 679.

31. Edward J. Jurji, *The Phenomenology of Religion* (Philadelphia: Westminster Press, 1963), 50.

32. It is significant that Santayana expressed mostly negative views regarding James's *Varieties of Religious Experience*. Santayana was suspicious regarding the possible mental state of the subjects whose experiences James depicted and not sympathetic to James's openness to paranormal religious and psychological events. Santayana's expressed views reflected in part his generally derisive attitude toward mysticism. See John J. Fisher, "Santayana on James: A Conflict of Views on Philosophy," *American Philosophical Quarterly* 2, no.1 (January 1965), 67–73.

33. Santayana, *The Idea of Christ in the Gospels*, 3.

34. Ibid.

35. Michael Weinstein, "Twentieth-Century Realism and the Autonomy of the Human Sciences: The Case of George Santayana," *Analecta Husserliana: The Yearbook of Phenomenological Research* 15 (1983): 124.

36. Santayana, *The Idea of Christ in the Gospels*, 25.

37. Santayana, *Realms of Being*, 58–58.

38. On the opening page of *Reason in Religion* (from the one-volume edition of *Life of Reason*), Santayana observes that "the enlightenment common to young wits and worm-eaten old satirists, who plume themselves on detecting the scientific ineptitude of religion—something which the blindest half can see . . . points to notorious facts incompatible with religious tenets literally taken, but it leaves unexplored the habits of thought from which these tenets sprang, their original meaning and their true function" (179).

39. Marlies E. Kronegger, "A. T. Tymieniecka's Challenges: From a Spiritual Wasteland to Transcendence," *Analecta Husserliana: The Yearbook of Phenomenological Research* 43 (1994): 84.

40. George Santayana, *Platonism and the Spiritual Life*, taken from *Winds of Doctrine and Platonism and the Spiritual Life* (Gloucester, MA: Peter Smith, 1971), 248. This is not to suggest that morals are not important, but only extraneous to the infinitely valueless Realm of Essence and the spiritual life. Otto's purpose in discriminating between morals and the religious experience is more specifically to deal with the religious experience (the "numinous tremendum fascinans") *per se*.

41. Da Silva, *The Phenomenology of Religion*, 27–29.

42. Dermot Moran, *Introduction to Phenomenology* (London: Routledge, 2000), 3.

43. Santayana, *Realms of Being*, 171–74.

44. John Passmore, *A Hundred Years of Philosophy* (New York: Basic Books, 1966), 291. McCormick provides the same reference in *George Santayana*, 271. In his endnote (fn18, 551), McCormick observes that Passmore provides no basis for his comment. I can find no basis for it either in Santayana's work or letters. In a letter to Justus Buchler dated October 15, 1937, Santayana indicates only familiarity with Peirce's theory of signs and indexes but suggests he frequently used in his writing "a classification he [Peirce] made . . . of signs into indexes and symbols and images" (Buchler, "One Santayana or Two?" 54). Peirce is also barely referred to in Santayana's autobiography, *Persons and Places*. Nevertheless, consideration of Peirce's phenomenological theory is instructive for our purposes here.

45. Buchler, "One Santayana or Two?" 54. From a letter to Buchler, October 15, 1937.

46. Jaegwon Kim, and Ernest Sosa, eds., *A Companion to Metaphysics* (Cambridge, MA: Blackwell, 1995), 393–94.

47. Edwards, *Encyclopedia of Philosophy*, s.v. "Essence," Alasdair MacIntyre.

48. Santayana, *Realms of Being*, 173–74; emphasis mine.

49. Husserl's conception of *evidence* means that impression grasped in the immediate, only through an intuition of essences or an "experiencing of something that is, and is thus." See Edmund Husserl, *Cartesian Meditations*, trans. Dorion Cairns (The Hague: Martinus Nijhoff, 1960), 12. Something that through intuition is evident is for Husserl, *apodictic*, or beyond doubt (i.e., one intuits what one intuits and at that instant can be certain of it). See Michael Hammond, Jane Howarth, and Russell Keat, *Understanding Phenomenology* (Oxford: Basil Blackwell, 1991), 20–21.

50. David Bell, *Husserl* (London: Routledge, 1990), 193–94.

51. Ibid., 196. "The datum of essential intuition is a pure essence . . . Essential intuition is the consciousness of something, of an 'object,' a something towards which its glance is directed." Edmund Husserl, *Ideas Pertaining to a Pure Phenomenology and to a Phenomenological Philosophy*, trans. F. Kersten (The Hague: Nijhoff, 1982), 55.

52. Santayana dedicates chapter 5 to "Complex Essences" in *Realms of Being*, 66–77.

53. Santayana, *Realms of Being*, 68–69.

54. Ibid., 68.

55. Richard Schmitt's article s.v. "Phenomenology" in Edwards, *Encyclopedia of Philosophy* equates "phenomenon" to "essence." Santayana clearly does so. This can be a subtle point and I am grateful for my discussions with Professor Charles Courtney in arriving at some distinction in the usage of these terms by Husserl.

56. Santayana, *Realms of Being*, 168.

57. Ibid., 168–69.

58. Ibid., 171.

59. Ibid.

60. It is not known for certain by the author if Santayana attended Peirce's lecture "On Phenomenology" at Harvard on April 2, 1903, in which he discussed this subject. It later was referred to in a Peirce manuscript titled "The Basis of Pragmatism" that was probably published in December 1905 as "Phaneroscopy." Tiller in his paper *Peirce and Santayana: Pragmatism and the Belief in Substance*, referring to Brent, suggests that Santayana did indeed attend the lecture(s) and, unlike William James, was able to grasp Peirce's concepts. See Nathan Houser and Christian Kloesel, eds., *The Essential Peirce: Selected Philosophical Writings*, vol. 2 (Bloomington: Indiana University Press, 1998), 361–70. Santayana otherwise would have only had access to Peirce's theory of *phaneroscopy* through Hartshorne and Weiss, *The Collected Papers*, after he was long a resident in Europe.

61. Robert Corrington, *An Introduction to C. S. Peirce* (Lanham, Maryland: Rowman & Littlefield, 1993), 136.

62. Nathan Houser and Christian Kloesel, eds., *The Essential Peirce: Selected Philosophical Writings*, vol. 1 (Bloomington: Indiana University Press, 1992), xli.

63. Houser and Kloesel, *The Essential Peirce*, vol. 2, 362.

64. Corrington, *An Introduction to C. S. Peirce*, 137. Quotation from Hartshorne and Weiss, *The Collected Papers*, vol. 5, par. 44.

65. Manley H. Thompson, *The Pragmatic Philosophy of C. S. Peirce* (Chicago: University of Chicago Press, 1953), 159. Quotation from Hartshorne and Weiss, *The Collected Papers*, vol. 1, par. 287.

66. Glenn Tiller, "Peirce and Santayana: Pragmatism and the Belief in Substance," *Transactions of the Charles S. Peirce Society* 38, no. 3 (Summer 2002): 371.

67. Corrington, *Introduction to C. S. Peirce*, 111.

68. Ibid.

69. Peirce's three (trichotomous) ontological categories may be defined briefly as follows. Firstness: "That whose being is simply itself and not referring to anything nor lying behind anything" (e.g., possibilities, randomness and essence). Secondness: "That to which it is by force of something to which it is second" (e.g., relational action,

dialectic and imaginative process). Thirdness: "That which is what it is owing to things between which it brings into relation to each other" (e.g., relationship, a synthesis and an integration). For the purposes of a religious or teleological perspective, Peirce's idea of "The starting point of the universe, God the Creator, is the Absolute First; the terminus of the universe, God completely revealed, is the Absolute Second; every state of the universe at a measurable point of time is the third." From C. S. Peirce, "A Guess at the Riddle," in *The Essential Peirce*, ed. Houser and Kloesel, 1:248–51.

70. Corrington, *An Introduction to C. S. Peirce*, 118–41. Corrington provides a clear and extensive depiction of the semiotic character of Peirce's theory of ontological categories.

71. Edie, *William James and Phenomenology*, 33–34.

72. Rosensohn, *The Phenomenology of Charles S. Peirce*, 99.

73. Edie, *William James and Phenomenology*, 69.

74. Da Silva, *The Phenomenology of Religion*, 53.

75. Ibid., 54–55.

76. Santayana, *Realms of Being*, 172.

77. Husserl's *transcendental idealism* is defined by Husserl himself as "explication of my ego as subject of every possible cognition, and indeed with respect to every sense of what exists, wherewith the latter might be able to *have* a sense for me, the ego." In this the Kantian transcendent *noumenal* realm of "things in themselves" is obviated. Husserl recognizes no transcendent realm and equates his notion of *transcendental idealism "eo ipso"* with his systematic phenomenology. Husserl, *Cartesian Meditations*, 86.

78. Santayana, *Scepticism and Animal Faith*, 252–61. Santayana contrasts scientific psychology as part of "physics," or the study of nature and the record of how animals act, and literary psychology which is the art of imagining how animals feel and think. (In my view, the concept of "immediacy" in relation to the nature of lower mammalian experience vs. human intuition is an interesting subject for further study.)

79. Bell, *Husserl*, 158.

80. Moran, *Introduction to Phenomenology*, 127. Kant attempted to link the appearance of phenomena with that hidden order of existence that he postulated lies behind it, the *noumena* or *the things themselves*. Paradoxically, in Kant's system, this dualistic notion results in a pursuit of knowledge of a substantial underlying order. Husserl, on the other hand, seeks no order "behind" the phenomena, but only those experiences directly accessible to consciousness (i.e., *these* are the *things in themselves*). These may be *noumenotic* in the Kantian sense, but the concern is only with the immediate phenomena. See J. M. Edie, *Edmund Husserl's Phenomenology* (Bloomington: Indiana University Press, 1987), 86, 138n. Also see Steven William Laycock, *Foundations for a Phenomenological Theology* (Lewiston, NY: Edwin Mellon Press, 1988), 13–15.

81. Santayana, *Life of Reason: Introduction and Reason and Common Sense* (volume 1 of six volumes of the first edition, 1920), 163. See the one-volume edition of *Life of Reason* (Scribners, 1952) for a revised version subsequent to publication of *Realms of Being* when the theory of *essences* was fully developed.

82. Santayana, *Scepticism and Animal Faith*, 202–3; emphasis mine.

83. Moran, *Introduction to Phenomenology*, 132.

84. Hammond, Howarth, and Keat, *Understanding Phenomenology*, 29.

85. Moran, *Introduction to Phenomenology*, 135–37.

86. Hammond, Howarth, and Keat, *Understanding Phenomenology*, 19.

87. Moran, *Introduction to Phenomenology*, 128. From Edmund Husserl, *Philosophy as a Rigorous Science*.

88. Moran, *Introduction to Phenomenology*, 128.

89. Hammond, Howarth, and Keat, *Understanding Phenomenology*, 29.

90. Da Silva, *The Phenomenology of Religion*, 40.

91. Santayana, *Realms of Being*, 174.

92. Ibid., 172.

93. Ibid., 4–5; emphasis mine.

94. There are many references in Santayana's works indicating his view on his acceptance of empirical science as an approach toward the nature of matter and its limitations—for example, *Realms of Being* (440); *Scepticism and Animal Faith* (252); "A Brief history of My Opinions," Edman, 19; and "A General Confession," Schilpp, 8. Husserl's teaching in regard to science (*Wissenschaft*) in phenomenological and empirical practice is addressed in his *Ideas: A General Introduction to Pure Phenomenology*, trans. W. R. Boyce Gibson (New York: Macmillan, 1931), 78, 93–97. Also see Hammond, Howarth, and Keat, *Understanding Phenomenology*, 15.

95. Hammond, Howarth, and Keat, *Understanding Phenomenology*, 25.

96. Ibid., 57–59. In any case, such "evident verification," exacted in the phenomenological attitude, may provide more confirmation regarding the existence of an object and the relationship arrived at between perception and reality while in the "natural attitude," but, it seems to me, absolute confirmation remains beyond the scope of Husserl's claims whatever the evidence.

97. Santayana, *Scepticism and Animal Faith*, 34.

98. Daniel Moreno, "The Pathetic Fallacy in Santayana," *Overheard in Seville* 16, no. 22 (Fall 2004): 16. Moreno gives an excellent review and commentary on Santayana's various references to the "pathetic fallacy" (first mentioned by Santayana in *Interpretation of Poetry and Religion*) and its significance in his overall philosophy.

99. Ibid., 18; my italics. From Santayana, *Realms of Being* (463). The term "fallacy" is used in a correct philosophical sense by Santayana and pertains to an error in reasoning resulting in a false belief (see *The Penguin Dictionary of Philosophy*, s.v. "Fallacy").

100. Santayana, *Scepticism and Animal Faith*, 167.

101. Santayana, *Dialogues in Limbo*, 37.

102. Da Silva, *The Phenomenology of Religion*, 27–28.

103. Ibid., 36–37. More detail in delineating Husserl's method is omitted here due to space—for example, the modes of bracketing or reduction (i.e., historical, existential, transcendental, eidetic). The intent of this chapter is simply to argue for Santayana's phenomenological approach and to lend it some basic characteristics.

104. Santayana, *Scepticism and Animal Faith*, 74.

105. Ibid., 76.

106. Ibid., 49.

107. Santayana, *Realms of Being*, xxvi.

108. Hammond, Howarth, and Keat, *Understanding Phenomenology*, 18–21. Husserl postulates that "any evidence is a grasping in the mode that of 'it-itself,' with a full certainty of its being." Husserl, *Cartesian Meditations*, 15–16. That is, evidence is an experiencing something that is and is thus; it is precisely a mental seeing of something itself (12). Santayana's project pursues the same goal of reconciling evidence to what is perceived. Short of his pragmatic reconciling of the perceptions arrived at through experiencing essences with the reality of the world, he proposes that "the evidence of data is only obviousness" (Santayana, *Scepticism and Animal Faith*, 99), but "the obvious is only apparent" (43). Ultimately, for Santayana, the only certain "evidence" is the experience of the *essence* in the *sopm* and all else is based upon *animal faith*.

109. Santayana, *Scepticism and Animal Faith*, 252.

110. Ibid.

111. Ibid., 257–58; italics mine.

112. Sprigge, *Santayana*, 182.

113. Santayana, *Scepticism and Animal Faith*, 258.

114. John Lachs concisely differentiates the two cognitive stages of "pure intuition" and *animal faith*, as without and with intent, respectively. See Lachs, *George Santayana*, 108.

115. Santayana, *Scepticism and Animal Faith*, 258–59.

116. Hammond, Howarth, and Keat, *Understanding Phenomenology*, 2–4.

117. Charles T. Harrison, "Santayana's 'Literary Psychology,'" *Sewanee Review* 61 (1953): 213. Harrison emphasizes the character of Santayana's writing as reflective

rather than dialectic and the poetic and aesthetic character of Santayana's entire philosophical project.

118. Santayana, *Scepticism and Animal Faith*, 173.

119. Evidential claims made in the "natural attitude" of a certain behavior have through experience proven predictable. If one recognizes in the immediacy of the pre-cognitive state (i.e., intuitively), a complex of *essences* presented before, one then recognizes them and can intuit the consequences. See Hammond, Howarth, and Keat, *Understanding Phenomenology*, 54–55. Also see Husserl, *Cartesian Meditations* regarding "the intentional object as 'transcendental clue'" (50).

120. Santayana, *Scepticism and Animal Faith*, 173–74.

121. Moran, *Introduction to Phenomenology*, 175.

122. Moran, *Introduction to Phenomenology*, 177. From Husserl, *Cartesian Meditations*.

123. Moran, *Introduction to Phenomenology*, 177.

124. Santayana, *Scepticism and Animal Faith*, 173–74.

125. Hammond, Howarth, and Keat, *Understanding Phenomenology*, 47. See also da Silva, *Phenomenology of Religion*, 32–33.

126. My primary reference regarding Husserl's descriptive process is Hammond, Howarth, and Keat, *Understanding Phenomenology*, chap. 2, "Intentionality and Meaning." The primary source as to method is Husserl, *Cartesian Meditations*.

127. Santayana, *Realms of Being*, 67.

128. Ibid.

129. Ibid.

130. Santayana describes the symbolic character of the *essences* and hence their "vagueness" due to lack of signification. It is only through arriving at some *perception* of this instantaneous phenomenon (recall the nature of the *sopm*) that one assigns it signification. But in doing so Santayana affirms that "Perception *is* faith; more perception may extend this faith or reform it, but can never recant it except by sophistry." See Santayana, *Scepticism and Animal Faith*, 68–69. Further, he proposes that "perception is a stretching forth of intent beyond intuition; it is an exercise of intelligence" (282). I acknowledge here my good fortune to have been enlightened by Dr. Herman Saatkamp on the nature of the subtle transition from *essence* to *perception*.

131. Husserl, *Cartesian Meditations*, 50.

132. Spiegelberg, *The Phenomenological Movement*, 697. Spiegelberg's chapter "Essentials of Method," unlike many phenomenology texts, is a particularly concise and helpful description of the methodical descriptive aspect of the phenomenological process.

133. Santayana, *Realms of Being*, 14.

134. Hammond, Howarth, and Keat, *Understanding Phenomenology*, 62–63.

135. Santayana, *Realms of Being*, 4.

136. Ibid., 3–4.

137. Santayana, *Scepticism and Animal Faith*, 28.

138. Santayana, "Apologia Pro Mente Sua," Schilpp, 514.

139. Letter to Justus Buchler, July 1,1936, in *The Letters of George Santayana*, ed. Daniel Cory, vol. 5 (New York: Scribner, 1955), 354.

140. Spiegelberg, *The Phenomenological Movement*, 123. Spiegelberg, as I indicated earlier, confines his comparison of Husserl's method only to Santayana's radical skeptical method. However, his observation here can safely be referred to Santayana's broader concept of the contemplation of *essences*.

141. Ibid.

142. Santayana, *Realms of Being*, 11.

143. Ibid., 659. "In this book I am deliberately taking the point of view of spirit fully awake, contrasting itself with other things, and aspiring to its own freedom and perfection."

FOUR

The Coherent Nature of Santayana's Philosophy of Religion

> Mythical thinking has its roots in reality, but, like a plant, touches the ground only at one end. It stands unmoved and flowers wantonly into the air, transmuting into unexpected and richer forms the substances it sucks from the soil.
>
> George Santayana, *Reason in Religion*

Santayana's philosophy of religion must be thought of as more a description of the "disposition of the mind" and a "phenomenology of the spirit," in regard to the spiritual experience, rather than a phenomenological description of the anthropological and cultural aspects of religion.[1] There is indeed an evolutionary and historical trajectory characterizing *The Life of Reason* with a somewhat broader perspective on religions other than Christianity (Hinduism, Buddhism), but this broader approach is for the most part only intermittent in *Realms of Being*, his ontological *summa*. There the symbolic language of Christian theology interjects as the grammar describing the character of the human experience of Being. I referred in chapter 1 to Santayana's statement in "A General Confession" that religion "is the head and front of everything,"[2] and with only limited consideration we can see why this must be. In the life of the spirit the grammar of *essences* is of the eternal realm, of the Realm of Essences—the ideal images that are evident especially in the symbols of religion. The prominence of the Realm of the Spirit in Santayana's ontology as the realm that encompasses the most meaningful aspects of human existence underlies such a positioning of religion. His approach, as I earlier claimed, particularly for his later works, is substantially phenomenological, naturalistic and descriptive, and ultimately directed toward freedom and enlightenment of the spirit. The following from the introduction to

Realms of Being describes his method which is a summary of an approach to the life of the Spirit.

> After having cleared my mind as much as possible of traditional soph-
> istry, I have endeavored to recover the natural and inevitable beliefs of
> a human being living untutored in this world, but having a reflective
> mind. He need not be ignorant of the systems of mythology, religion or
> philosophy that ingenious or inspired wits have constructed . . . but all
> of this will merely complicate for him in a challenging fashion the
> landscape of nature; and his allegiance need not begin to be engaged to
> anything speculative until he has seen its place, as an arbitrary or as an
> inevitable conception, in the life of mankind.[3]

Certainly, as discussed at length earlier, the triadic complex of Santayana's captivation with Roman Catholicism in his youth, his intellectual
decision to leave Catholic belief behind and his mourning of the loss of all
but the *kultur* and the moral tenets of Catholicism has a great bearing on
his viewpoint. One is reminded, in regard to this last point of the development, of his natural psychological disposition and of his claim that his
philosophy is "the result or sediment left in my mind from living."[4] We
can readily capture with confidence a number of additional major reasons for Santayana's "privileging" of the importance of religion based
upon a perspective that remains for him essentially unchanged from the
early *Interpretations of Poetry and Religion* and *The Life of Reason* through
Scepticism and Animal Faith, Realms of Being and his later work, *The Idea of
Christ in the Gospels* and *Dominations and Powers*.

(1) Religious dogma and doctrine reflect the moral aspirations and
ideals of the human race as developed over time through individual and
social experience and religion, as a repository of the ideal, and should not
be evaded or compromised except for the dispensing of an objective referent.[5] In the perspective of history and tradition of the West, Catholic
Christianity especially represents a deep spiritual thread that reflects human nature and desire from the time of the Greeks.[6]

(2) In spite of this positive character, the hypostatization of religious
myths, legendary figures and the idealistic images at large in the imagination is likely the most threatening manifestation of the "pathetic fallacy" to both human spiritual freedom and the longevity of religious doctrine.[7]

(3) Nevertheless, religion opens "another world to live in," and an
escape from the mundane and the realization of the relative impotency of
the individual in the world of matter.[8] Further, "a dogged allegiance to a
particular temperament or country or religion, though it be an animal
virtue, is heroic; it keys the whole man up to sacrifice and to integrity so
that persons devoted to such a specific allegiance attain a high degree of
spirituality more often, perhaps, than sceptics or original philosophers."[9]

(4) Religion, then, is integral to the life of reason (along with reason in society, art and science). On its own, in a singular sense, it fails in realizing the life of reason but it "sanctions, unifies and transforms ethics," and as in reason 3 emancipates man from his personal limitations.[10]

As I stated earlier, it is my position that although the humanistic character of *The Life of Reason* lost some emphasis in Santayana's later works by his own admission, the essential structure of the model persisted throughout his later philosophical development where more emphasis was put upon the life of the spirit.[11] The importance of faith in Santayana's philosophy also has a somewhat obvious bearing on the importance of religion. It is through *animal faith* that we strive to attain a semblance of knowledge of the world, just as we may strive, in this case to little avail, to assume to approach knowledge of a supernatural world through religious beliefs. In faith, according to Santayana, we contrive both our material world and, if we are conventionally religious, our supernatural one. The belief in the reality of a supernatural world and the objectification of religious doctrines and myths beyond the framework of poetry Santayana would consider the exercise of the "easy faith" he refers to in his essay "Ultimate Religion," which I will discuss further on. The fruits of *animal faith*, on the other hand, are presumed by Santayana to be ideally the fruits of reason, and of particular importance to us here is Santayana's inclusion of religion as explicit in the ideal of the life of reason.

From chapter 1, recall my comment on Morris Grossman's opinion that Santayana's philosophical positions seem to be played out on a "double moral grid," wherein declarations are made on both sides of any given issue and Santayana "characteristically gives us not arguments for viewpoints, which would be lean and insufficient, but intellectually passionate cases for them as he makes intellectually passionate cases for their opposites."[12] This seeming ambiguity contributes, in my view, as I suggested in chapter 1, to a sympathetic view on the part of many scholars and philosophically inclined members of the Christian religious community and an inclination to find in Santayana, after all, a theistic disposition or inclination.[13] Such declarations as the following from Santayana's *Winds of Doctrine* may, on being read out of context, augur hope for eventual inclusion of the philosopher in the community of the faithful.

> It is not those who accept the deluge, the resurrection, and the sacrament only as symbols that are the vital group, but those who accept them literally, for only these have anything to say to the poor, or the rich, that can refresh them. In a frank supernaturalism, in a tight clericalism, not in pleasant secularization, lies the sole hope of the church.[14]

In making such statements, which upon closer examination turn out to be objective and accurate in relation to Santayana's beliefs, the contrast between this statement and Santayana's apparent position may seem to be great, even to the extent of a contradiction. Hence, the seeming paradoxical and even confusing aspect of interpreting where he stands. One tends toward a careful reading in an effort to detect, behind his more extreme naturalistic statements, a glimmer of hope and of the possibilities for the "unseen."

On Santayana's gravestone in the *Cimitero Monumentale al Verano* in Rome is an inscription in Spanish of a quotation taken from *The Idea of Christ in the Gospels* which, in its finality, would give any semi-initiated visitor to the grave site (e.g., the pious Spanish widow whom Daniel Cory refers to in making the same point) the sense that a deathbed conversion had taken place: *Cristo ha hecho posible para nosotros, La gloriosa liberatad del alma en el cielo.*[15] Since I refer to Santayana's comments on *Christ in the Gospels* above, I will take for a "summary" of Santayana's disposition on religion a quote from a letter written near the end of his life to Warren Allen Smith, the popular skeptic and secular humanist of the period, dealing with the question put to him by Smith as to whether this work was an example of "theistic humanism."

> Those professors at Columbia who tell you that in my *Idea of Christ in the Gospels* I incline to theism have not read that book sympathetically. They forget that my naturalism is fundamental and includes man, his mind, and all his works, products of the generative order of nature. Christ in the Gospels is a legendary figure. Spirit in him recognizes its dependence on the Father, not on monarchial government; i.e., the order of nature; and the animal will in man being thus devised, the spirit in man is freed and identified with that of the Father.[16]

From this declaration we are clear that Santayana's causative world remains only in nature and that the Gospel of Jesus Christ is categorized as legend and mythology derived from the imagination of man. The symbolism, however, contains the idealistic teaching of man liberated from the domination of society, government and other earthly claims on his spirit, and with and through Jesus, claimed and freed by God the Father. If we plumb even deeper to the core of Santayana's philosophical disposition, we find in this same letter that there is nothing romantic in Santayana's materialistic naturalism, as he proclaims, "Mine is the hard, non-humanistic naturalism of the Ionian philosophers, of Democritus, Lucretius and Spinoza." Further, he affirms that "the most brutal form of naturalism is materialism, and I have repeatedly confessed that I am a materialist."[17] Howgate's observation that Santayana retained "the sterner rather than the gentler side of Christianity" is generally true and reflects a disciplined and uncompromising "adamant underneath," leaving any romantic notions regarding theistic religious belief behind.[18] This will be more apparent when I address further on his attitude toward the symbols of Christian orthodoxy. It is within this seemingly stark framework and confines, then, that I will approach Santayana's philosophy of religion, which we will discover is not in itself irreligious. In a more positive sense, as appropriately suggested by Elisio Vivas, "Santayana also took religion from the hands of the apologists and theologians and enabled us to see its significance for humane living."[19]

AN ULTIMATE RELIGION

In September of 1932, Santayana presented the paper "Ultimate Religion"[20] on the occasion of the Spinoza tercentennial meeting at the *Domus Spinozana* in The Hague, and was pleased to have paid homage to his "hero" on this occasion.[21] Santayana's presentation reflected upon the greatness of Spinoza and "the magnificent example he offers us of philosophic liberty, the courage, firmness and sincerity with which he reconciled his heart to truth," and he proceeded to explore with his audience "what inmost allegiance, what ultimate religion, would be proper to a wholly free and disillusioned spirit."[22] In a letter to Mrs. C. H. Toy on March 12, 1932, as Santayana was working on his lecture for The Hague on the requested topic of religion and philosophy, he expressed his intent to give his paper the "special title" of "Ultimate Religion" and to "make it an integral part (with few modifications) of *The Realm of the Spirit*, on which I have been doing a little work this winter, as well as on the *Realm of Truth*."[23] Daniel Cory points out that Santayana did not finally incorporate "Ultimate Religion" in the Realms, but rather in the volume of essays *Obiter Scripta*. However, the clear association, as indicated by Santayana in his letter to Mrs. Toy, with the paper and his concurrent development of *The Realm of the Spirit*, I consider both fortuitous and validating for using "Ultimate Religion" as a relatively concise "platform" to elaborate on his mature philosophy of religion. James Gouinlock provides some support for this decision, suggesting that "Ultimate Religion" "faithfully represents the main conclusions" of *Platonism and the Spiritual Life*, *The Realm of the Spirit*, and *The Idea of Christ in the Gospels*.[24] I will comment further on some of these later works, particularly on *The Realm of the Spirit*, and its relationship to "Ultimate Religion" as we progress.

A Phenomenological Examination of Consciousness

After extolling to his audience at the Hague the philosophy and "moral victory" of Spinoza in courageously and rigorously solving "the problem of the spiritual life after stating it in the hardest, sharpest, most cruel terms," Santayana singled out the nature of the relatively uncomplex environment of Spinoza's seventeenth-century world. In this world, "every man had a true and adequate idea of God," revealing "a virgin sense of familiarity with the absolute." It is in this environment that Spinoza derived his straightforward and "unmysterious" idea of *Deus sive Natura*, the threatening force of nature that must not be opposed, but accepted as "a decidedly friendly and faithful object of the mind."[25] It is this hypostatization in Spinoza's philosophy of the elemental force behind all that has being that Santayana takes issue with in his paper. He suggests that the assurances of influence on Spinoza and people of the seventeenth century (i.e., the notion of absolutes) are on more shaky ground still, in the environment of the twentieth century. It is on this premise that Santayana invites his audience into a phenomenological exercise he depicts as an "examination of conscience," in effect, an *epoché*, wherein an "abstention from all easy faith"[26] entails a suspension of all "ulterior reasonable convictions."[27] In some sense, Santayana's "building-block" approach from "scratch" is reminiscent of his skeptic antecedent David Hume's quest for a *de minimus* philosopher's religious belief, and indeed the scholarly probing for traces of theism in Hume can remind one of the same scholarly inclination toward Santayana.[28] There is another interesting parallel both in method and intent when Friedrich Schleiermacher in his *On Religion: Speeches to Its Cultural Despisers* addresses his audience through an approach that Thomas Reynolds characterizes as "proto-phenomenological suspension or bracketing that disassociates the erroneous from the essential."[29] In the case of Santayana, the philosophical basis for such an approach is that rebuilding process wherein skepticism destroys beliefs and *animal faith* restores them based on experience in the world. Santayana proposes that the exercise of this attitude of observation will bring us to that "denuded" state of "standing [spiritually] unpledged and naked, under the open sky."[30] Given my phenomenological claims for Santayana and the phenomenological character of the exercise he proposes in "Ultimate Religion," I will initially organize my discussion of Santayana's philosophy of religion around his essay, using some of the language and conclusions arrived at in the exercise he puts forth in his essay as benchmarks and headings under which I will address the nature and "coherence" of his views.

FAITH FOR THE DISILLUSIONED

"The Omnificent Power of the Doer of Everything"[31]

Santayana's concept of "God" as a symbolic term for that *essence*, the descriptors of which include "creator of the world," "dispenser of good fortune" and "omnipotent judge of all creatures" is consistent with the popular notion of such a divine power.[32] Despite his claim that his atheism is like Spinoza's,[33] Santayana's concept of the "omnificent" force that energizes the universe—"the wonderful and immense engine"[34] —is observable and unexplainably present, but not in any sense equivalent to God, nor is this power characterized by either those attributes associated with the popular notion of God or those broader and less personal aspects attributed by Spinoza. Santayana is indeed an atheist, in the classical sense of having arrived at a belief that the popular notion of God and all his traditional attributes is not reasonably tenable.[35] Further, having acknowledged the mechanistic power that is the "doer of everything," Spinoza's God as it is, *sans* personality, intellect, will and purpose, is a notion that is so remote from the traditional litany of attributes that it seems hardly necessary for the "wholly free and disillusioned spirit."[36] One can surely be tempted by the "Lorelei" when Santayana suggests that "my atheism like that of Spinoza is true piety towards the universe,"[37] when, in fact, Spinoza's position is rather one that is theistic, or more specifically, one of monistic pantheism.[38] However, in *The Idea of Christ in the Gospels*, Santayana makes his position quite clear regarding the lack of any "special advantage" to humans of pantheism,[39] and further, in *The Realm of Matter*, proclaims that pantheism "is more materialistic than materialism, since it assigns to matter a dignity which no profane materialist [as Santayana clearly purports to be] would assign to it, that of having moral authority over the hearts of men."[40] In all of this, however, I am in accord with H. T. Kirby-Smith when he claims, "If God is dead, Santayana had nothing to do with it," and I will return to this insightful claim as we proceed.[41] In regard to Spinoza's notion that this "stripped-down" God is necessary and his predetermination of all creation is by necessity and not by will, we can fall back on Santayana's philosophical *Grund* to justify his opposition to such a notion.[42]

Santayana's brief but provocative definition of truth can then be brought to bear here (i.e., "Truth is the complete ideal description of existence").[43] Further foiling the attribution of teleological powers in Philosophical Idealism, Santayana addresses the subcategory of "necessary truth": "So that truth being descriptive of existence and existence being contingent, truth will be contingent also."[44] Later he continues,

> Are there no truths obviously necessary to common sense? If I mislaid my keys, must they be somewhere? . . . The necessity asserted foolishly parades the helplessness of the mind to imagine anything different. Yet this helplessness on which dogmatism rests, is shameful, and is secretly felt to be shameful. Spirit was born precisely to escape such limitations, to see the contingency and finitude of every fact in its true setting. Truth is groped after, not imposed by presumptions of the intellect.[45]

There are then no claims by Santayana for the apodicticity of anything beyond the immediate intuition of an *essence*. If there is one philosophical principle that underlies all of Santayana's "uncertainty" it is the nature of the non-existence and powerlessness of *essences* and their uniqueness in constituting the only objects that we experience as phenomena in intuition. Therefore, it is not only God and the "unseen" that fall into uncertainty, it is everything in the empirical realm as well, for all knowledge is virtual except through *animal faith* and its belief in an interface of phenomena and *essence* with matter. With this underlying principle, it only follows as consistent that Santayana can logically derive from the basis of his naturalism that "the existence of God is therefore not a necessary truth":

> For if the proposition is necessary, its terms can only be Essences; and the word God would then designate a definable idea, and would not be a proper name indicating an actual power. If, on the contrary, the word is such a proper name, and God is a psychological moral being energizing in space and time, then his existence can be proved only by the evidence of these natural manifestations, not by dialectical reasoning upon the meaning of terms. [46]

Here then is a rigorous logical proposition that underlies his unbelief not only in the popular notion of God but also in that more "reasonable" notion of Spinoza. Beyond this convincing opposing rationale to absolutism based upon no "necessary truths," we find, on the basis of the principle of contradiction, an equally convincing philosophical basis. This is as a consequence of Santayana's confinement of causative "power" or "force" to the realm of matter and the consequent "powerlessness" of spirit to act. *Essences* cannot be hypostatized to existence, therefore God is a definable idea rather than a power and Santayana runs up hard against Anselm's ontological argument. In *The Realm of the Spirit* he calls our attention to the Judeo-Christian notion that God is both power and spirit, whereas Santayana places "spirit and power at opposite ends of the ontological scale." [47] Of the power in the universe, which he deigns to call omnificent but does not know enough to call omnipotent, he "profess[es] to know nothing further." [48] If the Realm of Truth provides no necessary truths, then, in fact, Santayana has disclaimed any justification for the traditional quest for metaphysical disclosure. [49] By the truth, Santayana means a complete ideal description of existence, eternal and given in the language of *essences*, infinite, omnimodal and totally enveloping. Since truth then is contingent, one cannot be certain of it, and we further see a firm basis for Santayana's starting point of skepticism in dealing with the "real" world, the Realm of Matter. Ultimately, then, Truth, in Santayana's epistemological philosophy, is an identity between knowledge and object, or "the identity of a fact asserted and the fact existing." [50] In the case of humans this knowledge, however, can only be rough, approximate and short of complete, and one then can act only on these approximations through a "leap" of *animal faith*. To disclose the Truth of the Realm of Matter, the only existential Realm, in Santayana's view, is not possible. Contrary to William James, and the Pragmatic school in general, where truth was more subjective and subject to utility, he believed that truth should remain an ideal, and as an ideal, it was morally good although all truth was not good. [51] Moreover, the concept of Absolute Truth, consistent with Santayana's claims above, "is not merely by accident beyond the range of particular minds."

> It is incompatible with being alive, because it excludes any particular station, organ, interest, or date of survey: the absolute truth is undiscoverable just because it is not a perspective. Perspectives are essential to animal apprehension. [52]

The Human Plight in the Solitude of a Naked Spirit[53]

Santayana appeals to classical images of solitude (e.g., "a man in the night, in the desert . . . alone with Allah") to depict that "nakedness" of the "suffering spirit" overtaken by the multitude of "accidents" that leave us vulnerable before an "alien and inscrutable power." Having abstained from all "easy faith," and our "easy home" of self-pleasing and protective constructs, we are "subjected to an utter denudation and supreme trial."[54] The ancient image of the barrenness of the desert, where one meets both reality and God, is a sacred symbol of spiritual discovery. We can see the symbol manifested in the image of Bellini's painting *St. Francis in the Desert*, with the saint, eyes uplifted and arms opened in the *orans* position in appreciation of his dependency and vulnerability. There is in this state of solitude a condition of Heideggerian "attunement" wherein all distractions are forsaken and ontological awareness is sensitized to a high pitch so that we powerfully sense the dependency of the spirit. Santayana's notion of the power of the universe and our dependency upon it is reminiscent of both Schleiermacher's isolation of a "feeling of absolute dependence"[55] as the essence of religious belief as well as his own comments in *Reason in Religion* more than thirty years before his address at the *Domus Spinozana*. He proposed then that "whatever is serious in religion, whatever is bound up with morality and fate, is contained in those plain experiences of dependence and of affinity to that on which we depend."[56] In "Ultimate Religion" Santayana, indeed, brings us to the edge of what clearly is the Existential abyss for the ultimate realization not only of Heideggerian *Dasein*-like awareness but of the full extent of our vulnerability. In this state, even existence remains "bracketed," and we can make no claim to any certainty, either of future events or of our own very personal destiny.[57] The result is that the spirit is helpless in the face of eternity where "it has perceived that though it is living, it is powerless to live; that though it may die, it is powerless to die; and that altogether, at every instant and in every particular, it is in the hands of an alien and inscrutable power."[58]

From this fearsome silence and dependency there can be salvation, but Santayana still presents, in Jungian fashion, the dangers and pitfalls of what we could safely call a self- individuation process as he warns that "there may be dark abysses before which intelligence must be silent, for fear of going mad." Here, we find in Santayana's empathy for this state a seeming contradiction in regard to his denial of Existential despair and *Angst* (in "healthy" people), and indeed, in his general antipathy to the Existential project in general. In a letter to an inquirer of Santayana's reaction to Kierkegaard and Christian Existentialism, he crankily responds with attributions to his nemesis, Protestantism: "Is not such *Angst* a disease, an emotion produced by Protestant theology after faith in that theology has disappeared?"[59] He suggests in another letter written late in his life that his quarrel with the concept of *Angst* is a "temperamental" one and that, by virtue of their egotism, Existentialists "do not seem healthy themselves."[60] Although Santayana's general disposition, in my view, was one naturally adapted toward the power of personal will (i.e., toward discipline) in overcoming any degree of Existential despair, he did have some grasp of the difficulty in transcending this state of mind in others. Woodward also suggests that "transcendence of *Angst*-ridden contingency always seemed possible to Santayana even within the context of his own materialism."[61]

There must be, then, an escape in transcendence from this potentially terrifying awareness arising from "the solitude of the naked spirit," and having dismantled or discarded all comforting assumptions and constructs, a rebuilding, block-by-block, must ensue. There is philosophical consistency in such a "rebuilding" in that the entirety of Santayana's project, since beginning from the platform of that sole certainty, the *sopm*, our personal construct of the world—its objectivity, behavior and predictability—is rebuilt as I indicated above, on *animal faith*. John Lachs observes that "Santayana's manner of proceeding has the advantage of symmetry: while skepticism gradually destroys beliefs, *animal faith* little by little restores them," and belief after belief is added to "the cognitive austerity of the skeptic."[62]

Love, Harmony and Health in the Actuosa Essentia of the Universe[63]

There is in Santayana's raising up of the "ultimate religion" a "therapeutic" or "healthful" character in which he perceives a balance of virtue, a kind of "golden mean," wherein the spirit, through a process of personal will and discipline, finds harmony and happiness. We are reminded that for Santayana, his philosophy claims, as the Ionians and Lucretius do, a singular goal of happiness for the individual. Despite the helplessness of the spirit in the flux of nature, Santayana introduces possibilities for personal will in achieving such a "tuned" balance of virtue. This seems at first contrary to his concept of non-causation or impotency of the spirit and the general deterministic character of nature until one realizes that the total exercise of will (i.e., in a mentalistic sense) and discipline takes place entirely in the life of the spirit and is powerless in the material world. It is the life of the spirit that we are dealing with solely within the concept of "ultimate religion" or any religion. It comes finally to a matter of belief and faith as well as that of religious *praxis*, wherein those actions (not beliefs) associated with liturgy, worship, exercising charity and so forth, which are acts in the world—that is, motions, relocations and interactions that are neurophysiologically initiated through the *psyche* and reflected by signs and symbols (intuited *essences*) connotative of our spiritual life—are acted out. These latter are not manifestations of the spirit but of the body and the life-force implicit in Santayana's epiphenomenol theory.

Santayana, then, has the spirit stripped of presumptive notions, facing the omnificent power which "comes down upon me clothed in a thousand phenomena; and these manifestations of power open to me a new spiritual resource."[64] This cathartic process to achieve awareness opens the door to the reality of the world, and the spirit becomes newly activated to new perceptions and "occasions for intellectual delight."[65] Any terror is to be left behind in a new freedom. We realize our place in the order of things, the contingency of our existence, and the overwhelming power of the flux which carries us. In this realization Santayana, with the model of Spinoza's arrival at a pious acceptance of the *Deus sive Natura* in mind, proclaims, in spite of this power, the joyful aspects of the "greatness" and "victory" of the world. In Spinoza as in Santayana's derivation of the ultimate religion, this is presented by Santayana as an epiphanic moment, and from this platform one passes into what Spinoza terms the *scientia intuitiva*[66] or final stage of knowledge. However, the two philosophers arrive at different religious endpoints. For Spinoza, the arrival is at the intellectual love of the all-powerful and impersonal God-Nature, and for Santayana the process continues beyond Spinoza, passing through stages of ascetic yielding of the "troubled thought of ourselves" to "something more rich in life."[67] At this juncture, Santayana, while still proclaiming the wonder of arriving "on a mountain-top" and the ecstasy of freedom and boundless sympathy with the universe, reveals the shortcoming of arresting the process as Spinoza does, in an intellectual sanguinity with the *Deus sive Natura*, while the emotional and moral needs of the essence of man, of his "animality," Santayana claims, are not sufficiently considered.[68] Much earlier in *The Life of Reason (Reason in Religion)* Santayana reflected that "the spiritual man needs . . . something more than a cultivated sympathy with the brighter scintillation of things."[69] Subsequently in "Ultimate Religion," he similarly proposes that it is not enough to satisfy the spiritual need of most humans to only share "the movement, the *actuosa essentia* of all the universe." Despite the healthful and heroic stance of Spinoza, more is needed than just his intellectual love of God.

Contemplation of the Truth of the Universe and the Pursuit of the Universal Good[70]

Santayana's philosophy, as we have noted in earlier chapters, rests upon a high level of confidence in the "common sense" or "orthodoxy" of the natural man. In spite of a tendency toward self-rationalization on the basis of the *pathetic fallacy* and "normal madness" in the natural man, there is an intuition of falsity and even danger in radical departures from tradition or convention. In "Ultimate Religion," Santayana draws our attention to the failure of Spinoza's rational arrival at the religious end-point of *Deus sive Natura* to satisfy the need for a moral component in an ultimate religion. This component is absent not only in Spinoza's religion, but so far in Santayana's phenomenological process in "Ultimate Religion" in that he has taken his audience at The Hague only to that point of "a boundless sympathy with the universe."[71] This experience of standing "as on a mountain-top,"[72] for the purpose of making a point of contrast here, is one of feeling and therefore can be claimed to have the character of a religious experience, although the path to this point entails a rational and descriptive process. Santayana has reached a juncture in "Ultimate Religion" wherein the emotional or "feeling" component of religion is differentiated from the moral component. As mentioned earlier, Rudolf Otto, in *The Idea of the Holy*, directing his phenomenological concern particularly at the emotional aspect of religion, specifically the "numinous feeling," designated the importance of this subjective state of mind and differentiated it from the other essential component of religion (i.e., the rational and the moral or ethical component).[73] As Otto recognizes the essential importance of the moral component, in addition to the rational and "feeling" component, Santayana does also, suggesting that "the problem" is not solved for mankind at large, which remains no less distracted than it was before."[74] Further, "nor is it solved for the individual spirit [where] there is a radical and necessary recalcitrancy in the finite soul in the face of all this cosmic pomp and . . . cosmic pressure . . . to which Spinoza was less sensitive than some other masters of the spiritual life, perhaps because he was more positivistic by temperament and less specifically religious."[75] Man may have rationally reached the "mountain-top" but unless he or she is particularly rationally disposed and of a particularly courageous temperament, the "dark abyss' looms threateningly below. Santayana points out that "reason may be the differentia of man; it is surely not his essence" which "at best, is animality qualified by reason . . . and from this animality the highest flights of reason are by no means separable."[76] Since the intellect and the possibility for an ecstatic mountain-top experience are not seen by Santayana to be emotionally sufficient for a lasting religious position, Santayana proceeds to seek that essential additional component (i.e., the missing moral component which for him is the "Universal Good"). Santayana, while claiming himself a moralist and moral philosophy as his "chosen subject,"[77] recognizes the unlikelihood of a materialist, such as he was, who proclaims morals are relative to the happiness of the individual, to "justify moral ideals, morally." This philosophical principle of moral relativity immediately poses the impossibility of imposing universal moral judgments when people and social groups are given philosophical license to live by their own morals and ethics. Nevertheless, even on the basis of this relativity, Santayana is able to define the parameters for the necessary moral component of an ultimate religion (i.e., the "Universal Good"), and in doing so, clearly and logically delineates the value aspect of this moral "amendment" to Spinoza's intellectual religion. In his final work, *Dominations and Powers*, Santayana will observe that "there is also something slack and destitute about having nothing to defend, something unmoral in loathing nothing." Religion then without morals (i.e., "a moral nonentity") is incomplete, and it is "steadied when it becomes moral, and morality is liberated when it becomes spiritual."[78]

To Move with the Object of Love toward Happiness[79]

I discussed in chapter 2 the Platonic and Aristotelian legacy to Santayana and the aspect of morality as it is incorporated by the Greeks into the life of reason. Aristotle in particular, and his concept of virtue as an expression of reason, is the example for Santayana as he elaborates on the moral aspect of the "ultimate religion." In Santayana's "amendment" to Spinoza's intellectual religion, two essential components of the "ultimate religion" are presented—the "good" and love. Spinoza's seemingly egotistical concept of love as "an epithet we assign to whatever increases our perfection" is interpreted by Santayana as logically justified in a life of moral value and "a greater charter of liberty and justice than ever a politician framed."[80] The concept of perfection, an ideal, can be traced first from Plato's Eros, where love is the love of beauty and the perfect form of this love is the love of the Form of beauty, and then more precisely from Aristotle, who, in elaboration on Plato, broadens love as the desire of the imperfect for the perfect. Hence, love as the erotic desire by the lover for the perfection of the object of love becomes doctrine in Santayana's post-Spinozan model of religion. He returns to Spinoza's "epithet" of the "good" as the ultimate object of that love and elaborates the praxis and broad-reaching consequences of this love and its object for both the individual and society. However, in order to achieve the goal of happiness in the recognition and love of Good, Santayana introduces a *caveat* which in turn will bring the lover to a point of some personal sacrifice.

> That the intellect [here we are still at the level of Spinoza's intellectual love] might be perfectly happy in contemplating the truth of the universe, does not render the universe good to every other facility [and

> hence the recalcitrancy in the finite soul]; good to the heart, good to the
> flesh, good to the eye, good to the conscience or the sense of justice . . .
> [Therefore the] universal good by which the spirit, in its rapt moments,
> feels overwhelmed, if it is not to be a mystical illusion, cannot fall short
> of being the sum of all those perfections, infinitely various, to which all
> living things severally aspire.[81]

Therefore, one must not be parochial in one's perceptions of good, but
despite all possible or existing conflicts of goods, one must love those
goods that universally are loved everywhere. This is tantamount to charity, in the most universal sense, that is beyond any conflict: for example,
between interpretations of what is good in Christianity, Islam, Buddhism
or Marxist Communism. In the quotation above, Santayana sets in place
the cornerstone of his moral philosophy.

At this point, given Santayana's moral relativism, I will address before
proceeding what I think can be an excessively rigorous and therefore
misleading interpretation of Santayana's prospects for finding solace in
the "good." This involves the interpretation of "goods" in relation to the
universal "good" or the collective "good" which Santayana chooses as
the object of love. Professor Gouinlock, from his reading and critique of
"Ultimate Religion," puzzles over Santayana's admonition that one "love
things spiritually, intelligently and disinterestedly . . . to love the love in
them, to worship the good which they pursue, and to see them all pro-
phetically in their possible beauty . . . and the implicit inclusion of some
particularly unlovable hearts we are asked to love (e.g., Charles Manson
or the murderer of Polly Klaas).[82] Gouinlock's issue seems to be related
also to Santayana's failure to discriminate as to the "goods" that would
make up the true good or the universal good resulting in an impartiality
as to what makes up the "eternal beauty in the heart of all things." I do
not puzzle over this issue of love for love of the universal "good," as it
seems to me both profound and comprehensible. Indeed, it seems to
circumnavigate the problematic issue that Gouinlock is essentially concerned with—that is, the practicality of what he calls the extravagantly
high requirements of the "ultimate religion" and the likely prospect that
"no free and disillusioned spirit could demand them, much less satisfy
them."[83] Why, I ask, should it be perceived as more demanding than the
rigors of Orthodox Christianity? Another perspective that could be
brought to bear in response to Gouinlock's critique of Santayana's "Ultimate Religion" is found in a quotation taken by Levinson from *Reason in
Religion* revealing what I suggest is an important insight into Santayana's
"ideal" in its religious context and in relation to religious *praxis*, its contingency.

> After adopting an ideal it is necessary . . . without abandoning it, to
> recognize its relativity. The right path is in such a matter rather difficult
> to keep to. On the one hand lies a fanatical insistence on an ideal once

arrived at, no matter how many instincts and interests (the basis of all ideals) are thereby outraged in others and ultimately also in one's self. On the other hand lies mystical disintegration, which leads men to feel so keenly the rights of everything in particular and of the All in general, that they retain no hearty allegiance to any human interest. Between these two abysses winds the narrow path of charity and valor.[84]

Herein lies Santayana's philosophical basis for the contingency of even ideals! He is not suggesting compromise here in relation to our ideals, but seems to be affirming both a charitable and understanding attitude regarding other "ideal" concepts, and to avoid the brittle and even pathological extreme of certainty (e.g., in mysticism). The ideal, contrary to the view of Christianity and other world religions, is not the actual, and such a view of idealism, as mentioned earlier, is the basis for conflict and misunderstanding. Santayana continues in developing the concept of the ultimate religion in providing a key axiom of his moral theology that further defines the nature of the universal good which we are asked to love.

> A glint or symbol of this universal good may be found in any moment of perfect happiness visiting any breast: but it is impossible unreservedly to love or worship anything, be it the universe or any part of it, unless we find in the end that this thing is completely good: I mean, unless it is perfect after its kind and a friend to itself, and unless at the same time it is beneficent universally, and a friend to everything else.[85]

There is then no license in this to love willy-nilly, without discrimination, all that simply seems good to us, but rather there are specific conditions for our love—the criteria for a "good" that is "beneficent universally" and compatible with a complex world. Santayana does not ask us to love an apparent good or a little good, but rather the ideal, "the completely good," and this independent of border squabbles in "the press of the world" over these "varied perfections" and whose is best;[86] for "charity is a second birth of love, aware of many wills and many troubles."[87] Ultimately we can say that for Santayana, not unlike for Husserl, the concept of God is one of an *ideal*, and Santayana's *ideal* is the absolute "good" (i.e., God is [the] Good, and seems to reflect the Platonic ideal).

A Synthesis of Piety, Spirituality and Charity Directed toward "That Eternal Beauty"[88]

Finally, in this section, I wish to direct attention to associations in Santayana's "Ultimate Religion" with the elements of *piety, spirituality* and *charity* that Santayana proposes, respectively, as the categories of "religious emotions" and "imaginative morals" in *Reason in Religion*.[89] If these, as Santayana suggests in *Reason in Religion*, are characteristic elements of religion in general, the following "apologetic" is offered by

Santayana for any of an orthodox bent who would challenge the religious integrity of his "Ultimate Religion" for the "free and disillusioned spirit."

> If then any of us who are so minded should ever hear the summons of a liturgical religion calling to us: *Sursum corda, Lift up your hearts,* we might sincerely answer, *Habemus ad Dominum, Our hearts by nature are addressed to the Lord.* For we recognize universal power and respect it, since on it we depend for our existence and our fortunes. We look also with unfeigned and watchful allegiance towards universal truth, in which all the works of power are eternally defined and recorded; since in so far as we can discover it, the truth raises all things for us into the light, into the language of spirit.[90]

In Santayana's religious formula for the "disillusioned" we find implicit the common emotional features and moral values of religion he identifies as *piety, spirituality* and *charity.*[91] It is the notion of these tenets as values rather than the object of their intention that Santayana seems to emphasize. In piety we are recognizing and honoring that which we see as given, as "gifted": the "universal power, the "historic nutriment" that nurtures our "existence and our fortunes."[92] It is what we hold in awe as Otto's *mysterium tremendum fascinans,* and it is what we worship and direct our piety toward—it is the *Deus sive Natura* of Spinoza and for Santayana, the eternal perfection and "goodness" in matter.

Spirituality is seen by Santayana as more noble than *piety* and as a "higher side" of religion "which looks to the end toward which we move as *piety* looks to the conditions and to the sources of life."[93] As a common feature in religion it is a reaching of consciousness toward the "truth," an effort toward clarification and security or even certainty. It is deliberate and optional just as *piety* is, and as Santayana suggests above, it seeks the truth which "raises all things for us into the light, into the language of spirit."[94] In Santayana's religious world of disillusionment, there is no reaching through the mystery to a supernatural resolution, but instead, he suggests in *Realms of Being* that spirituality is *"an exercise in self-knowledge, an effort on the part of the spirit to clarify and to discipline itself."*[95] There is a finer point in distinguishing between *spirituality* and *the life of the spirit* which is the question of what precisely constitutes such a life. I will address this important issue at length later in the chapter, particularly in relation to Santayana's concepts of "contemplation of the *essences*" and the meaning of the *ideal.*

Charity, the third aspect of religion, leads us toward a certain selflessness in legitimatizing the needs and ideals of others and perceiving the relativity of our own in relation to the world's. It is from this principle, philosophically based upon the undiscoverability of the absolute, that Santayana's moral relativity is derived, and hence, the virtuous element of *charity.*[96] To act out this charity is to be blind to all divisions between institutions or cultures for "to relieve suffering in anyone's body is an immediate mercy to the spirit there."[97] However, in the world, the compatibility and harmony of varied perfections is as impossible as full attainment of any ideal (e.g., loving your enemy, turning the other cheek or living in full compliance with any and all Christian doctrine). As in Christianity, the potential energy generated in the differential between the imperfect and the ideal drives the lover in "love of the universal good," and it follows that "charity is a second birth of love, aware of many wills and many troubles."[98] Therefore, there is more in Santayana than the love of an ideal and an abstract Catholic notion of Christian charity since the admonition has broad consequences. As Woodward points out, art may also be a form of charity, or any good—that is, a good for the spirit, of oneself or another, that contributes to a move toward spiritual perfection and relief from suffering of the material world.[99] From the platform of Spinoza's stark "epithet" of love, Santayana logically derives a Christian ethic *in nuce* in "Ultimate Religion" as he concludes, "Thus the absolute love of anything involves the love of universal good; and the love of universal good involves the love of every creature."[100]

The model of *praxis* for these "virtues" which I proposed as Santayana's "dispositions" in chapter 1 can be interpreted as derived from the teachings and practice of Roman Catholic moral theology. Santayana further defines the elements of religion as "specific ideas, hopes, enthusiasms, and objects of worship; it operates by grace and flourishes of prayer."[101] With the exception of prayer, which I will address further on, we can recognize all of these elements in Santayana's "Ultimate Religion." However, the sphere of influence bearing on all hopes, grace, prayer and worship emanating from the spirit is confined only to the realm of matter. The spirit remains powerless. At the same time, Santayana denies any suggestion by a hypothetical empirical critic who would suggest that through reduction, he has arrived at a de-supernaturalized religion, and those elements in his "meager inventory" are only those bare elements of the original. He claims to leave faith and religion alone for those who would choose it in any form, supernatural or otherwise, and leaves religion's forms to those who make them objects of faith. For in his "Ultimate Religion" the tenets have been arrived at through "examination of conscience" and not through faith, unless it be *animal faith*.[102]

THE LIFE OF THE SPIRIT AND THE CONTEMPLATIVE LIFE

The Life of Reason and Spirituality

There has existed in some scholarly quarters a misunderstanding in regard to Santayana's concept of the life of reason as first defined in his work *The Life of Reason*, in relation to what he later defined as "the spiritual life" in *Realms of Being* and *Platonism and the Spiritual Life*. There is a need, for the purposes of this book, to carry the argument one step further concerning the question "One Santayana, or Two?" in order to consider the coherence of Santayana's early model for the life of reason and his later writings on the spiritual life. The question warrants more space than I have here, so I will make my argument brief.

One example of a view of "discontinuity" between the model of the life of reason" and Santayana's later position on the spiritual life is Sterling P. Lamprecht's view that "the life of reason and the spiritual life are different in nature. As one is a temporal career toward ideal goods, and the other is withdrawal from time and indifference to goods."[103] I do not believe that Santayana ever intended to suggest anything other than that the religious and spiritual aspect of the life of reason is an essential and foremost aspect of it, and that within that frame, the spiritual component remains important. Indeed, they are different in nature in respect to the question of *spirituality*. Granted, there are what could be considered evidential suggestions from Santayana (e.g., in his preface to the second edition of *The Life of Reason*) that his concept of this way of life had decreased in importance relative to his mature ontology. However, even acknowledging Santayana's admission of his "humanistic" bent in *The Life of Reason*, there is no evidence, on the whole, that those spiritual or spirituality aspects of the life of reason were substantially disclaimed either in the revised and abridged one-volume edition published in the year after his death in 1952, or in his other later works.[104] Granted that Santayana's own religious perspective is non-theistic and naturalistic, and there is a shift from a preoccupation with the history and human experience of traditional religions in *Reason in Religion* that was displaced by his exploration of his naturalistic ontology in later works. Of course, he had not fully developed his theory of *essences* at the writing of *The Life of Reason* nor even fully his concept of the spiritual life. To separate the two and compare them, as Lamprecht has done, it seems to me, is only to attempt to compare the part with the whole! To further suggest, as he does, that Santayana, in *The Realm of Essence*, totally disclaimed a spiritual life for the preferred life of reason is, I believe, to confuse the difference between an extreme life devoted to contemplation of "Pure Being" and that spiritual component of the life of reason that is more harmonious to the whole.[105] Santayana only suggests in *The Realm of Essence* that he is following these "spiritual minds" who excel at such a "rare vocation," *non passibus aequis*.[106] That suggests his understanding that a transcendence into contemplation of *essences* is an intermittent or periodic delightful episode in removing one from the cares of the world, but still a part of, rather than an alternative, to the life of reason. There seem to be, therefore, degrees of the spiritual life, in Santayana's view. To carry this one step further, he similarly suggests in his preface to the second edition of *The Life of Reason* that the life of reason itself is intermittent in its practice and definition and is not a rigid model.[107]

In a similar critical vein to Lamprecht above, Milton Munitz questioned the consistency of Santayana's definition of the spiritual life and "parsed" and summarized definitions derived from different Santayana works. He consequently accused Santayana of "a radical shift" in his moral philosophy, abandoning the morality of the life of reason.[108] Santayana responds to Munitz's "positivistic" attack on his moral philosophy and theory of essences, suggesting that Munitz searched "in the most out-of-the-way corners for something of mine that seems to contradict me" in the manner of a "prosecuting attorney."[109] I only briefly summarize these positions of Lamprecht and Munitz in regard to Santayana's disconnect of spirituality from the life of reason, in order to contrast my own view. Despite a wish that I may share for more conciseness in Santayana's integration of the spiritual life and the life of reason, I hold the viewpoint that little or nothing of Santayana's humanistic approach in *Reason in Religion* (particularly in the revised one-volume edition) is not consistent with and complementary to his more developed philosophy of the spirit in his later works. Indeed, it is clear that *The Life of Reason* turns outward, addressing the historical and evolutionary development of the human spirit, while *Realms of Being* turns inward as a phenomenology of a naturalistic spirit which, of necessity, can only be that consciousness of Santayana.[110] Finally, in regard to this matter, a similar dialectic to my own above arose in Horace Friess and Henry Rosenthal's paper "Reason in Religion and the Emancipated Spirit: A Dialogue" regarding the continuity and conjoinment of Santayana's religious philosophy as presented in the historical and humanistic vein of *Reason in Religion* and in his later works.[111] In exploring this issue they effectively draw on a quote from Santayana that, it seems, supports both their view and mine that there is not an "either-or" question regarding the life of reason and the spiritual life in Santayana's more mature philosophy.

> There is a certain option and practical incompatibility between spirituality and humanism . . . but the conflict is only marginal, the things are concentric, and spirit merely heightens and universalizes the synthesis which reason makes partially, as occasion requires, in the service of natural interests . . . Between the spiritual life and the life of reason there are accordingly no contradiction: they are concomitant: yet there is a difference of temper, and level, as there is between agriculture and music.[112]

In a letter to Justus Buchler, July 1, 1936, Santayana responded to Buchler's inquiry regarding the part that spirituality might play in the life of reason and if the life of reason was somehow subsumed by the spiritual component. Santayana strongly indicated that this was a misconception held by many, particularly at Columbia. I quote in small part a paragraph that expresses the gist of his response:

so that the rationality of his [man's] life and its spirituality might be called to concomitant dimensions of it, the one lateral and the other vertical. The vertical is the spiritual dimension in what inward religion has always added to life in the world, or in the cloister, which is part of the world.[113]

Santayana speaks here of "inward religion," and there is in his view a marked difference between this and organized religion. The relation of organized religion to the life of reason is a different question altogether.

There can be an impression that the life of reason, at its ultimate *praxis*, is a pathway of logic and science deliberately undertaken to attain knowledge of the natural world. It seems rather that Santayana viewed it in broader terms. In *Reason and Common Sense* he defined it as

simply the unity given to all existence by a mind *in love with the good*. In the higher reaches of human nature, as much as in the lower, rationality depends upon distinguishing the excellent; and that distinction can be made in the last analysis, only by an irrational impulse.[114]

Indeed, for Santayana religion falls short of rationality in "its texture and in its results" since it "pursues rationality through the imagination." However, he affirms that religion exercises a function of the life of reason in striving for the ideal (i.e., the unity of all existence). Granted, from the viewpoint of philosophy, another sphere from religious thought, Santayana points out the "difference in tone and language" of religion. While still extolling the pursuit of the life of reason by religion as superior relative to the spheres of society, science or art, he confesses that in religion, the life of reason "has been singularly abortive." So as in all spheres of society that Santayana addresses in *The Life of Reason*, in the great pursuit of the life of reason there are shortfalls all around in pursuing the ideal.

Life in the Ideal and the Semiotic Condition for Ideals

If, as Santayana suggests, "a man is spiritual when he lives in the presence of the ideal, and whether he eat or drink does so for the sake of a true and ultimate good,"[115] it is important to understand his concept of the "ideal." Are *essences* ideals, and if not, where do ideals originate? We have already discussed in an earlier section the symbolic representation of ideals in religious myth and dogma (i.e., dogma has value as a conveyer of moral "truths" or ideals). We have also discussed Santayana's claim that ideals are subject to individuality and to arrive at a fully universal ideal is beyond human capability. In this light alone, an understanding of Santayana's concept of the *ideal* is important. We find in *Realms of Being* the notion of *contemplation of essences*[116] which on first impression suggests that if spiritual life is life in the ideal, then we are contemplating ideals. As we shall see, this is not the case and I will address this question below, first attempting to arrive at Santayana's definition or concept of the ideal. As one might anticipate, the concept of the ideal is an important element to be understood in aesthetics. In fact, it is in *The Sense of Beauty*, a series of essays based upon Santayana's course in aesthetics at Harvard, that we first find his concept elucidated. He states that "the ideal means that environment in which our faculties would find their freest employment, and their most congenial world. Perfection would be nothing but life under these conditions."[117] Earlier in the same work, he suggests that to encounter an "incongruity with the formed precept [the ideal], is the essence and measure of ugliness."[118] Clearly then, we gauge our expectations vs. an ideal that we have personally concocted to serve our deepest needs and our happiness, and the "surprise" of something less (i.e., most things in life), to one degree or another, is "ugliness." Hodges and Lachs helpfully suggest that "the motto of *The Life of Reason* is that everything natural has an ideal completion and everything ideal a natural ground."[119] There is then, nothing universal, permanent or other-worldly in Santayana's concept of the ideal. This idea is of course consistent with the Lucretian goal of "happiness" in Santayana's philosophy where one must, as far as possible, find the freedom to meet one's needs in satisfying one's personal "goods" in reaching full potential as an individual. McCormick suggests that Santayana's concept of the ideal is "an ideal of condition or achievement" directed at satisfaction and, quoting from *Reason in Common Sense*, "Satisfaction is the touchstone of value."[120]

It is desirable to clear up the question I raised above regarding any congruence between ideals and *essence*. Intuition of *essences* in itself, first of all, is a pre-reflective act, and therefore any response to the sign or symbol that the *essence* would represent to the subject has not occurred. In other words, the intuition itself is pre-semiotic, as the spirit, either in an effortless "dream" or in a disciplined intentional focus, imposes "brackets" on all reflection or response to the *essence*. In order for an ideal to be formulated, the semiotic response to the *essence* as sign or symbol must provoke reflection and then perception, and from this the thought process that goes into formulating an ideal follows. An ideal is a theory concocted in the imagination, and therefore it falls into the realm of *animal faith*. Ideals, as products of the imagination, are only formulated following a semiotic response to an essence, hence ideals and essences are not identical. At the same time, *essences are* ideal (in a descriptive sense) in that in a "pure" contemplation of *essences*, which I will discuss below, we are intuiting a "formal" or "ideal" reality.[121]

Levels of the Spiritual Life and Contemplation of the Essences

For Santayana, there are two modes of the life of the spirit or consciousness: that of day-to-day life in the world based upon *animal faith*, and that of transcendence to intuition of the *essences*—tantamount to an escape from the anxieties, cares and problems of animal life. The second of these, Santayana makes clear, is an option—a release into the eternal realm through contemplation that results in a harmonious life in the spirit (i.e., an important component of the life of reason as indicated above). If one can frame all components of the spiritual life into a religion that avoids the dark side of the world's organized religions, then there is a convergence that approaches an ideal, and reason and religion in a life of reason become conjoined. Santayana's "lay religion" as derived in "Ultimate Religion" seems to approach that ideal for Santayana. His "Ultimate Religion" explicitly contains all three components of a "religion," as presented in *The Life of Reason* (i.e., *piety*, *spirituality* and *charity*). Friess and Rosenthal observe also that those elements from *Reason in Religion* making up "a reasonable discipline of religion" (e.g., piety and "symbols of the eternal good") are carried over into the "Ultimate Religion." They also observe, supporting my argument vs. Lamprecht above, "that ecstatic contemplation [i.e., a high form of spirituality]" is a "moment" in the development of man's humanity, again suggesting the compatibility of Santayana's earlier and later philosophy of religion.[122] Further, if one understands Santayana's treatment of religion as a "phase" in *The Life of Reason* (i.e., a passing from traditional religion to something further evolved), then one can view "Ultimate Religion" as a transition in phase.[123] Hodges and Lachs capture well this line of thought in their chapter "Religious Belief" in *Thinking in the Ruins*, a comparative study of Santayana and Wittgenstein. A quotation from the end of their final chapter seems generally to support my argument.

> The ultimate religion is closer to what flourishes in India than what is everyday in the West. Yet there are traces of it in primitive religion, and mystical, joyous, and celebratory reaches of the Judeo-Christian tradition give ample insight into its nature. It is a religion without explicit theology . . . no theory and . . . no descriptions of fact. It provides instead the privileges of spectatorship, of taking joy in seeing the contest from a great distance or under the form of eternity. Though they were not religious men, Santayana and Wittgenstein shared the attitudes, the insights and the pleasures of this religion of the mind.[124]

It's likely more than coincidence that chapters on "Distraction" and "Union," respectively, are the longest in *The Realm of the Spirit*, for in these chapters Santayana probes deeply into the criteria for a meaningful spiritual life.[125] As indicated earlier, for Santayana, all sense experience is prompted by *essences*, and all thought as a function of the imaginative spirit is intuitive. Therefore, it would follow that any experiences of spiritual life involve primarily the intuition of *essences*. Further, Santayana's depiction of the attainment of a spiritual life is in many respects a process which proceeds through a removal from distraction and the cares of the world, and at the same time tends toward the goal of a personal reconciliation between the spirit, nature and the ideal. In and through this non-reflective process one attains the ultimate reconciliation of the world with personal ideals and the investiture of self in the universe. This process, as is evident in *Realms of Being,* to a greater or lesser degree, parallels the path in the Christian tradition (e.g., monastic life) toward a spiritual life of worldly detachment dedicated to a union with the divinity in the Christian tradition. In chapter 4, "Pure Being," of *The Realm of Essence,* Santayana probes the inner core of his ontology and, at the same time, the ultimate goal, the highest achievement in the spiritual life. He also draws close, in his concept of pure Being to the contemplative object of mystics and saints in traditional religions (i.e., God), but carefully draws the philosophical barriers to any identity.[126]

There are, however, as I mentioned above, degrees of spiritual life short of the ideal, just as there would be in the scope of a spiritual life circumscribed by traditional religion (e.g., even in a monastery). Angus Kerr-Lawson, Michael Brodrick and others have addressed this question and have designated levels—in the case of Brodrick, three levels—which transition vertically from a day-to-day contemplation of essences to a more extended profound state of removal from existence in the case of some Buddhist or Indian masters. Kerr Lawson also provides a particularly insightful perspective on the role of the spiritual life in the life of reason and the aspects of social responsibility in Santayana's project despite his personal alienation from contemporary society.[127] In regard to levels of spirituality, it bears repeating that Santayana himself falls below a "ten" and by his own admission follows those more rigorous spiritual minds, *non passibus aequis.* He also declares, not unexpectedly, that this "emancipation and impartiality of the spirit . . . can be reached only in moments of perfect equilibration and internal harmonious movement."[128] Not unexpectedly, we find that anything but a modicum of spiritual life ("very limited flights")[129] is "optional" in the sense that consciousness can remain subject to the distractions of the day-to-day world ("the proper nature of existence is distraction itself")[130] through choice (the Will) or through weakness or helplessness. The consequences Santayana attaches to such distractions as limitations are dire:

> In such discord, spirit suffers horribly and is indeed, morally, the only sufferer in all camps . . . Sometimes consciousness seems to make cowards of us all; life is spoiled by responsibility for life; care, fear, and indecision poison the innocent pleasure of seeing and feeling and playing the game.[131]

If indeed there are levels of spiritual life, albeit all of them involving varying degrees of intensity and intermittence, how must we define the approach and method for participating in it? Since we are determining Santayana's mature view of the spiritual life, we would best consider first his views in *Realms of Being.* If indeed, all of spiritual life involves intuition of *essences*, the first consideration we need to briefly revisit are Santayana's various approaches to *essences* discussed in chapter 3 which are *skepticism, dialectic, contemplation* and *spiritual discipline*.[132] Clearly, to exercise any of these approaches in discriminating *essence* involves an initial act of the intention and therefore, as indicated above, they are optional. Since all of these approaches are involved in different ways and degrees in the life of the spirit, it is helpful to understand these approaches to *essence* as they ultimately apply to the spiritual life. Recall that Santayana would reject *skepticism* as a tenable approach to life, since the life of the intellect is, in effect, obviated. The *dialectic* approach was rejected based on its relegation of *animal faith* and experience in the world or the *a posteriori*. In Santayana's view, the dialectician was left trapped in his imagination and in the realm of *essences*. A Peirceian perspective would leave the dialectician permanently immersed in "secondness" or the semiotic realm where *essences* take on symbolic significance. The third approach to *essence* is through *contemplation*, and it is in this approach that we are nearing that mode of ideal spiritual activity that Santayana suggests is an intuition of "pure Being." It is a mode that is juxtaposed to the world of concerns, confusion, hope, fear and other "distractions" of animal life. Santayana reminds us of biblical and Platonic admonitions, as well as phenomenological "retrenchment" and conscious intent when he suggests, "The difference between the life of the spirit and that of the flesh is itself a spiritual difference . . . [more] in the quality of their attention: the one is anxiety, inquiry, desire and fear; the other is intuitive possession."[133] As we come to understand *spiritual discipline*, the integrating effort of the Will in achieving the spiritual life, its close relationship to *contemplation* becomes evident. If one chooses any of the pathways to *essence* that Santayana designates, there is a common avenue, attention, that determines one's progress in the spiritual life; we recall his admonition quoted earlier, "Awaken attention, intensify it, purify it into a white flame."[134]

Here Santayana, even in the first chapter of *Realms of Being*, reveals both the "wakefulness" needed for contemplation of the *essences* and the difference between interpretation of the *essence* as a symbol (passage into semiosis) and resultant action, and the pre-semiotic nature of contemplation (i.e., intuiting the *essences* only for their inherent value in a suspension of intellectual and emotional involvement with the world). Contemplation may mean different things to people; therefore, we need to clarify Santayana's precise meaning which is implicit in the above quotation. To put this briefly and clearly, I can again do no better than John Lachs in first delineating the spiritual life from that balance in the realm of the spirit that may not be considered purely spiritual, and further describing Santayana's concept of contemplation.

Every type of consciousness belongs in the realm of the spirit, but only intuition free of intent or animal faith is truly spiritual. Feeling, belief, and memory are forms of consciousness, but they do not possess the spirituality of pure intuition. Unbiased and uncommitted contemplation, aesthetic enjoyment of the immediate reveals most clearly the inner, spiritual nature of the spirit. Spirituality is freedom from the concerns of animal life, release from the anxious selectivity of the psyche, liberation from the practical intelligence which is incessantly at work adapting means to ends. [135]

Therefore, we see again in this summary description what I discussed in chapter 3 regarding the parallels in contemplation and intuition of *essences* and the *epoché* and transcendental phase of the Husserlian phenomenological method. [136] As I also mentioned in chapter 3, Santayana perceives that children, and even animals, in their ability and inclination to draw upon the immediate, that is, those *essences* in the flux that strike them as first impressions of the world without reflection or analysis, are better initiated than adult humans into the nature of *essence*. [137] It is only later for children (and likely never for lower animals) that the natural ability to be cognizant of *essence* becomes obscured by cognitive experience and the practical thought of living (i.e., with distraction). Therefore, unless spiritual discipline is exercised, *essences* will remain "thin abstractions to those absorbed in action." [138] Lachs draws attention to possible misconceptions regarding Santayana's idea of the spiritual life, in particular the notion that there is more to it than the pre-reflective intuition of *essences*. [139] Santayana's relativism provides for an infinite and unrestricted scope of essences that may be given to intuition, unlike the preferential objects of religion for contemplation by mystics, saints and religious people in general. Such liberty in contemplation is likely a disappointing prospect for many who would find a more noble or worshipful intent in a spiritual life. However, it seems as Lachs suggests that "the spiritual life is thus an optional perfection: for those whose nature predisposes them to the quiet enjoyment of the immediate, it is the finest and freest human act." [140] If contemplation of *essences* is so integral to the spiritual life, how then can we put it in perspective in relation to the whole of spiritual life, or is the contemplation of *essences* the whole of it? Is prayer somehow related to contemplation or is it rather meditation, and in what degree of importance, if any, does Santayana hold it, given his non-theistic philosophy?

Prayer and Union with the Good

The role of prayer in the life of the spirit is clearly more dialectical than contemplative and therefore would not be considered by Santayana to be at the highest end of the spiritual life. In the case of prayer, unlike in contemplation, aspects of morality and belief are intermingled in attentiveness to life in the world and its problems. We could further conclude that given the "immediate" intuitive aspect of the spiritual life, from Santayana's standpoint, prayer may fall outside of it. Also, without a God to pray to, from a rational standpoint, prayer would seem on first consideration to be useless. From the standpoint of traditional religion, this would, of course, be the case, since prayer would be perceived as having or influencing power. Santayana proposes that prayer in this sense "could not be efficacious except magically if incantations . . . could compel nature [or influence God] to obey our commands."[141] Nevertheless, Santayana still affirms that prayer "constitutes something spiritual." In the final pages of *The Realm of the Spirit* he reaffirms its importance first defined in *Reason in Religion* thirty-five years earlier and if anything, seems in his reaffirmation to think of it as even more important. In *Reason in Religion* he proposes,

> In rational prayer, the soul may be said to accomplish three things important to its welfare: it withdraws itself and defines its good, it accommodates itself to destiny, and it grows like the ideal which it conceives.[142]

And further:

> Prayer, in fine, though it accomplishes nothing material, constitutes something spiritual. It will not bring rain, but until rain comes it may cultivate hope and resignation and may prepare the heart for any issue, opening up a vista in which human prosperity will appear in its conditioned existence and conditional value.[143]

The concept of prayer in traditional religions presented in phenomenological description by Santayana in *Reason in Religion* relates the act of bargaining or compelling God to meet our wishes and desires.[144] This conception of prayer is believed by Santayana to be not only "incompatible with Christianity" and unspiritual—that is, it is rather like a practical and worldly transaction—but also sacrilegious.[145] In *The Realm of Spirit*, as earlier in *Reason in Religion*, Santayana treats the subject of prayer at length, ultimately characterizing it as "oratio, the eloquence of destiny," addressed to no one, as "we are recollecting, digesting, purifying our conscience."[146] "Prayer . . . abounds in regrets, praises, aspirations, laughter and curses, but all transposed from the plane of action to that of reflection and prophecy."[147] There is resignation on one hand as expressed in the Lord's Prayer, "thy will be done," and also there is hope.[148] Santayana rhetorically asks how we might be united in spirit with the "good," the ideal that may never be a reality, and at the same time "be at peace with a power that is perhaps destroying us.[149] He finds the answer in prayer, and further affirms that "thus, strange as it may sound to a rationalist who thinks prayer ridiculous, the only rational form of life for a spirit that has attained self-knowledge is the life of prayer."[150] Prayer, then, is dialectic and ratiocinative and gathers in from experience, and, although it takes place in the realm of the spirit, it is undertaken in the mode of *animal faith*. One could also argue that prayer is not only dialectical, reflective and even meditative, it is also practical in considering our approach to life in our environment in the world in Santayana's sense, as deep reflection rather than contemplation.

A Naturalist's Immortality

In the preface to *The Realm of Truth*, Santayana reflects that "man alone knows he must die,"[151] and sets the stage for that cruel truth that one reaches in mature disillusion where such a truth can be loved. The foundational realization of Santayana's naturalism is expressed early in *Interpretations of Poetry and Religion* (i.e., "The existence and well-being of man upon earth are, from the point of view of the universe, an indifferent incident"), and this understanding persists throughout his mature thought. Santayana considers teleology at length in chapter 7 of *Realms of Being* and recognizes the interplay of tropes, or repeating forms in nature, and does not deny their underlying causality. He does not deny that final causes exist for human beings, but any underlying final causes or natural forces he proposes "we may darkly assign to fate or matter or chance or the unfathomable will of God."[152] These deep forces of nature are inaccessible to human intelligence and are more likely assigned human theological or poetic descriptives. This naturalistic view is not inconsistent with the acceptance of suffering and calamity in the Christian cosmology, but the form of salvation in Santayana's religion of disillusion entails another form of resurrection and immortality. The form of immortality may indeed be a disappointment in the light of Christian expectations regarding the survival of the "soul," and Santayana depicts it concisely in the preface to *The Realm of Truth* in the form of a quotation from an introduction to Spinoza's *Ethics*.

> A man who understands himself under the form of eternity knows the quality that eternally belongs to him, and knows that he cannot wholly die . . . for when the movement of his life is over, the truth of his life remains. The fact of him is a part forever of the infinite context of facts.[153]

First, the achievement of life, he says, remains undeniable, even if forgotten by the world and resides eternally in the Realm of Truth. However, his foundational philosophy as ontologically depicted in *Realms of Being* does not allow for immortality in the conventional sense of the word, for as he states in *Scepticism and Animal Faith*, "whatsoever, having once arisen, never perishes would be *immortal*. I believe there is nothing immortal."[154]

However, the idea of eternity is particularly pertinent to the truth because "it is contemporary with all times" although, as an *essence*, it does not exist and only characterizes facts that occur in time. Truth is, he says, "frozen history" and outside of time, having passed from the temporal to the eternal in the flux of history.[155] Santayana's concept of immortality, therefore, has its foundation in the idea of truth and the repository in eternity for truth, and carries the essence of our lives into eternal Being. Such an immortality is reminiscent of Whitehead's eternally retentive Consequent Mind of God wherein all the truth that ever was resides in this ever-building, everlasting divine consciousness.[156] It can't be denied that for many this is a harsh understanding of immortality, but for Socrates, Spinoza and Santayana, human life is seen and accepted as a manifestation of everlasting truth. In the message of the Gospels and the risen Christ, Santayana finds a symbolic representation of the ideal cycle of life, death and resurrection—for example, "Having finished his mission, [Christ] transmitting his work without regret or anxiety, into other hands."[157] Resurrection for Santayana is an ontological and symbolic parallel to the Passion story. We are born into the alien natural world in which its very vitality imposes suffering. In this environment of suffering and trials our spirit is liberated, finding solace in the ideal. Our life is acted out for good or evil and our memory is interrupted by death, and the *essence* of this unique life passes into eternity.

Explicit in Santayana's concept of *essences* are infinite possibilities for their actualization in matter, and the consequent contingency of nature is evident in the inability of animal life to ascertain either the truth *or* the future. Could God or a transcendental life in the supernatural be possible? As a naturalist he would deny the supernatural, but if God plays a role in Nature as matter, this could not be denied by Santayana since in his philosophical system he makes no claim to have ascertained truth. He has only his belief consistent with his metaphysics, and that would only allow for a God that was substance (matter + *essence*) which would need to be in the natural world where the divine psyche could survive. Hence, in the frame of Santayana's metaphysic, the only surviving element is the truth of the actualization of the animal *essence*. In all of this, one could suppose that there is at least one possibility for another manner of "survival," and this possibility relies upon the eternal nature of *essences* which are beyond time and hence can be actualized in matter simultaneously. Based upon this premise, a human or any animal could be essentially replicated at some time in the future within the biological frame of another psyche. Obviously, one cannot say that the *essence* or the original human was "cloned" since there is no relation between the existence of the original psyche and the newly actualized one. Although that possibilities are infinite is never denied, we are confident that Santayana would recommend that we not speculate on such a possibility and rather address ourselves to the spiritual and practical demands of this existence.

Life then is seen by Santayana as a "self-repeating trope," and life is perpetually renewed in forms and shapes that are the platform for the individual spirit. Implicit in the life of reason is a preparation for death and the acceptance of an "ideal immortality [that] is implied in the truth of every finished life."[158] The "immortality" of the species is played out in the spontaneous rebirth or resurrection of new spirit in the natural generation of new souls. If then, our ideal immortality is in the eternal Realm of Truth, how then might there be some soteriological aspect, some notion of salvation in any sense within the frame of Santayana's philosophy?

Salvation and Liberation

Chapter 8 of *The Realm of the Spirit* is titled "Liberation" and is in effect Santayana's depiction of a pathway to a kind of salvation. This salvation would play out only in the Realm of the Spirit and be limited by our death. If we accept freedom as a consequence of liberation and salvation as somehow related to a "release" or to some degree of freedom from the suffering and anxiety of life, we can logically return to the concluding words of chapter 5 of the *Realm of the Spirit*, titled "Freedom," and find the stage for the nature of this freedom.

> The freedom and glory of the spirit comes from its impotence . . . Its essence is to be light, not to be power; and it can never be pure light until it is satisfied with an ideal dominion, not striving to possess or to change the world, but identifying itself only with truth and beauty that rise unbidden from the world into the realm of the spirit.[159]

If, as Santayana claims, there is no escape from nature and no immortality except in history and the realm of truth, the only salvation from suffering must be found in this life. For him in a "lay religion," as depicted in "Ultimate Religion," is disillusion from transcendental expectations, and salvation lies in a recourse to a disintoxication from the anxieties of the world and even from values themselves.[160] Again we see here the separation of "feeling" and "morality," and then salvation consists of both an attitude of acceptance, a disillusionment and a sensitivity to the place of the individual in the light of eternity. The high road of this awareness finds expression in contemplation of those elements proper to eternity, the *essences*. In this manner, one loses preoccupation with facts and intuits the "purest reality."[161] Salvation is therefore found for Santayana in acceptance and contemplation. The ideal conditions, he claims, for this transcendence of the world through this "contemplative habit" is rather "in solitude than in society, in art than in business, in prayer than in argument. It is stimulated by beautiful and constant things more than by things ugly, tedious, crowded or uncertain."[162]

Finally, in regard to such an approach, Santayana draws comparisons as to what traditions are most inclined to incorporate it in their traditional praxis.

In fact, the great masters of the spiritual life are evidently not the Greeks . . . but the Indians, their disciples elsewhere in the East, and those Moslems, Christians and Jews who have surrendered precisely that early, unregenerate claim to be enveloped in a protecting world designed for their benefit or vindication.[163]

Then, setting up a hierarchy of contemplative dispositions, Santayana, not surprisingly, suggests that the contemplative habit "is more freer in the East than in the West, among Catholics than among Protestants [and], among Muslims than among Jews."[164]

IMAGINATION, DOGMA, MORALITY AND POETRY

Imagination

Santayana's Darwinian view of man as one with nature projects an image of the primitive, dominated by hunger, disease, war, the general fight for survival and death. Through the genius of the race, man emerges from these pressures both as an individual with a mind as "a turbulent commonwealth" seeking to satisfy its desires, but still in a tenuous balance and compliance with rules and sanctions perceived best for the group or the powers-that-be. Santayana proposes that the ultimate aim for both the individual and society is a balancing of aims and desires. This is the "Good [which] is harmony to be established by the perfect definition and mutual adjustment of all natural functions, both in the individual and the state."[165] Such acceptance and harmony as a goal can even remind one of the "reality principle" and the accommodating goal of the Freudian psychotherapeutic. In this process of achieving harmony, Santayana views the role of the imagination as paramount.[166] At the same time, the imagination which generates poetry and religious ideas is the same organ of consciousness that, in the less gifted, or under the press of the day-to-day world, "yields vulgar perception."[167] Imagination, then, is that relational organ of the spirit that builds, in conjunction with *animal faith*, individual and collective reality upon the only certainty of the *sopm*. But the imagination or the poetic perspective in Santayana's philosophy of religion is also the great redemptive power that can allow one to dwell *sub specie aeternitatis* while living in the world.[168] Santayana's reverence toward imagination as a vehicle for life in the eternal can give the reader a sense of transcendental intercourse between the individual consciousness and the universal powers. From this same organ of imagination arises the human moral function, and from the individuality of imagination arises also the bias associated with moral concepts; that is, what is "right" in meeting my desires for perfection and, therefore, sometimes contentiously, right for others as well.[169] All of this is a translation of signs occurring in the imagination "to be interpreted as effects produced in the animal psyche by the revolutions of matter within and without that animal." [170] Santayana's philosophical principle that absolute truth is unattainable to animal life and hence no knowledge is certain translates readily to his belief that a universal truth of morality is, hence, unachievable, and in this he is consistent with William James and the Pragmatists.

> To reach moral truth, which like all truth is eternal, we should have to remember or foresee with absolute clearness the aspirations of all souls in all moments; and confronting these aspirations with their occasions, we should have to measure their relative vanity and physical compatibility. [171]

Dogma and Morality

If, as Santayana claims, doctrine and dogma have value as conveyers of moral ideas and human yearnings, is there truth in them? Just as he proclaims the absurdity of the commonly stated function of modern philosophers to disclose absolute truth by "reading nature into their private idioms," [172] he impugns inspired myth- and dogma-makers as barking up the same tree. Nevertheless, he perceives "their myths as a whole are wisely contrived" [173] within the social and religious microcosm in which they are generated. He offers the apologetic that "devils and semi-bestial gods, nymphs and muses were no empty fancies. They were inspired dreams of what existence might be and almost is, either beyond us or in ourselves." [174] They are he believes "symbolic representations of moral reality" that have an important function as vehicles of the lessons of experience but at the same time are a "deception" to the extent they are represented as literal facts in traditional religions [truths]. [175] The importance of imagination and the moral and poetic nature of religion are the sole "theme" Santayana proclaims and addresses in *Interpretations of Poetry and Religion*. [176] In phenomenological perspective, a vision of reality "flashes like sheet-lightning broadly but unseizably, and only for a moment in every intuition of the spirit." [177] Mythology and dogma are simply that imaginative construction, fallacious, but in good faith, beyond the *sopm*.

Santayana suggests that "truth" in myth is reflected as rather a quality of perceived moral excellence of beneficence (e.g., a god dispensing grace and benefits). [178] What must be emphasized here, however, is the phenomenology of the experience of the immediate, that is, that "an animal vision of the universe . . . is, in one sense, never false: it is rooted in the nature of that animal" and justifies the claim to be true in having a phenomenon as a real object. [179] On the other hand, as discussed in earlier chapters, Santayana's philosophical position based upon the unattainability of *certain* knowledge is that life and the world are subject to the chaos or, if you will, Peirce's Firstness in flux and are therefore contingent. The translation of this intuition or vision to myth, dogma or doctrine that Santayana suggests can be "wisely contrived" is still based upon the "truth" of the phenomenal object of inspiration, but it has been taken from the "immediate" to the semiotic stage of reflection and perception of the *essence* to an interpretation of the vision. As the synthesizer and conveyer of inspiration, "the imagination, therefore, must furnish to religion and to metaphysics those large ideas tinctured with passion, those supersensible forms shrouded in awe, in which alone a mind of great sweep and vitality can find its congenial objects."[180] However, there can be nothing permanent in dogmas, despite the claims for them as eternal truths by the magisteria of orthodox faith, for "the imagination in its freedom abandons these errors for others simply because the prevalent mood of mankind has changed, and it begins dreaming in a different key."[181] Dogma or doctrine, whether philosophical or religious, cannot be considered "true" but only a reflection of an individual or group-generated formula for organizing apparent manifestations of order and continuity in the flux of experience.

> Each new gospel attributes a unique and final authority to one type of value and to one passionate interest. Nevertheless, each religion is the source and only sanction of a special morality, coloured and heightened by that special enthusiasm; so that each religion, from the point of view of human reason, carries with it a moral heresy. To undermine that religion is to undermine this bias in morals; a bias which custom or ignorance or narrowness of temperament causes believers to identify with morality itself.[182]

Poetry and Religion

Santayana even disclaims his own philosophical theory as "not true, nor meant to be true [but] a grammatical or possibly poetical construction having . . . a certain internal vitality and interest.[183] It is, in other words, personal in its emanation; parochial, even as dogma is. There can be no certainty in humankind of an identity between knowledge as an object or the congruence of an asserted fact and the actuality of that fact in existence. Santayana opens the preface to his *Interpretations of Poetry and Religion* with two of his own philosophical tenets that I suggest henceforth reflect his lifelong perspective on religion and dogma.

> This idea is that religion and poetry are identical in *essence*, and differ merely in the way that they are attached to practical affairs. Poetry is called religion when it intervenes in life, and religion, when it merely supervenes, is seen to be nothing but poetry. It would naturally follow from this conception that religious doctrines would do well to withdraw their pretensions to be dealing with matters of fact. That pretension is not only the source of the conflicts of religion with science and of the vain and bitter controversies of sects; it is also the cause of the impurity and incoherence of religion in the soul, when it seeks sanc-

tions in the sphere of reality, and forgets that its proper concern is to express the ideal.[184]

The poetry from which religion is built is descriptive and of immediate experience of the natural world in those terms and symbols that are natural to the subject, be it primitive innocence, or aesthetic sophistication. Its purpose, as Santayana suggests, is to draw from reality materials for an image of the ideal. We discussed in chapter 3 the inherent phenomenological character of a poetic response to the *essences* of immediate experience, not as facts but as phenomena. I argue, as I think Santayana would have, that the generative process of doctrine and dogma arise through phenomenological description by the spirit(s) that witness the world. Such description relies, beyond the *sopm*, on *animal faith* and imagination. In the case of the mythical form, "it is an ideal interpretation in which the phenomena are digested and transmuted into human energy, into imaginative harmonies."[185] Foundational to Santayana's claim for the non-factual content of dogma is his (and Husserl's) phenomenological tenet that "nothing given exists."[186] In summary fashion, Santayana depicts the role of imagination in attempting to discern reality, but adheres to his own dogma:

> My matured conclusion has been that no system is to be trusted, not even that of science in any literal or pictorial sense; but all systems may be used, and up to a certain point, trusted as symbols . . . Philosophies and religions, where they do not misrepresent these same dynamic relations and do not contradict science, express destiny in moral dimensions, in obviously mythical and poetical images: but how else would these moral truths be expressed at all in a traditional or popular fashion? Religions are the great fairy-tales of the conscience.[187]

Nevertheless, if systematic religion offers, in its proclaimed wisdom, nourishment for the needs of the soul, it must be respected, as in Santayana's civilized view, moral tolerance obviates conflicts and enhances individual freedom to satisfy its unique needs. As he suggests in *Dominations and Powers*, the language of science, that of observation of the physical world, and that of the imagination in all its modes, must coexist, one not condemning the cultivation of the other.[188] Such a familiar note Santayana strikes here in anticipating that great ongoing debate between science and religion and its only possible ultimate resolution.

DOMINATIONS OF ORGANIZED RELIGION

The Philosophical Compromise of Dogma and Tradition

Freedom in disillusion is to "move gladly with the world." Woodward recognizes Santayana's rationale for orthodox religious tradition:

"'It is all make-believe,' when taken literally, but as a help to steering a steady course amid the currents of existence under the tutelage of hallowed ideals that are the fruits of ancient spiritual insight, it is an admirable discipline and essential component of the Life of Reason."[189] Santayana's expressions of distaste for what he perceives as the whimsy and self-serving logic of Protestantism are almost "harping" in their persistence as he decries the compromise of orthodox dogma.[190] As I have indicated above, for Santayana, dogma is an expression of a humanistic *ideal*, not to be taken literally, but still of utmost importance. It is not to be cast aside, as in what Santayana saw as the great compromise of Protestantism and modern philosophy in general, but respected as a vehicle of the human quest for the ideal. Santayana's sympathy for the moral as well as the aesthetic value of dogma was indeed counter to the trends apparent in Western philosophy from the seventeenth through the twentieth century. Evidence of Santayana's departure from the trajectory of the *Zeitgeist* in philosophy can be dramatically demonstrated in a comparison of Santayana and Hume (1711–1776) in regard to their respective attitudes toward religion. There are obvious similarities held by the two philosophers in regard to rejection of a supernatural realm, the potential distraction from life of a doctrine of immortality, miracles, the importance of the moral component of religion and the potentially suppressive character of religion. I intend no in-depth comparative analysis here but only wish to make a particular point by comparison of their important differences in regard to Christian dogma. Hume, the Scottish empiricists in general and most philosophers of Protestant origins since Kant have rejected not only orthodoxy but also its associated dogmas. Hume, for example, unlike Santayana, saw little of moral value in doctrines such as the threat of punishment in hell or immortality of the soul. The liberal Protestant weakening of the more gloomy aspects of Christian doctrine would be substantially in accord with Hume's preference.[191] I will further address Santayana's dispute with both Protestantism and the Roman Catholic Church later in this chapter.

Dogma, Religion and Domination

If there is moral value in dogma and doctrine, where then, other than the claim of the church for its literal truth, is there a further aspect to its dark side? Despite Santayana's contrarian view on religious dogma, he affirmed that religion or philosophy, as it is obsessed with a single criteria for truth, its own formulated dogma, imposing its will in a way that distracted from a person's individual response to the world, is anathema. Dogmatic emphasis for Santayana, as Kirkwood suggests, could "turn bigotry into a principle."[192] Hence, his distaste for dogmatism was more in its manifestation as "domination" than the fact of its formulation. In this way, religion as a domination can be a threatening opposition to those powers of individuals and society that derived from and are in accord with nature (matter). Santayana construes a domination as a compulsive force "that begins when free action in one direction [e.g., that to satisfy the individual's needs and desires] collides with free action in another [e.g., another individual, church or state]."[193] The individual life of the spirit, as a result of such opposition, is consequently restricted in its freedom to fulfill its nature. There is, Santayana suggests, a cost in the form of sacrifice in seeking harmony in society and "a strong and well-knit nature, brave with perfect harmony within, will despise and detest harmony on a larger scale; it will refuse to [or resist] sacrifice [of] any part of its chosen good."[194] A simple example provided by Santayana from Roman Catholic doctrine relates to marital divorce.

> If divorce is possible, the union remains free; but where divorce is out of the question, the vows once made become a fatality . . . .because Will in men and women contain many other impulses besides the impulse to live together . . . Therefore, if no divorce is allowed, the marriage contract loads the dice in every subsequent decision and exercises a real constraint over the other impulses of the Will.[195]

Santayana's perspective on religious dogma, as I hope I have made apparent by now, seems to be through the "lens" of his Roman Catholic experience. Levinson correctly categorizes Santayana's naturalism as "culturally catholic."[196] At the same time, Santayana's perspective is balanced, reflecting irony and paradox as it plays across juxtaposed value judgments on what Grossman termed Santayana's "double moral grid."[197] Santayana's views on the detrimental aspects of orthodox dogma seem to vary minimally over his lifetime from his earlier views expressed while at Harvard—for example, *Interpretations of Poetry and Religion*; various essays during that period—for example, "The Present Position of the Catholic Church" (1892) and *Reason in Religion* (1900); and later works—for example, *Winds of Doctrine* (1913), *Scepticism and Animal Faith* (1923), *Realm of the Spirit* (1940) and *Dominations and Powers* (1951).[198] His view on dogma, throughout his works, it seems to me, is clearly synoptic, just as is his view on the poetic nature of religion.

In *Dominations and Powers*, published in 1951, the year before his death, Santayana's attention is directed in a broad sense at the political relationship between the government, religious and other and institutions and the interests and way of life of the individual and society. Ultimately, it is a study of the dichotomy between precepts of the individual and that of institutions and the restraining dominations of unrestrained moral dogmatism.[199] In this, his terminal work, Santayana addresses that side of religion that impinges on personal freedom, and "has become the most tyrannous element in that hostile, hopeless world from which it has come to deliver us."[200] Here is the other aspect of the dark side. Santayana proposes that the "function of religious commands is precisely to load the dice, to load them with mystical authority and disproportionate fears, so that no temptation should overcome the force of the official precepts." As such a command becomes social convention and public conscience, the individual is coerced and his reason compromised.[201] Essentially all of Santayana's observations regarding the potential for domination by religion, with the exception of limited observations on the militancy of Islam,[202] are directed at the power of the Roman Catholic Church. Although, as we have observed, this same church is also held up by Santayana as a valued repository of ancient traditions and ideals and its power that is derived from teaching a literal interpretation of doctrine redounds in domination of individual powers.

Charity and the Uncompromising Disposition of Santayana

When closely aligned with the government, the domination of religion in accord with the state can go beyond a spiritual threat (e.g., eternal damnation) and carry with it threats of imprisonment and death (e.g., as in the Inquisition or in militant manifestations such as the Crusades).[203] It is, of course, the maximizing of personal freedom to satisfy individual desires that is the unattenuated foundation of Santayana's resistance to dominating influences. The attenuations to this grounding principle that arise in the course of life in the material world are always in the nature of compromise that results in the "good" through harmony with nature: that is, with natural manifestations such as wind, rain and temperature, but also with the dynamics of political life and society. Of these attenuations, the dominations of political and religious powers and the sanctions they impose remain real, and the harmony between these dominations and the individual depends substantially on the will of institutions toward individual freedom. It seems to me that Santayana says next to nothing in regard to the compromise and adaptation (action in the material world) of an individual to the domination of religion, except to compensate by a full spiritual life. However, he pointedly states that "charitable" behavior exercised by individuals or institutions may minimize domination and conflict. From my discussion on charity earlier in the chapter we can relate to Santayana's admonition that "charity is a second birth of love, aware of many wills and many troubles."[204] To act out this charity is to be blind to all divisions between institutions or cultures for "to relieve suffering in anyone's body is an immediate mercy to the spirit there."[205] In fact, in their blindness, the philosopher suggests that "Justice and charity are identical."[206]

Some compromise regarding the material manifestation of one's personal ideals becomes necessary for harmony between the individual and the societal "good," or despair and death may reign. Santayana proposes that the texture of the natural world, the conflict of interests in the soul and in society, all of which cannot be satisfied together, is accordingly the ground for moral restrictions and compromises. Whatever the upshot of the struggle may be, whatever verdict pronounced by reason, the parties to the suit must in justice all be heard, and heard sympathetically.[207]

It is not only that "charity is a second birth of love, aware of many wills and many troubles,"[208] but, as has been stated earlier, Santayana perceives harmony as essentially equivalent to the good, and it follows that harmony is the *sine qua non* of the life of reason. To act out this charity is to be blind to all divisions between institutions or cultures for, as I quoted earlier "to relieve suffering in anyone's body is an immediate mercy to the spirit there."[209] It is then "harmony" that is sought, and ultimately, however, it is in the spiritual realm, in the privacy of consciousness, that one can "flourish without domination . . . to obey and develop your freest, most disinterested powers."[210] In other words, to be consistent with love, charity, justice, harmony and the life of reason, it is not, in the case of exercising Santayana's concept of charity, a compromise to compromise toward harmony!

THE FALLACY OF MODERNISM

"As to Modernism, it is suicide. It is the last of those concessions to the spirit of the world which half-believers and double-minded prophets have always been found making; but it is a mortal concession."[211] Thus Santayana's resistance to modernism, at the same time he proclaims himself a materialistic naturalist, can be construed as a substantial contributing factor to his seemingly paradoxical philosophy.[212] An excellent representation of his anti-modernistic views is the chapter "Modernism and Christianity" in *Winds of Doctrine*, which I will periodically refer to in this section. We have seen above some manifestations of this view in Santayana's disposition to uphold the value of Roman Catholic dogma and resist the "dilution" of Protestantism. T. J. Jackson Lears in *No Place of Grace* points out the concern for "a general uncoiling of the springs of moral action" around the turn of the century.[213] As an example of anti-modernistic response, he comments on Santayana's affirmation in *Interpretations of Poetry and Religion* that "the Christian doctrine of rewards and punishments is . . . in harmony with moral truths which a different doctrine might have obscured, affirming his belief that Christian dogma, as symbol, should not be diluted or ignored in the increasingly scientific Modernistic attitude."[214] Further, Santayana admonished modernists for their resorting to evasions and "cheap fictions" instead of confronting doubt as had the philosophers and poets of the Middle Ages.[215] In profile, here is a philosopher of a broad and liberal education who is a proponent of individual intellectual and personal freedom to satisfy individual needs. He is resistant to dominations of religion, politics and ideas and pluralistic in his view of society and religion but an unbeliever in the supernatural.

Indeed, these characteristics can be construed as dominant aspects of the modernist stereotype! However, in his essay "A General Confession," Santayana reveals his true colors:

> The liberal age in which I was born and the liberal circles in which I was educated flowed contentedly *towards intellectual dissolution and anarchy*. No atmosphere could have been more unfavorable to that solidity and singleness of conviction to which by nature I was addressed.[216]

Among some of Santayana's most vehement attacks and critiques were those directed at the fallacy of modernism, from the point of view of one who proclaimed himself "a materialist, cynic, and Tory in philosophy."[217] Manifestations of modernism that were highly suspect for Santayana ranged from the sincere efforts of Catholic liberals to modernize the Roman Catholic Church and the rejection of religious values as unscientific to the distraction and busyness of the modern progressive commercial state and democratic government itself. How can all of these characteristics be justified as philosophically compatible in what Levinson terms Santayana's "libertarian conservatism?"[218] For our purposes here, I will attempt to justify the philosophical compatibility and consistency of his anti-modernist views in religion by addressing two aspects which I will refer to as "fallacies" in the sense of Santayana's meaning of the term.

The Fallacy of Modernizing the Catholic Church

In *Winds of Doctrine* Santayana explores the conflict which we still observe in America and Europe today (i.e., the conflict between modernism and Christianity).[219] He observes that efforts of reform in the name of modernism which were characteristic of the times also were penetrating the Catholic church, "that institution which is constitutionally the most stable, the most explicit of mind, least inclined to revise its collective memory or established usages."[220] In Santayana's observations and critique of the discrepancy between what may be called the "essence" of Christianity and those adaptations to society and culture (*Zeitgeist*) throughout its history up through the modernist movement, we can see revealed again his distaste for compromise. Also revealed is the basis for his contempt for the most egregious compromise, the Protestant Reformation and its return to a Hebraic religious model. I will return to this. In his critique of modernism Santayana is particularly harsh on the well-intentioned intellectual modernist Catholics who wish to remain in the church. While they reject Protestantism *per se* as a religious path for themselves, they still wish to accommodate new rationalistic insight into biblical studies and mitigate the fear that comes from sin against the harsh rigors of Catholic moral doctrine. In particular, they find abhorrent the doctrine of eternal punishment in hell for those dying in a so-called state of mortal sin. Not only is such a doctrine abhorrent to the modernist Catholic, it is seemingly absurd and cruel in relation to the human concept of God's divine goodness and mercy. The modernist Catholic therefore wishes, in effect, to reconcile the Catholic Church to the perceptions of the modern world, and in this Santayana perceives a grievous intellectual and spiritual fallacy.[221]

In this conservative position we find he is totally consistent with his uncompromising naturalistic philosophy. We have already discussed above both the imaginative and moral character of dogma. For Santayana, the modernist Catholic falls from not only religious faith in his error, but also from reason. Further, he does not have the courage to recognize the extent of the compromise he wishes to implement and take instead an honest position outside the faith, presumably recognizing the symbolic, non-literal character of dogma. He has chosen "the path which must lead him away, steadily and forever from the church which he did not think to desert . . . He becomes, in principle, a Protestant."[222] As for any modernist inclination to soften the doctrine of hell and eternal punishment, unless the modernist takes it literally (in which case, how can one change it?), Santayana regards it as totally, as I indicated above, "in harmony with moral truths which a different doctrine might have obscured." Therefore, in regard to the liberalizing modernist Catholic, Santayana falls back on his Scholastic logic to reveal his contra-rationale:

> The good souls who wish to fancy that everybody will be ultimately saved, subject a fable to standards appropriate to matters of fact, and thereby deprive the fable of the moral significance which is its excuse for being . . . We are reduced for our moral standards to phenomenal values . . . These values are quite real, but they are not those which poetry and religion have for their object.[223]

If one is to tamper with the moral accretions of the ages, the doctrinal distillation of the highest ideals derived from human experience and coalesced in the human imagination of the faithful, one is on the downward path through heresy to "free-thinking." Santayana observes that the modernist "takes . . . a strangely long time to discover it," and ultimately he is out of sympathy with so much of the teaching of the church that "so as not be compelled to abandon it . . . [he] sets about to purge it of its first principles, of its whole history, and of its sublime and chimerical ideal."[224]

Where might there be an alternative for the liberal Catholic if a mission for change will not do? In respect to individual solutions, Santayana is never truly prescriptive but only presents his own views. In regard to any modernistic effort to reform the Catholic Church, he advocates no change that would be more accommodating to this world and that would lessen in any way the importance of salvation in the next.[225] For those who have become arrested in their spiritual life as true believers, there is a path of hope, happiness and salvation, while for those who are *disillusioned*, there is the symbolic and aesthetic wealth of the church sustained in moral lessons and dogma. Any religion, he proposes, opens vistas and propounds mysteries that are another world to live in and opens up an eternal world providing a spiritual harmony not available in the natural world.[226] Ultimately he saw the Catholic Church as in a separate theological frame from any worldly *praxis* and recognized from the outset that Christianity in its purest moral form as interpreted by the church fathers would always have minimal effect on society as a whole, "unless it turned the world into a monastery."[227]

It seems on first blush that in regard to orthodox Christianity and its protective repository, the church, Santayana would like to eat his cake and have it too! Rather, when one carefully sorts out his position, it is equivocal in regard to orthodox religions of the world. On one hand, the propensity of organized religion to ultimately interfere with individual spiritual freedom seems to leave little social value in its existence other than preserving dogma as repositories of moral lessons of the ages and providing an opportunity of spiritual respite from the contingency of the world. Organized religion, for Santayana, ultimately tends toward constraint of individual spirituality and freedom. On the other hand, for those true believers, it offers in the Gospels and in ritual a clear pathway to redemption. It is for Santayana and the *disillusioned* alone that this path is symbolic. In its formality, Santayana suggests, "Christianity is thus a system of postponed rationalism, a rationalism intercepted by a supernatural version of the conditions of happiness . . . its motive power is the impulse and natural hope to be and to be happy." Any social value of religious orthodoxy to Santayana seems obscured by the ranging idiosyncratic and contradictive beliefs and claims for absolute truth and the rational shortfall that ultimately lead to conflict, domination and suffering.[228]

The Fallacy of Leaving the Faith of One's Birth

We find that Santayana not only frowned upon religious heresy (partial or complete), but viewed apostasy in the same way. Apostasy for Santayana, however, was that sideways shift from the model of the Holy Roman Catholic Church and its ideals to a compromised Christianity divorcing "the history of the world from the story of salvation, and God's government and the sanctions of religion from the operation of matter."[229] Santayana recognizes the only "solution" for the unconvinced to be an uncompromising flight from Christianity *per se*, even while still admiring or even loving its unique incorporation of ideals. This position again is based upon his disposition of "no compromise," his philosophical position that one religious "truth" may be so only in the context of a given religion and the psychological insight that one is simply more comfortable in the religion of one's birth and should not depart from it to another for doctrinal reasons. If Santayana were to be perceived as prescriptive in this regard at all, he is saying, "Be what you are based on what you believe," with the caveat that if you call yourself a Christian, only be this entirely based upon foundational Christian tenets of a supernatural salvation and the rejection of the material world. As Faurot suggests, "Santayana inhabited his philosophy,"[230] as did Socrates his, and if Santayana is prescriptive at all, he is inclined to suggest others do the same uncompromisingly.

The core tenets of Christianity, Santayana claims, are to be found only in the Roman Catholic Church, although admittedly encrusted with theological, ritualistic and authoritative embellishments in a *"mise-en-scène"* far from the early church.[231] He addresses the issue initially in an opening chapter of *Reason in Religion* in suggesting that "travelers from one religion to another" lose their "spiritual nationality," and in capturing what they believe is some generic essence of all religion, may not remember "the graciousness and naturalness of that ancestral accent which a perfect religion should have."[232] Santayana admonishes the atheists and heretics for rebelling against "the poor world's faith" because they did not have the patience to understand it, and the apostates, fleeing to other religions, while not realizing their new beliefs are "vestiges of old beliefs."[233] Here, it is clearly not the atheism that Santayana finds objectionable, but rather the naive scientific critique of Christian orthodoxy and the consequent attack of its role in human experience. One will recall from the last section Santayana's attack on modernity and the liberalization of church doctrine. One must not confuse the science that addresses material factuality with the character of poetry.[234] On the other hand, Santayana recognizes a "dialectical science which elaborates ideas," and among the objects of study in this latter science is that of ethics and values present in religious doctrine.[235] This aspect of religion, independent of spirituality, is a work of the imagination and has been entailed in church doctrine from the time of the Greeks. I will return to this position of Santayana's in regard to "apostasy" in chapter 5.

THE CONSEQUENCES OF PROTESTANTISM: THE INTERRUPTED PATH

First, we can recognize that Santayana, as a cultural Catholic and admirer of the Catholic orthodox structure as a historical repository of moral ideals, would likely be less disposed to Protestantism of any stripe. It is rather the extremism of his disposition that captures our attention. Close to the root of the problem is the fact that Santayana considers the Protestant Reformation a fragmenting and destructive event of ongoing impact on both civilization and the spiritual life of both community and individ-

ual. The continuum from the Platonic construct through the naturalization of Plato's thought by Aristotle, the neo-platonic reforms and the
adaptation of Greek thought to Christianity by Augustine and Aquinas,
was ruptured. Protestant Christianity turned from tradition more to Hebraic roots antecedent to the Greeks and away from the spiritual truth of
the Neo-Platonic adaptation. The "dramatic wholeness" that Santayana
sought was lost in this rupture, as was the orderliness of that "whole
body of influences that can render civilized life noble and good; influences which they [the Greeks] beautifully pictured in the forms and worship of the gods."[236] Therefore, Protestantism is lacking the pagan roots
that Santayana became increasingly sensitive to after attending the lectures of Professor Paulsen at Berlin.[237] In a letter to Daniel Cory in 1936,
he states, "The source of what you call the Catholic view is really Aristotle and quite pagan, except that the early fathers who were Platonists
may have worked out Catholic doctrine in those terms."[238] Fathers Butler
and Munson, whom I discussed in chapter 1, perceived Santayana and
other "modern" philosophers as extending the rift in Christian and philosophical tradition beginning with Descartes, and of course saw the Protestant Reformation as disruptive as he did. In the ironical tension we
have come to appreciate in him, Santayana, in general agreement with
this viewpoint, only excluded his own project, and possibly Spinoza's,
from culpability. Despite the distance one might project between Santayana and the Thomist priest-scholars, there would likely be at least initial
consensus that, as the philosopher proposes, "the three R's of modern
history, the Renaissance, the Reformation, and the Revolution [French],
have left the public mind without any vestige of discipline."[239]

In regard to the disruption caused by the Protestant Reformation,
there seems to be, as implied above, evidence of what I will term an
"interrupted path" as a basis for Santayana's lifelong distaste for the
"compromise" of Protestantism. This becomes particularly evident in the
chapter "Modernism and Christianity" in *Winds of Doctrine*. Again, the
ironic contrast becomes manifest between Santayana's love of the Catholic Church and his desire for it to sustain itself vs. the nature of his own
logically arrived at position of the non-literal character of myth and dogma. His observation is that a particular scenario or "dream" *sans* Reformation had particular appeal to neo-Catholics or neo-pagans. In this scenario,

> if the humanistic tendencies of the Renaissance could have worked on
> unimpeded, might not a revolution from above, a gradual rationaliza-
> tion have transformed the church? Its dogma might have been insen-
> sibly understood to be nothing but myth, its miracles nothing but leg-
> end, its sacraments mere symbols, its Bible pure literature, its liturgy
> just poetry, its hierarchy an administrative convenience, its ethics an
> historical accident. *The Reformation prevented this euthanasia of Christian-
> ity*.[240]

Santayana is no neo-Catholic or even neo-pagan, both categories of the anti-modernist and liberalization movement he seems to despise in the Catholic Church. However, one quickly gathers from the above "dream" that the outcome of the scenario depicts the irony of Santayana's despised Reformation saving his beloved Church! Further, as irony would have it, Santayana recognizes that the Reformation he despises has, in fact, facilitated a retrenchment of a literal interpretation of doctrine and dogma, through the Counter-Reformation in the Roman Catholic Church. Hence, both the church *and* supernaturalism are sustained, and the "euthanasia" of what he considers to be the embodiment of Christianity, the Roman Catholic Church, is held at bay as he would wish it to be.[241] In this *nexus* of the neo-Catholic "wish list" and Santayana's beliefs that are essentially identical to theirs, we can gain further insight into the paradox of Santayana's desire to sustain the Roman Church as orthodox.

With the presumed scuttling of Catholic tradition by the Reformation was lost to Protestantism that rich traditional life of the imagination—the asceticism, discipline, austerity and sacred symbols of the ideal which open to all humans an aesthetic and poetic medium so satisfying to the soul. With the complete "crumbling away of Christian dogma and tradition, Absolute Egotism appeared openly on the surface in the shape of German speculative philosophy," and Protestantism, driven initially by the "willfulness" of the Teutonic races, began its continuous metamorphosis and fragmentation in a state of "reckless self-sufficiency."[242] Santayana perceives Protestantism as therefore left stark, bare and compromised and Christendom as left depleted and vulnerable. Where it has attempted to enliven the vestiges of Catholic orthodoxy, say in the Oxford movement of the Anglican Church, Protestantism cannot regain anything authentic, and Santayana looks with approbation and even mockery on the sad imitation undertaken by those "tenderer and more poetical spirits" of the Anglo-Catholic movement.

> They are trying to recover the insights and practices of mediaeval piety; they are archaistic in devotion. There is a certain romance in their decision to believe greatly, to feel mystically, to pray perpetually. They study their attitudes, as they kneel in some correctly restored church, hearing or intoning some revived early chant, and wondering why they should not choose a divine lady in heaven to be their love and their advocate, as did the troubadours.[243]

We can safely gather then that Santayana recognizes one holy Roman Catholic Church, and anything else or anything less, such as the English Church which engenders "a sham front of moral solemnity,"[244] is an abominable compromise. At the same time, he holds no great hope for the future of the Roman Church either, and as Faurot correctly suggests, "Santayana had no romantic illusions about Christianity [inclusive of Catholicism]. As a cultural force, it has had its day."[245]

SOME CONCLUSIONS

Santayana's placement of religion as "the head and front of everything" is an emphatic acknowledgment that there is no other influence of more significance that bears on sentient being. The richness of Catholic tradition is a great repository of *essences* carried forth from the pre-Socratic Greeks to the imaginative paganization of Catholicism in the Renaissance. It is this full-blown panorama of symbolic power, aesthetic richness and intellectually coherent dogma and doctrine, all a unifying representation of human experience, that Santayana would retain. On one hand, any fall from Christian orthodoxy is a compromise as an accommodation to the world. On the other hand, he asks that we see the folly in literal belief in religious or any other absolutes, and he bases this admonition on a human history of parochial claims resulting in strife and death. His religious genius, in my view, is his emphasis on the life of the Spirit and the translation of orthodox Christian symbolism and dogma to a theology for the disillusioned. For the enlightened ones, for the intelligence that is purged of illusion and standing in awe of the contingency of life, there is offered both a transcendence, a salvation of a kind, and an uncompromising morality that has roots in the Christian tradition. The illusiveness of both truth and the absolute does not hold Santayana from defining the value of ideals which not only serve the individual, but by instilling a love of the "Good," result in an accommodation to other individual "goods" for the good of society and serving harmony.

His naturalism holds uncompromising reign over his religious philosophy and the role of a religious attitude, yet he discovers the utility of the virtues in all religion, those of piety, spirituality and charity as applied in a naturalist philosophical religion, a "lay religion." The individual's ideals are primary only as they can be accommodated in reaching for the larger "Good." Where these respective ideals become polarized, as is most likely in life, the opportunity to transcend the cares of the world in contemplation is the salvational restorative that provides that separate world where all individual ideals can be realized independent of the limiting forces in the world. Despite Santayana's prioritization of individual freedom in his philosophy of religion, at the end of the day, a harmonious and happy life is likely dependent on a tolerable equilibrium which will never be stable for long. No honest life can be lived outside of one's beliefs, therefore one must "live" out one's beliefs in the world where one can. As I have endeavored to demonstrate, it follows that Santayana's religious perspective is entirely consistent with his metaphysics. Only the Christian story and the coherent nature of Roman Catholic doctrine and theology seem to hold for Santayana those symbols that translate to the human story and to the life of the spirit. He has found no better language and framework to express his non-theistic theology, his authentic theology of nature.

I have argued that Santayana's concept of the life of reason was never abandoned despite the emphasis of his philosophical project later in life on an ontologically-oriented phenomenology of the spirit as exemplified in *Scepticism and Animal Faith* and *Realms of Being*. Further, I have claimed his essay "Ultimate Religion" is essentially congruent with Santayana's personal formula and ideal for the exercise of a "religious" or philosophically religious life, and that the elements and conclusions of "Ultimate Religion" are consistent with his later elaboration of the spiritual life in *The Realm of the Spirit* and indeed, throughout *Realms of Being*. A major premise for this claim of a continuum and substantial degree of consistency in this earlier framework of the life of reason and the later works is that the essential elements of religion, as put forward in *Reason in Religion* (i.e., piety, spirituality and charity), remain as elements in "Ultimate Religion" and the spiritual life as elaborated upon in *Realms of Being*.

NOTES

1. See Horace L. Friess and Henry M. Rosenthal, "Reason in Religion and the Emancipated Spirit: A Dialogue," Schilpp, 364–65.
2. Santayana, "A General Confession," Schilpp, 7.
3. Santayana, *Realms of Being*, xxvi–xxvii.
4. Cory, *The Letters of George Santayana*, 38.
5. See the preface to Santayana, *Interpretations of Poetry and Religion* (vi, ix) in regard to the value of religion in reflecting experience, hopes and morals of the human race. This viewpoint is reflected throughout Santayana's work; for example, *The Life of Reason* (183–85, 241–48); *Realms of Being* (842); and *Persons and Places* (419–20). Also see Harry M. Campbell, "Religion as Illusion in the Thought of Santayana," *Thomist* 34, no. 4 (October 1970): 534; Howgate, *George Santayana*, 90; and Levinson, *Santayana, Pragmatism and the Spiritual Life*, 238–40.
6. Santayana, "The Poetry of Christian Dogma," in *Interpretations of Poetry and Religion*, 76–117.
7. Santayana, *The Life of Reason*, 183–84. Also *Interpretations of Poetry and Religion*, 266; and *Scepticism and Animal Faith*, 6–8.
8. Ibid., 180.
9. Santayana, *The Life of Reason*.
10. Ibid., 181.
11. Evidence of this persistence of the life of reason or one of "harmony" can be gleaned from *The Realm of the Spirit* and from the essay "Ultimate Religion."
12. Morris Grossman, "Interpreting *Interpretations*," *Bulletin of the Santayana Society* 8 (Fall 1990): 22.
13. My approach in chapter 1 in demonstrating Santayana's philosophical and religious position in his later years, as he enters into occasional dialogue with Roman Catholic clerics and Thomistic philosophers, is intended to demonstrate this "lure" as Santayana's philosophic and religious declarations give off signals of a personal Christian religious disposition.
14. George Santayana, *Winds of Doctrine: Studies in Contemporary Opinion* (New York: Charles Scribner's Sons, 1913), 56.

15. Cory, *Santayana: The Later Years*, 329–30. The quotation from *The Idea of Christ in the Gospels*, 167, is taken from the English text "that glorious liberty of soul which the passion of Christ has made possible for us in heaven."

16. Letter to Warren Allen Smith, Rome, February 9, 1951. Cory, *The Letters of George Santayana*, 408.

17. Ibid.

18. Howgate, *George Santayana*, 137.

19. Elisio Vivas, "The Life of Reason to the Last Puritan," Schilpp, 316.

20. George Santayana, "Ultimate Religion," *Obiter Scripta*, ed. Justus Buchler and Benjamin Schwartz (New York: Charles Scribner's Sons, 1936), 280–97.

21. Santayana, *Persons and Places*, 522.

22. Santayana, "Ultimate Religion," Buchler and Schwartz, 280.

23. Cory, *The Letters of George Santayana*, 269.

24. John Gouinlock, "Ultimate Religion," *Overheard in Seville* 16 (Fall 1998): 1–12.

25. Santayana, "Ultimate Religion," Buchler and Schwartz, 281–82. The *Deus sive Natura* (God or Nature) of the "God-intoxicated" Spinoza is rigorously derived logically, *a priori*, in a natural theology that concludes in a necessary God, a dual identity of God and substance (*natura naturata et natura naturans*) that could be a God of no other nature. Man's goal is "to live under the aspect of eternity" in "the intellectual love of God." See Harry Austryn Wolfson, *The Philosophy of Spinoza* (Cambridge, MA: Harvard University Press, 1962), chap. 9 passim. See William L. Reese, *Dictionary of Philosophy and Religion* (Atlantic Highlands, NJ: Humanities Press), 1996., s.v. "Spinoza."

26. Santayana, "Ultimate Religion," Buchler and Schwartz, 295.

27. Ibid., 282. In Levinson's response to Gouinlock's critique of Santayana's essay "Ultimate Religion" (Henry Samuel Levinson, "Charity, Interpretation, Disintoxication: A Comment on Gouinlock's 'Ultimate Religion,'" *Overheard in Seville* 16 [Fall 1998]: 13–18), Levinson quotes from Santayana's *Interpretations of Poetry and Religion*, 148: "Let the worst of truth appear and when it has once seen the light, let it not be wrapped up again in swaddling clothes of an equivocal rhetoric . . . That Nature is immense, that her laws are mechanical, that the existence and well-being of man upon earth are, from the point of view of the universe, an indifferent incident—all of this is in the first place to be clearly recognized." This statement by Santayana, twenty-seven years earlier than his lecture honoring Spinoza at The Hague, sets the stage for his "examination of conscience" and the stark foundation of an "Ultimate Religion."

28. Beryl Logan explores the question of Hume's "atheism" based upon an exegesis of Hume's *Dialogues Concerning Natural Religion* in *A Religion without Talking: Religious Belief and Natural Belief in Hume's Philosophy of Religion* (New York: Peter Lang, 1993). See also Celestine Sullivan's essay "Santayana's Philosophical Inheritance," Schilpp, 86–89, for a brief but concise comparison of Santayana and Hume. For a comparative study of Hume and Husserl arguing the affinity of Hume's skepticism and Husserl's phenomenological method, see Richard T. Murphy, *Hume and Husserl: Towards Radical Subjectivism* (The Hague: Martinus Nijhoff, 1980).

29. Thomas Reynolds, "Considering Schleiermacher and the Problem of Religious Diversity: Toward a Dialectical Pluralism," *Journal of the American Academy of Religion* 73, no. 1 (March 2005): 156.

30. Santayana, "Ultimate Religion," Buchler and Schwartz, 282.

31. Ibid., 285.

32. Santayana, *Realms of Being*, 838.

33. George Santayana, *Soliloquies in England and Later Soliloquies* (Ann Arbor: University of Michigan Press, 1967), 246.

34. Santayana, *The Life of Reason*, 263.

35. In the "General Review" at the end of the *Realm of Spirit*, Santayana suggests that when the question of God's existence arises, one is really asking if the reality signified by the notion of God, "if we better understood that reality, could still bear the name of God," or be otherwise designated. He follows by proclaiming, "Now in this verbal sense, and in respect to popular religion that thinks of God as the creator of the

world and the dispenser of fortune, my philosophy is atheistic." Santayana, *Realms of Being*, 838.

36. Ibid. Also in the "General Review," Santayana disclaims Spinoza's notion of God as follows: "So God in Spinoza becomes identical with Nature, speculatively magnified; and if I retained the word God, as I do not in this connection, my result would be even more scandalous, since God, conceived merely as a power, would become identical with matter, the omnificent substance and force in everything." Hence, Santayana's "technical philosophy" upholds his form of atheism.

37. Santayana, *Soliloquies in England*, 246.

38. Reese, *Dictionary of Philosophy and Religion*, s.v. "Pantheism."

39. Santayana, *The Idea of Christ in the Gospels*, 175.

40. Santayana, *Realms of Being*, 397.

41. H. T. Kirby-Smith, "Santayana's God," 9. The author builds an extensive but, in my opinion, unconvincing argument that Santayana is not atheistic "in the usual sense," but at the same time deals effectively and informatively with much of Santayana's commentary on the notion of God.

42. *Penguin Dictionary of Philosophy*, s.v. "Spinoza."

43. Santayana, *Realms of Being*, 420.

44. Ibid., 408.

45. Ibid., 417.

46. Ibid., 416.

47. Ibid., 839.

48. Santayana, "Ultimate Religion," Buchler and Schwartz, 284.

49. Levinson, *Santayana, Pragmatism and the Spiritual Life*, 234.

50. Ibid., 185. From George Santayana, *Character and Opinion in the United States* (New York: Charles Scribner's Sons, 1920), 156.

51. Ibid., 185.

52. Santayana, *Realms of Being*, xiii.

53. Santayana, "Ultimate Religion," Buchler and Schwartz, 287.

54. Ibid., 282–89.

55. Friedrich Schleiermacher, *The Christian Faith*, ed. H. R. Macintosh and J. S. Stewart (Edinburgh: T & T Clark, 1948), 15–16. It is highly questionable that Santayana ever read Schleiermacher, and books by "the father of liberal Protestantism" were not present in his library upon his death. However Schleiermacher's thoughts on the associations between art, aesthetics and religion, particularly evident in *On Religion, Speeches to Its Cultured Despisers*, might be presumed to have given Santayana pause at the disagreeable notion that the two had something in common.

56. Santayana, *The Life of Reason*, 193.

57. Santayana, "Ultimate Religion," Buchler and Schwartz, 283.

58. Ibid., 284.

59. Letter to Arthur A. Cohen, February 9, 1948. *Partisan Review* 25 (1958): 632–37.

60. Letter to Richard C. Lyon, August 1, 1949. Cory, *The Letters of George Santayana*, 381–82.

61. Woodward, *Living in the Eternal*, 19.

62. Lachs, *George Santayana*, 43.

63. Santayana, "Ultimate Religion," Buchler and Schwartz, 288.

64. Ibid., 286.

65. Ibid.

66. Reese, *Dictionary of Philosophy and Religion*, s.v. "Spinoza."

67. Santayana, "Ultimate Religion," Buchler and Schwartz, 287.

68. Ibid., 290.

69. Santayana, *The Life of Reason*, 268.

70. Santayana, "Ultimate Religion," Buchler and Schwartz, 291.

71. Ibid., 289.

72. Ibid.

73. Rudolf Otto, *The Idea of the Holy (Das Heilige)*, trans. John W. Harvey (New York: Oxford University Press, 1958), xvi, xvii, 6. Otto's project is directed at "the holy, *minus* its moral factor . . . and its 'rational' aspect altogether." However, he emphasizes the implicit meaning of *"good,* [and] *absolute goodness"* in the Hebrew, Greek and Latin words for "holy," but this component is made up of the "filling in with ethical meaning" of what was a unique original feeling-response. The two components (or three if we include the rational) make up the "holy" or what is essential in religion.

74. Santayana, "Ultimate Religion," Buchler and Schwartz, 290.

75. Ibid.

76. Ibid.

77. Santayana, *Soliloquies in England*, 257.

78. Santayana, *Dominations and Powers*, 154.

79. Santayana, "Ultimate Religion," Buchler and Schwartz, 293.

80. Santayana, "Ultimate Religion," Buchler and Schwartz, 290–91.

81. Ibid., 291.

82. Gouinlock, "Ultimate Religion," 6.

83. Ibid., 2.

84. Santayana, *The Life of Reason*, 270. From Levinson, "Charity, Interpretation, Disintoxication," 16. Levinson argues against Gouinlock's position that Santayana's later works fall from "the narrow path of charity and valor" into mysticism and holds that Santayana's philosophy, early and later, avoids both mysticism and fanaticism. Levinson also affirms that charity for Santayana is, although an ideal, more than an abstract notion, and that its practice in the world, as Santayana suggests in *Reason in Religion*, is practically necessary because "the texture of the world is constituted by conflicts of interest all of which cannot be satisfied together [and] is accordingly the ground for moral restrictions and compromises" (17; from *The Life of Reason*, 271).

85. Santayana, "Ultimate Religion," Buchler and Schwartz, 291–92.

86. Ibid., 292.

87. Santayana, *Realms of Being*, 795.

88. Santayana, "Ultimate Religion," Buchler and Schwartz, 297. "These goals of life that desired perfection, that eternal beauty, which lies sealed in the heart of each living thing."

89. Santayana, *The Life of Reason*, 258. Santayana addresses "Piety," "Spirituality and its Corruptions" and "Charity" in sequential chapters.

90. Santayana, "Ultimate Religion," Buchler and Schwartz, 296.

91. Santayana, *The Life of Reason*, chaps. 10–12, 258–76. Edman, in his introductory essay to *The Philosophy of George Santayana*, briefly and effectively summarizes the importance of these three aspects of piety, charity and spirituality (xxxv–xxxvii).

92. Ibid., 264.

93. Ibid.

94. In the chapter on "Distraction" in *The Realm of the Spirit*, Santayana reminds us that "it is by no means a duty in animals to be spiritual" and that they may be content with "a routine of appearances in lieu of the truth." Discipline is necessary for spirituality, and "distraction" must be overcome (*Realms of Being*, 717). There is an interesting parallel here in regard to the "naive" or "natural attitude" of Husserl, the "animal attitude" of Santayana and the more intentional "transcendental" or "contemplative" attitude of discerning or intuiting *essences*.

95. Santayana, *Realms of Being*, 551.

96. Ibid., 791–97, 806.

97. Ibid., 795.

98. Ibid.

99. Woodward, *Living in the Eternal*, 93.

100. Santayana, "Ultimate Religion," Buchler and Schwartz, 294.

101. Santayana, *The Life of Reason*, 181.

102. Santayana, "Ultimate Religion," Buchler and Schwartz, 295.

103. Sterling P. Lamprecht, "Santayana Then and Now," in *Animal Faith and Spiritual Life*, Lachs, 308. First printed in the *Journal of Philosophy* 25 (1928): 533–50.

104. Santayana affirms in "A General Confession," Schilpp, 1940, 23, that "the humanism characteristic of *The Sense of Beauty* and *Life of Reason* remained standing; but foundations were now supplied for that humanism by a more explicit and vigorous natural philosophy . . . These additions are buttresses and supports." Most importantly, he refers here to the ontology developed in *The Realms of Being*. "A General Confession" consolidated edited versions of two earlier essays, "A Brief History of My Opinions" (1930) and the preface to volume one of the Triton Edition of *The Works of George Santayana* (1936). Santayana rigorously edited ("severely mutilated" according to Daniel Cory) the chapter "Spirituality and Its Corruptions" for the one-volume edition of *Life of Reason*, but the essentials regarding spirituality remain in place.

105. Ibid.

106. Santayana, *Realms of Being*, 65.

107. Santayana, preface to *The Life of Reason*, vol. 1, 1922 edition.

108. Milton K. Munitz, "Ideals and Essences in Santayana's Philosophy," Schilpp, 207. My sense is that Munitz did not have available to him, or had not read, the *Realm of the Spirit*, which had probably just been published (1939) when he wrote this chapter. If he had read chapter 9, "Union," in *Realm of the Spirit*, for example, his argument for differentiation of the life of the spirit from the life of reason would be weakened.

109. Santayana, "Apologia Pro Mente Sua," Schilpp, 538.

110. Santayana repeatedly proclaimed the individuality of philosophical perspectives and that they were "a work of the imagination," and a unique vision (e.g., see *Realms of Being*, xvi). Further, we can say that his phenomenology, as Husserl's, is an observation of one's own conscious activity in response to *essences* (i.e., one is confined to one's own consciousness or spirit).

111. Friess and Rosenthal, "Reason in Religion," Schilpp, 373–75.

112. Ibid., 373. Quotation from the preface to volume three of the Triton Edition of *The Works of George Santayana*, xii, xi.

113. Letter to Justus Buchler, July 1, 1936, Cory, *The Letters of George Santayana*, Book 5, 1933–1936, 354.

114. Santayana's *The Realm of Essence* was published in 1927, and the essay "Ultimate Religion" was presented in 1932.

115. Santayana, *The Life of Reason*, 264.

116. Santayana, *Realms of Being*, 6–7.

117. Santayana, *The Sense of Beauty*, 160.

118. Ibid., 76.

119. Michael P. Hodges and John Lachs, *Thinking in the Ruins: Wittgenstein and Santayana on Contingency* (Nashville, TN: Vanderbilt University Press, 2000), 84.

120. McCormick, *George Santayana*, 149.

121. Santayana, *Realms of Being*, 7. Here Santayana describes the paradox of *essences* which he considers "the purest reality," which is "formal and ideal." He also provides an example of contemplation of essences, which I quoted in chapter 3, that is, of "jogging to market in my village cart" (7–8).

122. Ibid., 371–73.

123. Ibid., 361. See comment on "historic religion" as a phase in the life of reason.

124. Hodges and Lachs, *Thinking in the Ruins*, 86. "Religious" in the sense intended here seems to connote the traditional definition (i.e., some belief in a transcendental or supernatural world as opposed to a naturalistic viewpoint).

125. Santayana, *Realms of Being*. The chapters on "Distraction" (62 pages) and "Union" (57 pages) are approximately 50 percent longer than the next-longest chapter in *The Realm of the Spirit*.

126. Ibid., chap. 4, "Pure Being," 58. Santayana suggests that a religion may be possible that has pure Being as its object (e.g., Brahmanism), but that since it is *Essence*, and hence without power, it cannot be equated to the God of theism.

127. Michel Brodrick, "Three Stages of Spirituality," *Overheard in Seville* 26 (Fall 2008): 19–24.

128. George Santayana, "Why Does Spirit Aim at Its Own Purity?" Lachs, *Animal Faith and Spiritual Life*, 294–95. From the Columbia Manuscript Collection 9:14:II.

129. Santayana, *Realms of Being*, 675.

130. Ibid., 48.

131. Ibid., 676.

132. Ibid., 14.

133. Santayana, *Platonism and the Spiritual Life*, 260.

134. Santayana, *Realms of Being*, 16.

135. Lachs, *Animal Faith and Spiritual Life*, 268.

136. Santayana's concept of contemplation, it seems to me, is nearly identical to at least one credible scholarly perception of it "as a direct intuitive seeing, using spiritual faculties beyond discursive thought and ratiocination." Further, meditation may be thought of as a preparatory prelude to contemplation in that it is "the narrowing of the focus of consciousness to a single theme, symbol." This, for example, may be a work of art or a religious theme or object. Mircea Eliade, ed., *The Encyclopedia of Religion* (New York, Macmillan, 1987), s.v. "Meditation: An Overview," Frederick B. Underwood.

137. Santayana, *Realms of Being*, 16–17.

138. Ibid., 16.

139. Ibid., 797.

140. Santayana, *The Life of Reason*, 198.

141. Ibid., 200.

142. I cited in chapter 3 Daniel T. Padarske's "Santayana on Laughter and Prayer." In his short but thorough essay, Padarske effectively treats Santayana's theory of prayer as well as its relationship to laughter. Of particular interest is the author's observation that in Santayana's works extending from *Reason in Religion* through *The Idea of Christ in the Gospels* and *The Realm of the Spirit*, he demonstrates "a rather complete and sympathetic phenomenology of prayer rare in American philosophy" (145).

143. Santayana, *Realms of Being*, 797.

144. Ibid., 799.

145. Ibid., 800.

146. Ibid., 799–800.

147. Ibid.

148. Ibid., 798.

149. Ibid., 797.

150. Ibid., 801.

151. Ibid., 406.

152. Ibid., 319. For an extensive treatment, see Brian Jonathon Garret, "Santayana on Teleology," *Overheard in Seville* 28 (Fall 2010): 1–10.

153. Santayana, *Realms of Being*. From the introduction to *Spinoza's Ethics*, Everyman's Library (London: J. M. Dent and Sons, 1910), xviii, xix.

154. Santayana, *Scepticism and Animal Faith*, 271.

155. Ibid.

156. Alfred North Whitehead, *Process and Reality* (New York: Free Press, 1985), 345.

157. Santayana, *Realms of Being*, 764.

158. Ibid., 744.

159. Ibid., 643.

160. Santayana, *Platonism and the Spiritual Life*, 248–49.

161. Santayana, *Realms of Being*, 7.

162. Santayana, *Platonism and the Spiritual Life*, 251.

163. Ibid., 249.

164. Ibid., 251.

165. Santayana, *Realms of Being*, 770.

166. Kirkwood, *Santayana: Saint of the Imagination*, 65.

167. Santayana, *Realms of Being*, ix.

168. Kirkwood, *Santayana: Saint of the Imagination*, 66.

169. Santayana, *Realms of Being*, 483.

170. Santayana, *Dominations and Powers*, 21.

171. Ibid., 482.

172. Ibid., xiii.

173. Ibid., x. Dogma, particularly Christian dogma, is generally defined as consisting of a systematic ordering of creeds and doctrines [these likely consisting of myths interpreted as literally true, e.g., of divine objects or phenomena, as well as moral tenets] and creeds affirming belief in the doctrine (see Reese, *Dictionary of Philosophy and Religion*, s.v. "Dogma").

174. Santayana, *Realms of Being*, 594.

175. Santayana, *The Life of Reason* ("Reason in Religion"), 183–84. Santayana's view on the poetic nature of religious doctrine, its value as a vehicle for the high themes of moral teachings learned through human experience and its unfortunate depiction of these truths as scientific truth did not distinguishably vary from his early work of *Interpretations of Poetry and Religion* through his final works of *Dominations and Powers* and *The Idea of Christ in the Gospels*.

176. Santayana, *Interpretations of Poetry and Religion*, x.

177. Santayana, *Realms of Being*, 616.

178. Santayana, *Interpretations of Poetry and Religion*, 6.

179. Santayana, *Realms of Being*, 456.

180. Santayana, *Dominations and Powers*, 156.

181. Santayana, *Interpretations of Poetry and Religion*, x.

182. Santayana, *Dominations and Powers*, 156.

183. Santayana, *Realms of Being*, 418.

184. Santayana, *Interpretations of Poetry and Religion*, v.

185. Santayana, *The Life of Reason* ("Reason in Religion"), 203.

186. Santayana, *Dominations and Powers*, 274–75.

187. Santayana, "A General Confession," Schilpp, 8. This essay, edited by Santayana in 1940 for publication in Schilpp's *The Philosophy of George Santayana*, although it was derived from earlier publications, that is, the latter half of the preface of the *Triton Edition*, volume 1 (1936), and the preface to volume 7 (1937), and *Brief History of My Opinions* (1930), reflects, in my view, Santayana's conclusive view on the imaginative and poetic character of dogma. My bibliographical reference is Herman J. Saatkamp, Jr., and John Jones, *George Santayana: A Bibliographical Checklist, 1880–1980* (Bowling Green, OH: Bowling Green State University Press, 1982), 53.

188. Santayana, *Dominations and Powers*, 274–75.

189. Woodward, 44.

190. Santayana, *The Life of* Reason, 179.

191. John C. A. Gaskin, *Hume's Philosophy of Religion* (London: Barnes & Noble, 1978), 148–58. In *The Natural History of Religion*, Hume associated the religious principles of popular religion with "sick men's dreams." Santayana, although generally holding a more tolerant view of the human tendency toward the "pathetic fallacy" and consequent unreasonable religious convictions, does show evidence of some impatience with the more extreme manifestations of religious experience. In a paper by John J. Fisher based in part on the marginalia in Santayana's copy of James's *Varieties of Religious Experience*, Santayana seems even to fall back to a medical materialism in making the point that "these religious phenomena accompany *diseased organs*. Fisher also cites a passage from *Winds of Doctrine*, wherein Santayana refers to James's sources as "sentimentalists, mystics, spiritualists, wizards, quacks and imposters." John J. Fisher, "Santayana on James: A Conflict of Views on Philosophy," *American Philosophical Quarterly* 2, no. 1 (January 1965): 69–70.

192. Kirkwood, *Santayana: Saint of the Imagination*, 135.

193. Santayana, *Realms of Being*, 621–22. This is a matter of "Wills" disposed in particular directions in opposition to one another.

194. Ibid., 483.

195. Ibid., 627.
196. Levinson, *Santayana, Pragmatism and the Spiritual life*, 239.
197. Grossman, "Interpreting *Interpretations*," 18.
198. It is consistent with my claims, and that of other scholars (e.g., Edman, Lachs and Woodward) that Santayana's foundational philosophy remained essentially unchanged, except for a more spiritual shift and the elaboration of the theory of *essence* and other technical aspects in his later works (e.g., *Realms of Being* and *Dominations and Powers*) and from a more humanistic view in the earlier *The Life of Reason*. His philosophical principle of moral relativity and the unattainability of an absolute universal moral code was evident early in his thought and never changed. The philosophical differential between these three works was narrowed somewhat in Santayana's late-life revision of *The Life of Reason* for the one-volume Scribner's edition.
199. Santayana, *Dominations and Powers*, vii–ix. In the preface to *Dominations*, Santayana states, "Circumstances from the beginning had prepared me to feel this limitation in all moral dogmatism" (i.e., that "what . . . seemed absolute and permanent was in fact relative and temporary"). However, in recognizing the *Realpolitik* in the world, Santayana suggests that "he [one] should not expect the good or the beautiful after his own heart to be greatly prevalent or long maintained in the world."
200. Santayana, *Dominations and Powers*, 161.
201. Ibid., 156.
202. Ibid., 283–84, 286. For example, "Islam . . . although initially a religious gospel, at once became a military mission of conquest and domination . . . and belief itself was to be imposed on pain of death."
203. Ibid., 161.
204. Santayana, *Realms of Being*, 795.
205. Ibid.
206. Santayana, *The Life of Reason*, 271.
207. Ibid.
208. Santayana, *Realms of Being*, 795.
209. Ibid.
210. Santayana, *Dominations and Powers*, 151.
211. Santayana, *Winds of Doctrine*, 56–57.
212. While Santayana may be referred to legitimately as an "anti-modernist" or even a "Romantic" in regard to his resistance to the reductive inclinations of the Enlightenment, he still ascribed to science its prerogatives, and to religion its superstitions and detractions, and ultimately only fell short of being a scientific materialist. Just as Joseph Campbell or Mircea Eliade, for example, in regard to their elevation of myth to therapeutic and salvific status, may be conceived of in a similar vein, they were ultimately what Robert Ellwood calls "exemplary modernists," viewing the world from the modern university essentially dedicated to the tenets of modernism. Santayana viewed the world from the same venue for nearly half his career but true to his nature fled the atmosphere at Harvard he considered to be a "domination" relative to his own "good." For the observation on Campbell and Eliade, see Robert Ellwood, "Is Mythology Obsolete?" *Journal of the Academy of Religion* 69, no. 3 (September 2001): 681.
213. T. J. Jackson Lears, *No Place of Grace: Antimodernism and the Transformation of American Culture, 1880–1920* (Chicago: University of Chicago Press, 1983), 45.
214. Ibid.
215. Ibid., 156.
216. Santayana, "A General Confession," Schilpp, 21.
217. Santayana, *Persons and Places*, 392.
218. Levinson, *Santayana, Pragmatism and the Spiritual Life*, 170.
219. Santayana, *Winds of Doctrine*, 25–57.
220. Ibid., 25. More recent evidence of Santayana's assertion can be found in Edward Wakin and Father Joseph F. Scheuer, *The De-Romanization of the American Catholic Church* (New York: Macmillan, 1966).

221. Santayana addresses this issue comprehensively, and particularly in relation to the doctrine of eternal punishment and the impact of Protestantism, in *Interpretations of Poetry and Religion*, chap. 4, "The Poetry of Christian Dogma," 93–112. Thirteen years later in *Winds of Doctrine* in the chapter "Modernism and Christianity," he takes essentially the same position regarding the misguided trajectory of the modernist Catholic.

222. Santayana, *Winds of Doctrine*, 45–46.

223. Santayana, *Interpretations of Poetry and Religion*, 103. T. J. Jackson Lears uses the same quotation of Santayana to demonstrate "a general uncoiling of the springs of moral action" in America. He also places Santayana in a group associated with an "aesthetic Catholicism flourishing at Harvard around the turn of the century." Lears and others generally associate Santayana as an important figure in the American antimodernist movement. Lears, *No Place of Grace*, 45, 252.

224. Santayana, *Winds of Doctrine*, 50–51.

225. Ibid., 50–57.

226. Santayana, *The Life of Reason*, 180–81.

227. Santayana, *Dominations and Powers*, 158.

228. Santayana, *The Life of Reason*, 476.

229. Santayana, *Winds of Doctrine*, 34.

230. Faurot, "Santayana's Philosophy of Religion," 260.

231. Santayana, *Winds of Doctrine*, 52.

232. Santayana, *The Life of Reason*, 180.

233. Ibid., 179–80.

234. Faurot, "Santayana's Philosophy of Religion," 261. From the preface to *Interpretations of Poetry and Religion*, vi.

235. Santayana, *The Life of Reason*, 388–89. The treatment of the sciences of *dialectic* and *physics* covered in section 5, *Reason in Science*, is beyond the scope of this book. It is enough for our purposes to emphasize that *dialectic* is directed at the "truth" of ideas in the realm of the spirit, as *physics* is directed toward the "truth" of the material realm.

236. George Santayana, *Dominations and Powers*, 166.

237. Recalling Paulsen, Santayana affirms his importance: "Paulsen . . . was simply an excellent professor . . . This semester he lectured on Greek Ethics, and in the next winter semester on Spinoza. In both subjects he helped to settle my opinions for good. The Greek ethics wonderfully supplied what was absent in Spinoza, a virile, military, organic view of life, a civilized view, to keep the cosmic and religious imagination of Spinoza in its proper moral place." Santayana, *Persons and Places*, 257.

238. Cory, *Santayana: The Later Years*, 171.

239. Santayana, *The Genteel Tradition at Bay*, 8.

240. Santayana, *Winds of Doctrine*, 38–39; italics mine.

241. Ibid., 39.

242. Santayana, *The Life of Reason*, 238–40.

243. Santayana, *Soliloquies in England*, 88. The short chapter "The English Church" provides a wealth of perspective on Santayana's disposition toward the "compromise" of the Anglican Church and the "tragedy" of its nationalistic origins. He clearly sees it as an anomaly, neither Protestant nor Catholic, since its subjection to Parliament renders it incapable of either category (see *Soliloquies in England*, 84–85). Note: In fact, it claims to be *both*, and a "bridge" between both traditions.

244. Santayana, *Dominations and Powers*, 256.

245. Faurot, "Santayana's Philosophy of Religion," 263.

FIVE

Aspects of Santayana's Legacy to Religion in the Third Millennium

> The spiritual experiences that come to us are according to our disposition and affections; and any new philosophy we frame will be an answer to the particular problems that beset us, and an expression of the solutions we hope for.
>
> George Santayana, *Winds of Doctrine*

My intent in this chapter is to affirm George Santayana's broad profile as a philosopher of religion with a unique vision both materialistic and spiritual. This unique profile alone, in my view, provides sufficient rationale, particularly in the light of contemporary religious issues, to embrace his thought in the philosophical canon of American religious studies. I will further provide a basis for his importance by first identifying his unique profile as a "spiritual naturalist" and the range of his philosophical vision. I will discuss his preemptive "postmodern" vision, his contribution to constructionist theology, his early insight into the mind-body relationship as understood by modern neuroscience and some aspects of his metaphysics that bear upon the basis for process theology. Finally, I will address the pertinence of his project in relation to some contemporary religious issues (e.g., religious pluralism) and propose some potential radical applications of his thought to modern religious *praxis*. When evaluating Santayana's importance today, in general, I consider it essential to address the man and his work *in toto* in regard to what John Lachs terms Santayana's "unity of theory and practice." For Santayana, this unity or harmony is best articulated in an integrated approach to life—a life of reason. For the purpose of assessing his relevance in relation to the philosophy of religion, I consider his unique translation of Christian tenets and dogma to those individuals who are part of a religiously *disillusioned* modern world to be of foremost importance. There is indeed a nexus of Santayana's vision with the "residue of disillusion-ment" that Kenneth Gergen suggests is the outcome of the failure of modern philosophy and that in the context of a preemptive postmodern-ism, Santayana effectively addresses.[1] Possibly of even more importance is his insightful perception of the necessary balance of "liberal" and or-thodox thought in relation to religion. This insight constitutes a particu-larly original idea—a concept relevant to those sectors of humanity which are today entrenched in their perceptions of the world at either one of these partisan poles. In all of this, at the core of Santayana's wis-dom is his transcendence of the idealism and skepticism of modern phi-losophy and a striving through *animal faith* and spiritual discipline to-ward a harmony of consciousness with the sole objective of individual happiness. Nevertheless, in the later years of Santayana's life while he consolidated his philosophical vision in Rome, the time and the trajectory of philosophy on a number of fronts seemed to pass him by.

A FALL FROM GRACE

We find that Santayana is typically excluded from, or given short shrift in, the canon of philosophers generally included in the curriculum of American Religious studies.[2] Even if we consider many of those marginal theists ranked high in the canon from Kant and his compromised moral deism to Schleiermacher and his subtle agnosticism, there is little ques-tion that Santayana's blatant non-theism was a contribution to his fall in grace. Even Dewey's utilitarian concept of Divinity didn't fall as far short of apparent "belief" as Santayana's sincere theology did relative to the various theistic concepts of the Americans: James, Peirce, Royce and Whitehead. He was in direct conflict with the last strains of Calvinistic influence in American philosophy, but this is only part of the story. Le-vinson, in his comprehensive assessment of Santayana's achievements and substantial contribution to American philosophy of religion, ob-served in 1984, "Hardly any scholar that I know construes Santayana as part of his canon," and he goes on to indicate that the next generation is missing something by not reading him.[3] John Lachs provides a litany of frustrations that philosophers have had with Santayana, suggesting, "Some think him too poetic, others too deeply devoted to reason and to science. Positivists find him too metaphysical, metaphysicians too posit-ivistic . . . moralists condemn him for having embraced an aesthetic or spiritual life; religious people bemoan that he is not spiritual enough."[4] There is no doubt that by the early 1940s, Santayana had lost favor as a representative of both Pragmatism and critical realism as he held fast to his uncompromising opinion that modern philosophy has been in regress since the pre-Socratics to the Moderns, resulting in the "centering" of philosophy on the transcendental and psychological.[5] Indeed, Lachs and

Hodges observe that Santayana, along with Wittgenstein, was unique relative to contemporary philosophy in basing his philosophical projects primarily on pre-Kantian concepts.[6] Santayana was focused upon the ontological and spiritual aspects of human experience while sustaining the symbolic characterization of this experience over human history as having immeasurable value (his non-reductiveness) even in relation to science. It is this unlikely philosophical position, while Santayana still maintained a rigorous naturalism, that ultimately constitutes his contribution to philosophy on one hand, while on the other, contributes to his eclipse in the 1940s by the political Pragmatism of Dewey and the reductive approach of scientific positivism.[7] Levinson depicts the final blow to Santayana's thought as coming with the "linguistic and symbolic logical turns in the 1950s," and also points out that following the enthusiastic acceptance of *The Life of Reason* as a major contribution to American Pragmatism, the later works, especially *Realms of Being*, were perceived by many to fall outside the frame of both Pragmatism and American Naturalism.[8] Levinson also depicts the political nature of Pragmatism and Naturalism which constituted "communities of discourse" (from Peirce) in which Santayana, as an individualist and perceived nay-sayer to progress, science and modern technology (Santayana throughout his project respected empirical contributions of science and technology), fell outside of the popular trends in philosophy.[9] Samuel Levinson, David Dilworth and others provide helpful insight into the reasons for Santayana's "demise" as an influential philosopher in America by the fifth decade of the twentieth century. To begin with, as David Dilworth observes, Santayana's "culturally saturated, non-reductive materialism" was simply anomalous in relation to the "modern mind" and the accepted model of "progress" inherited from Enlightenment thought.[10] One could also surmise that he was more generally out of synch with the *Zeitgeist* throughout his long writing career.

At the same time, from a religious standpoint which is of particular interest to us here, despite Santayana's spiritual bent in the tradition of Thoreau or Emerson, his ideas were too naturalistic and unaccommodating to the common theistic bent of the Pragmatists of the period (e.g., Peirce or James). Levinson suggests that he "fell between the stools" in relation to the more prominent theologically oriented religious thinkers of his time.[11] Later on in the 1950s, his reputation would suffer from the same incongruity with popular religious thinkers such as Reinhold Niebuhr and Paul Tillich (with Tillich there are interesting similarities which I will comment on later),[12] both of whom, indications are, he never read. As a litterateur cum philosopher, Santayana was deemed by the philosophical community to be "neither fish nor foul," and contrarily Catholic in disposition to boot. While caught in a tide that ran against him of Enlightenment-motivated residual Calvinistic Protestant philosophy which he termed the "Genteel Tradition," Santayana saw his influence

ultimately wane. It is only now in the milieu of our contemporary world
that Santayana's vision is at a newly compatible nexus with issues of the
day. I therefore support and in a modest way join those champions of his
thought, such as Lachs, Levinson, Kerr-Lawson and Saatkamp, who have
taken to reclaiming his value in the light of the contemporary philosophical and religious dialogue. [13]

SOME PERSPECTIVES BEARING ON SANTAYANA'S RELEVANCE TO RELIGION

A number of scholars have argued well in recent years for a revival of
interest in Santayana due to the recognition of a seeming convergence of
his philosophy with both contemporary philosophical and religious issues. In my view, Levinson stands at the forefront of the field. One aspect
of this recognition which has received limited attention is that of Santayana's preemptive anti-foundational position in philosophy in relation to
the deconstructionist trends in postmodern thought, and I will address
this aspect further on. John Ryder addresses this in relation to Santayana
as well as Peirce, James, Royce and Dewey in the American philosophical
pantheon. [14] Lachs also raises issues with some aspects of Santayana's
philosophical tenets—for example, that of impotency of mind (Santayana's particular form of epiphenomenalism) and truth and matter as an
ontological category. Lachs has written extensively on the philosophy of
mind-body relationship and Santayana's epiphenomenalism in relation
to causation. [15] Angus Kerr-Lawson has drawn parallels with Santayana's
and Spinoza's body-consciousness concepts and contemporary research
in psychology, neurophysiology and brain chemistry. [16] Both of these
writers are helpful as I will return to the subject of Santayana's epiphenomenalism and neuroscience in relation to religion later in this chapter.
Lachs designates Santayana's relativism and toleration, his assignment of
more universal possibilities for spirituality and his belief in the centrality
of individuals as having enduring religious and moral value. [17] Levinson
has provided a particularly broad perspective on Santayana's contribution to religious thought, especially in relation to American pragmatism,
to which I have frequently referred. In the concluding words of his paper
"Santayana's Contribution to American Religious Philosophy," Levinson
provides a helpful summation after providing a rationale for Santayana's
"eclipse":

> Thus it should not be surprising that Santayana's work has been
> eclipsed. But I should find it more surprising if scholars in American
> religious studies continued not to read him, now that we have learned
> of the significance of aesthetic spirituality and the problems of religious
> exceptionalism; now that we know that religion is not exhausted by
> theism and not reducible to this or that belief. [18]

Of significance to my claims for Santayana in this chapter is H. T. Kirby-Smith's belief "that Santayana aimed at a restatement of Christian orthodoxy so as to place it on a firmer foundation."[19] I believe that this is true in one sense, particularly for those appealed to by the perspective of *disillusionment*, but also it is an oversimplification. Indeed, Santayana claims that a restatement of Christian orthodoxy (e.g., a de-literalization of doctrine) can weaken the church as an institution, a prospect which he does not deem desirable although possibly inevitable. I will return to this interesting dichotomy further on since it bears on the uniqueness of Santayana's legacy. Otherwise, I concur with Kirby-Smith's suggestion that Santayana is ultimately a theologian,[20] empathetic in his view of Christianity, its doctrine and its "true believers" as he personally remains constant in his firmly metaphysically-based non-theistic vision.[21]

AN INTRIGUING PHILOSOPHICAL PROFILE FOR CONTEMPORARY RELIGIOUS THOUGHT

When considering the interest and value Santayana may have relative to contemporary religious thought, it is helpful to capture initially his unique philosophical "profile." To begin with, *Santayana is the only materialistic philosopher in the mainstream of the past one hundred years of American, and probably European philosophy, who proclaimed the importance of living a spiritual life, and additionally, represented a spiritual component of his philosophical project, independent of theistic belief, more descriptively and extensively than any of his modern forbears.* As I indicated in my introductory paragraph to this chapter, I consider this unique composite vision alone to be enough to consider Santayana's importance to contemporary religious thought.

His critique of the "weightlessness" of modern industrial society and its fixation on progress, the fragility of religious doctrine that tests the credibility of the contemporary intellect, the dangers of claiming any certainty and the potential oppression of individual religion and minority religions by dominant religious institutions is particularly pertinent as we begin the twenty-first century. At the same time *his observations on the consequences of diluting or reducing Christian doctrine, compromising religious orthodoxy and underestimating the negative impact of religious liberalism provide an integrated perspective on the true "costs" of religious harmony in today's world.*

His own individual *disillusion* of "Ultimate Religion" is not to be imposed upon or interfere with those who maintain belief in orthodox religious dogma and the supernatural. He provided within the framework of the life of reason a possibility for living a religious and spiritual life and expressed it substantially relying upon the language of traditional Christian symbolism. Although there is little in Santayana that is specifically prescriptive for living one's life, his philosophical project is in fact integral to his own life, and his proposition is that this consistency can work for others. For those individuals who are at odds with traditional Christian or other religious beliefs, Santayana provided the religious alternative of *disillusion*, a "lay religion," which could culminate in a "salvation and rebirth . . . by gift of nature."[22] Explicit in this naturalistic alternative is a life of discipline directed at piety, spirituality and charity with the Epicurean or Lucretian goal of happiness and the Plotinian possibility of a healthful *ecstasis* and transcendence through contemplation. Further, in the Hellenic tradition that so influenced him, and in the discipline so characteristic of orthodox Catholic *praxis*, Santayana found little room for compromise in living his philosophy in the world. Santayana, as a scholar of religion, has an acute sensitivity to and scholarly aptitude for the psychological and anthropological aspects of religious life, as well as being a competent, albeit non-theistic, theologian, as evidenced in his early work *Interpretations of Poetry and Religion*, and later particularly in *Realm of the Spirit* and *The Idea of Christ in the Gospels*. In my view, he is not unlike the Canadian scholar of religion, Michel Despland, as he distinctly addresses three elements of religion: its nature, the social and ethical context of religion and the mythos of religion.[23] These elements correspond respectively to the ontological, moral and aesthetic character of religion. I expect that I have made this evident in the preceding chapters as a reflection of this categorization being particularly represented in Santayana's *Interpretations of Poetry and Religion*, *The Life of Reason* (Reason in Religion), *Realms of Being* (The Realm of the Spirit), *Dominations and Powers* and *The Idea of Christ in the Gospels*. What is it to be a "religious" person? What moral practices and perceptions have emerged in the cultural milieu of the religion as it is practiced? How do symbolic representations reflect the experience of a culture in mythology and dogma? What restriction of the human "inner" person can result from religion? To what use is a philosophical religion in response to the contingency of the universe and the fear of death? These are some of the important questions that Santayana addresses in the framework of his vision that religion "is the head and front of everything."[24]

Much of this, in Santayana's approach, I have claimed in my argument to be approached within a framework of a phenomenology of consciousness or of the spirit which I believe is evident in *Realms of Being* and other works. As I proposed in chapter 3, Santayana's phenomenological approach is significant in his generally non-reductive approach to religious dogma and religious practice. Given some understanding of religious elements as they are manifested as phenomena, Santayana enters into dialogue with structures and symbols of religion from the perspective of his own metaphysic. He then, by difference, arrives at the "remainder" of those characteristics of traditional religions, under the three categories I mention above that are compatible with his lay religion of *disillusion.* This process is related to his contribution to constructionist theology which I will address later. Richard Comstock, in drawing an insightful comparison of Santayana and Paul Tillich, perceives both figures as examining "critical human experiences in which the mystery and actuality of power are encountered," and "on the basis of these experiences . . . [seeking] to construct systems of appropriate ontological and religious symbols through which their meaning and significance for human life can be articulated and understood."[25]

Of particular importance in Santayana's project is the low expectation for humankind in the epistemological inquiry for certitude, truth and causation, a vision that can have profound consequences for a contemporary religious issue such as pluralism. Ultimately, Santayana's metaphysics, based upon his theory of *essences* and his epiphenomenalism, can be both helpful and irksome (e.g., to process theologians as we shall see), and cannot be overlooked in relation to concepts such as God, the soul and the mind-body relationship. With the preceding brief profile as a base, I will provide further basis for these claims for the applicability of Santayana's philosophy to contemporary religious and spiritual thought, and as Levinson and others have done, sign the petition for his unqualified inclusion in the canon of American religious studies.

HARMONY, HAPPINESS AND ACCEPTANCE: A LIVED PHILOSOPHY

The life of reason for Santayana incorporates the accretion of spiritual character since his earliest humanistic formula in *The Life of Reason* and as it is put forward in his philosophical maturity in *Realms of Being*. It is a legacy of human coping well-suited and even salvational for many in what seems a contemporary hegemony of uncertainty. Like Democritus, Aristotle, Lucretius and Spinoza, Santayana has a philosophical objective that is ultimately reducible to individual happiness. A philosophy so directed is both individualistic and still sensitive to the "other," seeking internal and social harmony. Aristotle, providing the broadest antecedent influence on Santayana's moral philosophy, taught that happiness (*eudaimonia*) or the "good life" can best be pursued through the development of one's reason. Although Santayana generally seems personally immune to existential terror or angst, it is in the face of causative conditions (i.e., when "in the hands of an alien and inscrutable power")[26] that a sense of harmony in the individual spirit is sought. What is essential for understanding the generally non-prescriptive Santayana, who is dedicated to the idea of the uniqueness of individual life-needs for an authentic self-development, is that there is indeed one "umbrella" prescription (i.e., to honestly live one's life consistent with one's personal beliefs). Santayana, throughout his life, seems to have held true to his philosophical belief that certainty or the absolute is unattainable by refusing to take a demonstrative stance in argument, or resorting to harsh judgment of others' beliefs. At the same time, he resisted self-compromise under pressure from any quarter. John Lachs, a well-known exponent of an authentic life lived out of one's philosophical stance and one's responsibility "to bring our lives in line with our beliefs," is an advocate of the honesty found in Santayana's integration of philosophy and life.[27] Lachs goes to considerable length in his book to characterize Santayana as a philosopher who not only claims one should live one's beliefs but seems to do so. In a few sentences which I don't feel I can improve upon, Lachs depicts that harmonious state which Santayana suggests we seek through the life of reason.

> The good life for an individual, then is one in which he or she is able to satisfy the richest set of most intense desires or attain the largest number of sought after compossible goods . . . The interest in this harmonious maximization is what Santayana calls "reason" . . . there is nothing compulsory about reason or uniform about its products . . . There is no legitimate moral criticism of those who opt against reason, so long as we are not asked to bear the cost of their choice.[28]

In the quotation above, Lachs links the "good life" with "compossible" or compatible "goods," suggesting that to seek harmony of life is dependent on a harmony of "goods." It is implicit then, in Santayana's vision, that one must extend beyond the individual to reach some accordance with others' "goods." This idea is not, therefore, a totally selfish or inconsiderate one, although it primarily is directed to serve the individual's needs. However, one must seek compatibility with one's relational environment, or one's own desires for particular "goods" will fly in the face of others' contrary notions of what is ideal and good in "the press of the world." We are reminded that ideals, for Santayana, are relative.

In chapter 4, since our emphasis is on philosophy of religion and the spiritual life, I discussed those elements of "Ultimate Religion" and consequently the life of reason that compose the "religious emotions" as first presented in *Reason in Religion*. These are *piety, spirituality* and *charity*, and Santayana's guidance in exercising these actions as an approach to happiness in the face of contingency, independent of religious belief, is indeed a legacy for the times. These "religious emotions" constitute first, in piety, recognition and honoring of the "given" universal power of nature and that contingent force which gave us birth. We are compelled to accept this power over against which we now must survive. Our awe at the universe and its power has an ideal response in our spirituality which strives toward self-development and perfection. This is an exercise toward truth. In exercising our spirituality, we derive our ideals and define our "goods" as well as open the door to a withdrawal from the pressures of the world into a contemplation of the eternal. Our charity reminds us

of our non-centrality in the natural world and leads us toward a selflessness where we are sensitive to conflicts of our "goods" and others'
"goods." It is a "check" on our selfness, and ideally makes us blind to
divisions between religions and cultures. "Charity is a second birth of
love, aware of many wills and many troubles."[29] Whether it is in *disillusion* or in traditional religious belief, the interrelatedness of personal acceptance and coping with contingency, spiritual development and constructive relationship with the world are integral to Santayana's life of
reason.

SANTAYANA AND THEOLOGY

An Empathetic Christian Theologian

In chapter 3, I associated aspects of Santayana's methodology with
those of Rudolph Otto in *The Idea of the Holy* (*Das Heilige*), for example,
distinguishing morality from religious feeling. Of primary importance is
Otto's claim that subjecting everything to reason in studying religion can
cause it to lose its mystery and supernatural character. At the same time,
he proclaimed, to shut reason out could be equally distorting.[30] This
notion can be similarly associated with Santayana and obviously exercised in *The Idea of Christ in The Gospels* and in his other works dealing
with spirituality and religion. Further, there is an empathy in Santayana's
study of religion that likely comes from his own experience as a Roman
Catholic, despite his claim of never being a "true believer." Otto, at the
beginning of his third chapter of *The Idea of the Holy*, "The Elements of the
Numinous," requested those readers who could not recall a "deeply-felt
religious experience" to read no further. The artist, however, who "has an
intimate personal knowledge of the distinctive element in the aesthetic
experience" (i.e., as related as it is to religious experience) may read on
with some understanding.[31] Santayana's artistic temperament and cre-
dentials are well documented, and although it is safe to assume that his
spiritual experiences associated with Catholicism were more aesthetic
than religious, he falls within Otto's criteria, unless his suspicion of mystical experience might make him borderline. *In any case, despite his own
disillusion, his sensitivity to the phenomena of religious life and profound respect
for religious belief and practice are unquestionable.*

Kirby-Smith speaks of Santayana's "accommodation" of other beliefs
to his philosophy and perceives him "as a theologian who is too skeptical
or modest to impose any god or gods whatever on us," and he characterizes Santayana's views on religious freedom as "democratic."[32] The
characterization of Santayana as "theologian" is significant to my argument that Santayana's application to contemporary religious thought
may indeed be significant in theology. *He has taken the dogmas of Christian*

theology as a vehicle for piety toward the evolution of morality and ethical learning from the past and a forward-directed spirituality for the individual development toward an ideal in the future. As Levinson points out, Santayana may have been exceedingly optimistic in regard to the end of controversy in religious matters as a more interpretive age set in. As religious controversy in the contemporary world has increased and intensified beyond any intelligent expectations, it is now that Santayana's philosophical theological insights may be at last acknowledged.[33]

A PREEMPTIVE POSTMODERNISM

In chapter 4 I discussed Santayana's general anti-modernist position most evident from the last decade of the nineteenth century, and in particular his anti-modernist position relative to the Catholic modernist movement of this period associated with figures such as Alfred Loisy and George Tyrrell. I also indicated that associated with this view is Santayana's inclination to retain much of tradition with its myths, symbols and rituals as an important repository of historical human experience and reflection of human ideals. Also associated with this "anti-modernist" perspective, in an anti-foundationalist sense, would be Santayana's questioning of Enlightenment values for arriving at absolute knowledge through reason, the certainty of truth attained through the scientific method, the practice of a scientific reductive approach toward religion or the value of "progress." With such a view he draws closer to characteristics incorporated in the blurred stereotype of a postmodern turn, not popularly manifested until decades later in the 1960s. Included in the stereotype would be a general contrariness to the quest for certainty or universal knowledge or expectations for arriving at the objective nature of reality along with a penchant, instead, for a relativistic paradigm. Such characteristics are foundational to Santayana's project and, not unexpectedly, similar to the postmodernistic critique and ironic parody of religion. There is no question that Santayana's approach can be interpreted by many as hostile to organized religion and religious belief, and that rather than a theologian, he might be considered by some as an "atheologian."

Santayana's claim that *essence*, when intuited, reflected upon, and symbolically interpreted, can only at best approximate a knowledge of truth, his undermines any expectations that reason, the most remarkable of our earthly human gifts, is a reliable epistemic tool. As Hodges and Lachs suggest in relating Santayana to postmodern thought, "Santayana shows how our attempt to understand everything is excessive."[34] Hence, objective reality and any substantial degree of knowledge about it is beyond our reach.[35] Therefore, the claims of Jacques Derrida (1930–2005), for example, that meaning would not be assuredly derived through signs or symbols nor that anything reasoned is stable or timeless, would be in accord with Santayana's views. At the same time, Santayana, in a post-modern stance, recognizes the symbolism of ideas.[36] Although I have defined Santayana as a realist and materialist, he takes the stereotypical postmodern view that, in general, the role of philosophy is not to define the objective nature of things. As John Ryder points out, the characteristics of postmodernism are very evident in pragmatism (e.g., in Peirce and James),[37] and while Santayana may be considered as having characteristics of pragmatism (e.g., value determined through experience), he falls wide of the profile in other respects and is generally critical of pragmatism's non-absolutist perspective on truth. Although he admits to a preliminary reductionist approach in regard to religion—for example, his treatment of the four Realms of Being regarded as "a reduction of Christian theology and spiritual discipline to their secret interior source"—it is more a constructive or transpositional approach.[38] There is still nothing in Santayana of what John Stuhr calls "the deconstructive temperament . . . dark, brooding, suspicious and accusatory."[39] Again, we can relate him to Tillich's characteristically postmodern methodology (also phenomenological in its approach) in reinterpreting "highly-charged Christian doctrine" (e.g., the incarnation or the crucifixion) in terms of metaphorical and dialectical meaning.

A BASIS FOR SOCIAL CONSTRUCTIONIST THEOLOGY

Levinson suggests that Santayana's work prior to 1900 established the basis for a "constructionist view" of theology and that by 1906 he had "articulated all the characteristics of Geertz's 1966 definition of religion as a cultural system." Such an insightful preemption by Santayana, so briefly noted by Levinson, should be acknowledged more at length and as important in hindsight. Certainly for Santayana, as we could say for Tillich, human beings are framed by and integral with or embedded in culture.[40] If Geertz proposes that culture is "an historically transmitted pattern of meaning embodied in symbols . . . by means of which people communicate, perpetuate and develop their knowledge about and attitudes toward life,"[41] we can indeed see Santayana, as Levinson suggests, not far afield from this position. One premise of constructionist theology is that reality is a local consensus attained through linguistic intercourse (i.e., it is relational and culturally attuned). Further, it springs from a local narrative rather than a metanarrative. If we accept Von Glaserfeld's definition of *constructionism*, a term coined by Seymour Papert, cofounder of the media laboratory at MIT in 1980, as "a theory of knowledge in which knowledge does not reflect an 'objective' ontological reality, but exclusively an ordering and organization of a world constituted by our experience," it is not a stretch to associate such a view with Santayana.[42] Constructionism and therefore constructionist theology is primarily epistemological and in my view consistent with the very basic metaphysical premise of Santayana that "nothing given exists," and further, it is consistent with the recognition of his notion of the *pathetic fallacy*. Therefore, in non-phenomenological parlance, one can say that no individual linguistic conception can be affirmatively associated with a real object or event in the world. The theory is hence anti-foundationalist at its core and resides in the milieu of the postmodern turn. This metaphysical foundation of Santayana's presumed basis for constructionist theology would not have been clear until 1923, in *Scepticism and Animal Faith*, which still would have been far ahead of the postmodern notion of social constructionism. However, as Levinson suggests, Santayana provided a basis for constuctionist theology prior to 1900 in *Interpretations of Poetry and Religion* (1900) and then further developed it in his constructive methodology of *The Idea of Christ in the Gospels*.[43]

In order to identify those insights that relate to constructionist theology in *Interpretations*, I will derive some assumptions generally shared in this methodology abstracted by Duane Bidwell from Kenneth Gergen's *Invitation to Social Constructionism*, which I have integrated with some separate characterizations of constructionist theology from other sources, such as Peter L. Berger's *The Sacred Canopy*.[44] These assumptions or characteristics are as follows:

1. There are many perceptions of reality which are all subject to time, place and culture and subject to consensus communicated through a common language. There is no common and comprehensive "absolute" in religions except experience.

2. Language (symbols) of a community acquire the sense of truth and objectivity within the community where religion is practiced. The value of religion can only be fairly determined by those within the common language and practice of the community. Theology is built upon human experience, language and imagination.

3. The language and approach of science in considering religious beliefs can be reductive and tend to take on a privileged insight into truth. Religious or spiritual language (e.g., that of Christianity) can be more reflective, on the other hand, of moral and religious reality at any given time.

4. In the constructionist view, emphasis normally placed on the individual mind is replaced by concern for relational processes from which rationality and morality emerge. Individuals must be permitted to attain religious or spiritual meaning in their own manner without suppression.

5. We respond to and characterize "threats" or powers in our world in various manners depending upon place, time, language and culture. These threats and responses are based upon, and reducible to,

perceptions and representations, frequently in the form of symbols, of individuals and ultimately of the social or religious group.

6. The practice and value of religion evolves and adapts depending upon the needs of the present and is an ongoing process ideally determined by human need in any given culture or sect.

Considering briefly only Santayana's *Interpretations of Poetry and Religion*, I believe that Levinson's claim is justified based upon the following ideas expressed by Santayana in this work.[45] (Note: I will designate the number of the specific "assumption" of constructionism from the above where it applies directly after the reference from Santayana's *Interpretations of Poetry and Religion* and my related comments.)

Santayana affirms a basic premise of his philosophy of religion that religious doctrine would do well to withdraw any pretensions to be dealing with matters of fact since "poetry is called religion when it intervenes in life"[46] (1). The pretension of religion to represent fact through dogma and doctrine is the main source of conflict between religion and science.[47] The positivist school overlooks "the highest functions of human nature . . . All observation is observation of brute fact[48] (3). Santayana cautions against tampering with or reductively "liberalizing" religious language which "by minimizing its expression, both theoretic and devotional . . . [is] merely impoverishing religious symbols and vulgarizing religious aims; it subtracts from faith that imagination by which faith becomes interpretation and idealization of human life, and retains only a stark and superfluous principle of superstition"[49] (2, 3). One approaches religious doctrine and dogma, as well as individual beliefs in an open and unbiased manner with sensitivity to the appropriate religious symbolism. Such an approach is consistent with the phenomenological approach I claim for Santayana (1, 2). The issue of language refers also to that characteristic imagination that is cultivated only within the religious community. Santayana observes that "for this reason the believer in a mature supernatural religion clings to it with such strange tenacity and regards it as his highest heritage, while the outsider, whose imagination speaks another language . . . wonders how so wild a fiction can take root in a reasonable mind"[50] (1, 2).

As a moral relativist, a position necessarily derived from his recognition of the needs of the individual spirit, its unique imaginative disposition and the human lack of epistemological access to the absolute, Santayana recognized the danger of "dominations." For example, in *Interpretations* he cites the early illegitimate incursion of the Roman church beyond her borders where the imaginative traditions and moral experience of the Teutonic Christian people were not compatible with the Roman doctrines (i.e., "The self-reliant and dreamy Teuton could spin out of the Biblical chronicles and rhapsodies convictions after his own heart").[51] Santayana, of course, is not unique in modern or postmodern philosophy in his

recognition of the potential oppression of authoritarian organized religion, but this recognition is joined with a respect for religious orthodoxy
and its symbolic value that is indeed unique (4, 5). For Santayana, it is
important for religion to sustain traditional symbols and doctrine for the
symbolic value they have for moral behavior and where they provide
meaning meeting the individual's and society's needs. However, religions and religious belief are not fixed and change to satisfy these individual and societal needs. Santayana's philosophy is unmistakably based
upon the fulfillment of the individual who, if living on the basis of reason, is striving toward a "good life" relative to that individual's needs.
Society's role is to enable such fulfillment, but when such fulfillment is
only for the few or for a dominating majority, then freedom in overt
practice may be lost. However, although spiritual life may go "under-
ground," or spiritual needs go unsatisfied, they remain secret or pent up
in the individual and in relationship to other souls of the same disposition and ultimately can spring forth when societal pressure eases or more
enabling societal and religious forms arise. In *Interpretations*, Santayana
describes the manner in which Christianity provided a more satisfying
"scheme for the unification of the natural and the moral. The harmony
which the old religion had failed to establish . . . the new sought to
establish in history and in time"[52] (6). For Santayana, a move toward
"harmony" is also always a move toward reason.

I provide the above few references from *Interpretations* as a basis for
Levinson's general claim for Santayana's constructionist approach. Lachs
and Hodges in *Thinking in the Ruins* compare Santayana and Wittgenstein
in relation to some very similar philosophical convictions, some of which
are constructionist.[53] This is particularly so in regard to the need to respect language as it expresses the "truth" of subcultures (e.g., religions).
In relation to the particular needs of a subculture (i.e., to those psyches
that reflect those needs), they reflect Santayana's viewpoint that "the
ultimate thrust of religious belief is to transform the life of the believer.
Such transformation is impossible on the basis of intellectual assent or
insight. A vital commitment is needed, and it can be attained only if the
ideal articulated is native to the psyche."[54]

A CONSTRUCTIONIST INTERPRETER OF CHRISTIAN DOGMA

The Trinity

The extension of Santayana's constructionist approach is also manifested in his symbolic approach to the interpretation of Christian doctrine. This can be of significant interest as a basis for alternative considerations and fresh possibilities in philosophical theology, constructive and
constructionist theology. Mark Wallace's following broad definition of

constructionist theology as a postmodern methodology serves to categorize Santayana's approach in *The Idea of Christ in the Gospels*.

> It is a self-consciously *constructive* enterprise that selects from previous works thought forms and vocabulary that can be usefully recombined and refashioned in an idiom expressive of the hopes and desires of our age. On another level, however, post-modern theology goes beyond historical quotation and stylistic pastiche with its explicit commitment to enabling transformative practice.[55]

Santayana in his exegesis of the Gospels defines the Christological concept of "God in man" and then proceeds to address this *idea* as "valid for all men in all religions."[56] He observes that "in the Gospels the idea of Christ seems to be emerging from traditional prejudices that do not allow it to manifest its ultimate [i.e., universal] implications."[57] It is from this foundational bias that Santayana breaks free, seeking a universal application, deriving a Christology where "Christ thus represents the intrinsic ideal of the spirit," and God, existing in Christ, also enters into all of us through the spirit.[58] His symbolic interpretation of the Trinity is of particular interest in this respect in that it "transposes the doctrine . . . into terms of pure ontology and moral dialectic."[59] Santayana is not resorting to metaphysics to design his own "philosopher's" God but rather is finding meaning in the words of the Gospels and the foundation theology of the church fathers. We can recall from chapter 4 that Santayana rejects any truth claims for religious dogma, deeming it the imaginative and poetic creation of myths that are "wisely contrived" to strive toward eternal truth.[60] Santayana's foundational idea is that the religion of the "true believer" is where "the fictitious object of datum [is] taken for evidence of the fact."[61]

The primary sources for Santayana's Christology and interpretation of Christian doctrine are the earlier *Realm of the Spirit* and the later hermeneutical work *The Idea of Christ in the Gospels*. The symbolic congruence of the Christian epic with Santayana's metaphysics and philosophy of religion can provide for a unique theological trajectory. Santayana's Thomistic Catholic conditioning and ontological perspective holds sway in the development of a symbolic Christology in *The Idea of Christ in the Gospels*. Although in this book I do not dwell at any length on this aspect of Santayana's legacy, I will provide here as an example a brief summary of his interpretation of the Trinity in relation to his ontology. John Robert Baker in his essay "The Christology of George Santayana" already provides an excellent exegesis of *The Idea of Christ in the Gospels* and Santayana's Christology and, further, extends the possibilities of Santayana's non-theistic position to a doctrine of God drawing from Lachs's essay "Two Concepts of God."[62] Such a theological construction is a case in point for the potential of extending and building upon Santayana's theology. Prior to *The Idea of Christ in the Gospels*, Santayana, in *The Realm of the*

Spirit, directly relates the doctrine of the Trinity as defined in the Nicene Creed to his metaphysic providing an alternative interpretation of *perichoresis.*[63] The broader hermeneutic of Christology in *The Idea of Christ in the Gospels* extensively addresses the symbolism of the salvational role of Jesus Christ and his Resurrection and is rather more existential than metaphysical. His symbolic interpretation of the Trinity in *The Realm of the Spirit,* however, holds to the "process" flow of the Nicene Creed. In dissonance with the Christian Gospel he introduces a role for Christ as symbolically associated with the Holy Ghost as separate from the Son. In such an interpretation he indicates he is providing a more logical association than traditional Christian theology which "has been much less penetrating in regard to the Holy Ghost than in regard to the Father and the Son."[64] The symbolic interpretation of the Trinity in the creative act is of particular interest.

> The assault of reality, in the force of whatsoever exists or happens, I call matter or the realm of matter; but evidently this very power is signified by the First Person of the Trinity, the Father, almighty creator of heaven and earth and of all things visible and invisible.[65]

He goes on to define the symbolic role of the Son through whom all things are created according to the Creed, and who is "thus an indispensable partner and vehicle for the life of the Father." Power must resort to form or "[it] would be annulled before it began to exert itself unless it did or produced something specific, something eternally distinct and recognizable in its character." Therefore, the Father represents power and the Son, form or *essence* (i.e., "To exercise power is to elect form").[66] The Son or *Logos* "begotten not made" of the Father symbolizes the generation of spirit from matter emphasizing that "*Logos* is only a selection from the realm of *essence.*"[67]

Santayana's symbolism is somewhat analogous to Whitehead's and Hartshorne's process where *eternal entities,* contained in the primordial nature of God, lend form to the creative force. I will return to this interesting comparison in the next section. His approach in terms of interpreting the symbolic meaning of Christian dogma has some parallels to Carl Jung's symbolic interpretation and hermeneutic of Christian doctrine. Of significance, in comparing the two approaches, one from a psychological perspective (in the case of Jung) and the other from an ontological one (in Santayana), is the significant difference in the respective doctrinal interpretation. Both Santayana and Jung, it can be argued, take a phenomenological approach directed at the ultimate spiritual development and self-realization of the individual. In the case of the Trinity, for example, Jung views the doctrine as a representation of evolving consciousness, Father, Son and Holy Spirit each representing a phase in the process.[68] He does resort to Incarnational language and the idea of human destiny, but his essential approach is to psychologize the doctrine.[69] Santayana, on the other hand, views the doctrine as essentially moral and symbolic of a soteriological and creative process defined within the logic of the four Realms of Being. Given that Santayana was steeped in Catholic doctrine, it is not unexpected that his philosophy of religion and metaphysic *ab initio* would be so symbolically consistent with Thomistic Christian theology as is ultimately demonstrated in *The Idea of Christ in the Gospels*. He has adopted the language of Christian theology in constructing his own naturalistic theology which he considers more applicable and emancipatory to contemporary humanity.[70] He demonstrates his objectivity early in *The Idea of Christ in The Gospels*, with the intention to "analyze and detach one original element in the inspiration of the Gospels, namely the dramatic presentation of the person of Christ," and indicates that his personal sentiments are put aside and his intent is not in any way to question the validity of the Gospel. I interpret this to mean, as far as his intent, that Santayana objectively considers the symbolic meaning of the doctrine of salvation initially for any given dogma, and then makes the association with his own metaphysic as a secondary exercise. This would, in effect, as I suggested earlier, constitute a claim for "bracketing" before the reflective comparison with Santayana's own scheme was enacted. Despite his *disillusion* in regard to dogma, this demonstrates the strong Christian tone of Santayana's philosophy and how conducive Christian symbols and theological language are for the expression of his philosophy of religion.

TROUBLESOME ESSENCES: SANTAYANA'S METAPHYSICS AND PROCESS THEOLOGY

Timothy Sprigge, in a rigorous comparison of the metaphysics of Whitehead and Santayana, declares that there is much in Santayana that would justify calling him a philosopher of "becoming."[71] One may be reminded from chapter 2 of the importance of Heraclitus as an inspiration to Santayana in regard to the sense of "immediacy" and the obviation of absolute moral judgment. At the same time, a common inspiration for both Santayana's philosophy and that of process thought is the concept from Heraclitus of change in the "flux" of existence and further, singularly for process thought, that substance itself is process. In chapter 3, I have noted Santayana's enthusiasm in the postscript to *The Realm of Essence* for Whitehead's concept of *eternal entities* and their similarities to Santayana's *essences*. It is upon the similar but still subtly different character of these logical elements that still hangs a metaphysical controversy involving the theological underpinnings of process thought. I do not mean to diminish the major differences between Santayana's philosophy and the concepts of process theology—for example, Santayana's aversion to pantheism (or panentheism) and his non-theistic viewpoint or his idea of substance vs. Whitehead's—but space is not available here to elaborate. Also, Sprigge has already substantially done the groundwork. Much of the metaphysical controversy I refer to above has been summarized by Robert Whittemore in his brief paper "Santayana's Neglect of Hartshorne's Alternative," with particular reference to two essays by Hartshorne written twenty-four years apart and one much briefer response by Santayana.[72] As Whittemore indicates, "The issue between Santayana and Hartshorne is of importance," since "[Santayana's] theory of essence is the heart of Santayana's system of philosophy," while "conversely the notion of the 'literally changing God with an unchanging necessary essence' is the keystone of Hartshorne's theological edifice."[73] Since no theological resolution, if one is possible, is yet forthcoming, I consider the dynamic of this debate to be, in one more dimension, evidence of the importance of Santayana's project to theological and philosophical thought. It is evident from Hartshorne's polemic against Santayana's non-existing *essences* that, as Whittemore observes, Hartshorne exhibits irritation with this apparently compelling issue. Compelling it is indeed, as the theological coherence of the bipolar God of process and of Hartshorne's "career commitment," as Whittemore calls it, rides on the outcome.[74] I will not repeat here Hartshorne's rigorous and even vehement argument given Whittemore's excellent summary, except to say that it seems to rest upon the very derivation of Santayana's theory (recall his discernment of *essence* through the skeptical method and the *sopm*) and Hartshorne's misattribution of the nature of Santayana's Realm of Essence. I will only briefly outline the basic issue and its consequences of concern to Hartshorne and process theology.

Hartshorne claims in "Santayana's Defiant Eclecticism" that Santayana has neglected an alternative theory (the "neglected alternative") in regard to his theory of *essences*. As I indicated in chapter 3, Santayana observes an essential congruence between his *essences* and Whitehead's (and therefore Hartshorne's) *eternal entities*, both of which are nonexistent qualitative properties or forms. In the process model of the bipolar God, there are two entities, the primordial nature and the consequential nature which together, as processes in one God, account for the internal process dynamics of God and the manifestation of God in/upon the world.[75] In Hartshorne's "alternative" we find *eternal entities*, to be thought of also like Santayana's *essences*, as non-existents, but located as well in the primordial nature of God. In Santayana, we find *essences* in the Realm of Essence, an eternal repository of all possible essential forms that have been or will be actuated in matter (i.e., will ingress into the world of matter and constitute facts and truth). Santayana's *essences*, as we have established, are "powerless" and non-existent as they fall, as *essences*, outside of the Realm of Matter where action, influence and power are manifest. Having restated these basic characteristics of the seemingly identical *eternal entities* and *essences*, we can address the question as to why Hartshorne finds Santayana's *essences* so disconcerting.

The primordial eternal nature of God, that "unconscious" aspect of the bipolar process God that is an abstraction from God's total functionality, process theologians identify with the *Logos*. The primordial nature, while the source of unconscious creative love and novelty in the world and ideals which this nature urges toward fulfillment, involves *eternal entities* in the actualization into existence of what Hartshorne and Whitehead term *actual occasions* and Santayana, simply *existents*. We now come to a subtle but critical difference between *essences* and *eternal entities*, both in relation to function and properties, and it is this difference that bears upon the concept of Hartshorne's process God. In the process of generating or creating a "novel order " and an "ordered novelty," the primordial nature is "lured" to those forms, the *eternal entities*, which are apprehended by the primordial nature as being most favorable to ingression as *actual occasions*, or what Santayana would deem existents or *substance*. The *eternal entities*, in effect, are given the attribute of causality in their capability to "lure" the primordial God's apprehension. Santayana's *essences*, on the other hand, have no such causative property and are absolutely without power of causation. One must now speculate as to what the consequences would be of "non-luring" *essences* located in the primordial nature of God. If God cannot apprehend those *essences* of value without being lured toward "value," then one imagines a more random ingression of forms in *actual entities*. In this event, it would seem that both the "novel order" and "ordered novelty" would suffer and as a result, the "goodness" of creation would diminish.

Santayana's response to Hartshorne's initial essay is replete with good humor but cuts to the core of Hartshorne's argument by indicating, as part of a much longer response, that he does not neglect Hartshorne's argument at all but "merely expresses it in other words and regard[s] it, not as a dogma, but as a free speculation, essentially theological and mythical, like those of the Indians and the Neo-Platonists."[76] After all then, despite Hartshorne's claimed logic, whose theory, at the end of the day, could be deemed the more speculative? My sense is that Hartshorne would claim his logical model of God as speculative but still logical and more rationally and coherently derived than myth. However, such an abstraction of the internal workings of God would be lost to Santayana in principle. Of significance is that the construct of the bipolar process God has been logically derived and becomes logically dysfunctional when the causal power of *eternal entities* is sacrificed. Santayana's "defiance" therefore leaves unresolved a critical debate for future metaphysicians of process theology.

SANTAYANA'S EPIPHENOMENALISM AND NEUROSCIENCE

Of particular significance relative to contemporary religious thought in
relation to modern neuroscience is Santayana's *epiphenomenalism* or theory of the spirit-body relationship and the "powerlessness" of thought. As
early as 1913, Santayana called attention to the "deaf ear" that people
have turned toward the materialistic idea that

> the mind [consciousness] is not the cause of our actions but an effect,
> collateral with our actions, of bodily growth and organization [psyche].
> It may therefore easily come about that the thoughts of men, tested by
> the principles that seem to rule their conduct, may be belated or irrele-
> vant, or premonitory.[77]

Santayana's epiphenomenalism and the resultant theory that *essences* and
therefore thought are powerless has been substantially controversial and
counterintuitive to all but the most careful readers of his work. Some
interesting questions can be posed. How can consciousness and thought
not have influence over our actions and what about "the power of ideas"?
What about the concept of soul and the resurrection of the body, for is
this not traditionally associated with consciousness and with spirit? Does
the Enlightenment-inspired mechanistic model of the human organism,
including the brain, hold true? If one needs a body's processes, in Santayana's terminology, a *psyche*, to manifest action and power, what happens
to our dualistic reference of body and spirit, and for that matter, to the
mind of God? The orthodox God is omnipotent, but analogically considered, a spirit with no body unless one considers that God and world are
equivalent or are, as Sallie McFague proposes, a panentheistic model in
which the world or universe is "the body of God."[78] Does such a theory
make more logical the idea of the universe or world as both process and
product, *natura naturans* and *natura naturata*, as indeed seems the case in
Spinoza's model and those disposed to philosophical naturalism today?
Santayana's epiphenominalism indicates that the individual psyche (i.e.,
the tropes or inherent functionalities of the biological human organism) is
the source of all human action and power and that the spirit, its *entelechy*,
is powerless in the world. He points out the "horrid confusion in attributing to spirit the dogged conservatism and catastrophic evolution of the
natural world."[79]

Remarkably, Santayana's controversial epiphenomenal theory now
seems very much in accord with the theoretical model of mental function
developed by contemporary brain scientists such as Antonio Damasio,
MD, former founder and director of the Institute of Neuroscience at the
University of Iowa Medical School.[80] In Santayana's theory, there is an
element of dualism in the separation of "spirit" and body, but from a
functional standpoint it is a benign duality—that is, the manifestation of
spirit from organic body is powerless, being only concerned with the

terms of language (i.e., *essences*). For Santayana, "mind" is a nebulous term since "mind may be dissolved into a confused unconscious substance still paradoxically called feeling, out of which organic bodies and centers of apprehension may be composed."[81] The implication evident from Santayana's sense of "mind" is that mind involves "body" in some way and any idea of distinction between body and "mind" is not helpful. In a conventional definition, mind may mean "spirit" in Santayana's sense of spirit, but for Santayana, "mind" is simply not definitive enough to suggest, as he does for spirit, that it is powerless in the world. Therefore, when one considers any distinctions between mind and body, in fact an Aristotelean notion, wherein mind is equivalent to "soul," *epiphenomenal* theory would obviate such a notion.[82] Angus Kerr-Lawson addresses the relationship between Santayana's epiphenomenal theory and the current neuroscientific mind-body theory of Damasio and Daniel Wegner in his paper "Two Philosophical Psychologists."[83] Santayana's epiphenomenal theory is obviously grounded in that of an even more prescient Spinoza who perceived in the seventeenth century that activities of mind originated in unknown bodily functions and that the idea of consciousness as the cause of our actions is illusory.[84] The consequences of Santayana's epiphenomenalism and its accordance with modern neuroscience will not be addressed here, but two observations might be made regarding the nexus I claim for Santayana and contemporary religious thought. First, Santayana's categories of *Spirit* and *Matter* and their characterization as "powerless" and "powerful," respectively, take on even greater importance in relation to the scientific world than during his lifetime. Also, Santayana's metaphysical model opens a door to dialectic in theology and philosophy of religion in regard to panpsychic concepts of God, omnipotence of God, the understanding of "will" and theologies of the immortality of the "soul."

RELATIVISM, UNCERTAINTY AND THE ABSOLUTE

Santayana's "relativism," its epistemological and ontological basis and its relation to religious pluralism, inter-religious dialogue, fundamentalism and the domination of institutional religion can be of importance in considering these contemporary issues. We have already seen evidence of this above in relation to constructionist theology. Santayana's claim for the human epistemological weakness and the futility of seeking absolute certainty has been extensively discussed in earlier chapters. This claim is reflected in general in the postmodern critique of foundationalism and is consistent with the Humean skeptical tradition. Santayana's premise takes us beyond the confines of "inclusivism" defined by Gavin D'Costa in relation to Christianity "as holding to the definitive truth of Christianity, but recognizing that other religions may be 'lawful religions' (Rahner), even if in a provisional manner."[85] Exclusivism acted out in the world is a manifestation to Santayana of all that is counter to reason and is the source of anxiety, repression, conflict and war.[86] Religious fundamentalism of any form, Catholic, Protestant or Islamic, would be seen by Santayana as that religious disposition particularly prone to exclusivism, but such a disposition also must be accepted to the extent it doesn't dominate or restrict individual freedom of others. The philosophical basis for this view is that "the forms of good are divergent," and by acting on this premise, one can, as Santayana did, "overcome moral and ideal provinciality."[87]

Santayana's views on "domination" of religious views and institutions are pertinent to contemporary issues—for example, the politicization of Christianity by the conservative American "Right," the aggressive temperament of fundamentalist Islam or the religious suppression of women. The conservatism of fundamentalist religious views (e.g., Christian or Islamic, sexist and absolutist doctrine, racism and any suppressive political movement) would for Santayana be dominations potentially limiting individual freedom, development and happiness.[88] As I have pointed out earlier in the chapter, this recognition of absolutism and potential oppression by organized religion is not by any means unique in the philosophical canon. However, Santayana has a metaphysical basis for such a view which is not grounded simply on materialistic scientific reasoning as for example in most post-Enlightenment philosophers, but rather upon the inaccessibility of certainty and truth. In *Dominations and Powers* Santayana illustrates that personal religion exists in the face of the orthodoxy of the moment. He suggests that "religions are social, but religion is private" and that "sources of religion in the soul . . . lie in that unused residuum of life which the animal soul still feels within itself after social institutions and intellectual conventions have hemmed it in."[89] From the perspective of his "double moral grid" (described in chapter 1), Santayana points out the legitimacy of a systematic religion that presumes to be "true" and also presumes that it is legitimate for it to intrude into politics because this "is the work it comes to do in the world." On this premise of "truth" then, the imposition upon personal freedom can begin, and if an honest believer claims to "know by inspiration the conditions of life and the needs of the soul," then it's not surprising that he or she acts upon it.[90] Such an imposition is bound to result in conflict in a society with heterogeneous religious dispositions. Once a religion lays down "the principles of politics in the higher sense, and supplied maxims for personal conduct" of its own constituency, it is impossible for it to abstain from political participation and indeed, that is what Santayana seems to propose.[91] The danger that Santayana doesn't address is that which occurs when representatives of government are present in such number as to result in a hegemony (e.g., as might be the concern in the contemporary issue in America of the influence of Evangelical Christians in the Republican Party). The self-assumed role of America of spreading democracy around the globe would naturally fall under Santayana's admonitions regarding imposition of *ideals* upon others in disparate cultures (it would be additionally suspect based upon his own view of the limitations of political democracy).

Only out of a form of pluralism would Santayana conceive the path to a rational and peaceful world. Although he provides no formula for optimizing identity and tradition, his view is consistent with Ninian Smart's perspective on a philosophy of world order that "we need to avoid a homogenized globe. Differences should be preserved . . . We should not, even if we could, bulldoze cultures in the service of some global goal."[92] There is in this regard a congruence with the pragmatic view of William James that one must be "hands off: neither the whole of truth nor the whole of good is revealed to any single observer . . . It is enough to ask each of us that he should be faithful to his own opportunities."[93] Santayana takes the tension out of religious differences in a truly non-reductive pluralism that is in every way not antagonistic to religious belief. This is despite his own preference for a naturalistic "Ultimate Religion" free of metaphysical and transcendental pretensions (i.e., fallacies of hypostatization). The idea of relativity does not imply that there is not absolute truth, and Santayana presents the absurdity of such a contingency in the preface to *Realms of Being*. Here he logically reasons that, in the absence of an absolute, the "desultory views of individuals . . . would themselves be absolute." Truth is, as he claims, "no living view" but "merely that segment of the realm of *essence* which happens to be illustrated in existence."[94] However, humans cannot attain knowledge of the entirety of truth or of any certainty beyond immediate intuition. Even God, as variously conceived, is only unlikely in Santayana's scheme but still, as he suggests in the final pages of *Realms of Being*, "divine spirits may nevertheless exist."[95] However, Santayana's relativism is not relativism "run free." Within his broader vision of tolerance, there is a recognition of the inspiration, wisdom and even rational intent in the formation of religious doctrine, an awareness of deep human needs for cosmological explanation and, indeed, an awareness of the need for individual compromise in the spirit of charity.

In *The Idea of Christ in The Gospels*, Santayana's recognition and empathy for the fruits of religious inspiration are evident.[96] Implicit in "Ultimate Religion" is the basis for religious tolerance and a pluralistic view: "Thus the absolute love of everything involves the love of universal good; and the love of universal good involves the love of every creature."[97] As I noted in chapter 4, it is charity that provides the "check" for unbridled satisfaction of individual desires and introduces a "selflessness" that entails a blindness toward divisions between institutions and cultures. Charity, it would seem, of the elements Santayana puts forward in the practice of religion (i.e., piety, spirituality, charity and discipline), is the vehicle to engage Santayana's relativism with constructive religious pluralism. Ninian Smart proposes that it is no longer the goal of philosophy to be conceived as a path to an integrative worldview of human knowledge and identity.[98] His view is fully in accord with Santayana's vision of individualistic philosophy based upon unique human needs and desires. Santayana, like Smart, would avoid homogenization of global culture and religious views and preserve difference. If indeed we would share Smart's conviction that philosophy of religion is vital in cross-cultural and inter-religious relations,[99] Santayana's non-theistic, tolerant and non-reductive vision would seem to be a common denominator in developing a paradigm of pluralistic dialogue.

THE DELICATE BALANCE OF ORTHODOXY AND LIBERALISM

Santayana is neither a classic religious liberal nor a rationalizer of liberalism. Rather, the rationale for religious and spiritual freedom in the modern world inherent in Santayana's project holds traditional Christian orthodoxy, religious symbols and traditional doctrine and ritual in high esteem. I suggest that this paradoxical view of a materialistic naturalist is especially relevant to contemporary religion. Foundational to Santayana's view on the value of religious symbols is a bipartite perspective on the value and power of these symbols in doctrine and dogma to both the religiously *disillusioned* and the "true believer." There is a potential for the "swords" of both liberalism and orthodoxy to cut both ways, either one profoundly affecting the other. Manifestations of this view are found in Santayana's criticism of Protestantism for diluting or deleting orthodox Christian doctrine and symbols, and in his antipathy toward the reductive vision of the modernists in the Roman Catholic Church. For an understanding of Santayana's disposition toward orthodoxy we must recall at the same time his view toward the "compromise" as might be evident in a reduction of Christian dogma based upon a rational perspective. At the same time, it is helpful to appreciate that the tension between modernism and conservatism evident in the later part of the nineteenth and earlier part of the twentieth century is still manifest and gives every evidence of continuing. The conflict between the liberalizing views of Vatican II and the more conservative orthodoxy of the subsequent Roman Catholic Magisterium and the wave of evangelical and fundamentalist Christian movements running counter to liberal Protestantism are examples. Santayana's views in regard to orthodoxy vs. modern liberal views, therefore, remain pertinent. They also provide a dilemma when seeking, as I am here, some valuable ongoing lesson from Santayana that may mitigate this tension.

To begin with, we must recall two basic and problematic positions that he holds:

1. "To divorce, as the modernists do, the history of the world from the story of salvation, and God's government and the sanctions of religion from the operation of matter, is a fundamental apostasy from Christianity."[100] "The very motive that attaches them to Christianity is worldly and un-Christian."[101]
2. "What is this whole phenomenon of religion but human experience interpreted by human imagination? And what is the modernist, who would embrace it all, but a freethinker, with a sympathetic interest in religious illusions."[102]

From these admonitions, one would deduce from Santayana's viewpoint that there is little room for a "halfway" Christian. At the same time, a de minimus interpretation of his viewpoint could be that any claim one makes for an authentic Christianity requires adherence to its strictures or an admission that a derivative of Christianity is what is practiced. Santayana has reminded us that the true original concept of Christianity is of a supernatural, salvational religion opposed to those things of the world such as "emancipated science, free poetic religion, optimistic politics and dissolute art." After all, it was "the needful salvation from these follies, [that] Christianity went on to announce, had come through the cross of Christ."[103] A quite similar contemporary "reminder" in the same vein may be found in Garry Wills's *What Jesus Meant*, published in 2006 for the popular press.[104] Further, Santayana is not a member of the Roman Catholic Church and consequently is not trying to align his own beliefs and that of the church from within the fold. He is an apostate, not a heretic, and additionally he has no desire to compromise the orthodox doctrine of the Catholic Church since it is an ideal. It is the weakening and compromise of the Christian ideal, theologically and doctrinally "encrusted" as it may be in the Roman Church, that he wants to avoid. However, when the ideal is imposed and penalties result from individuals wandering from doctrinal strictures, Santayana is opposed to such a domination. Hodges and Lachs draw many meaningful comparisons between Santayana and the later Wittgenstein in relation to their respective attitudes toward religion. Of particular interest is the attitude held in common by the two philosophers that philosophy and reductive rationalization should not interfere with the religious beliefs of people and that the paradigm for the study of religions should be primarily one of description.[105] In effect, Wittgenstein and Santayana would subscribe to a Hippocratic oath in regard to religion (i.e., "To do no harm") both from the standpoint of not challenging religious doctrine and from that of condoning religion's domination of human freedom. The practice and beliefs of religion stand on their own, not upon scientifically or empirically established evidence and with their own rationale as a "passionate commitment" to moral authority. Santayana takes the view that "dogmas are at their best . . . when nobody denies them: for then their falsehood sleeps, like that of an

unconscious metaphor, and their moral function is discharged instinc-
tively."[106] This would assume that their moral function is positive.

As we consider Santayana's admonitions against a compromised
Christianity we soon enough realize that it is more than a semantic issue
for the philosopher: that is, if you're not a traditional Christian in the
fullest sense, then call yourself something else! In my view this is but a
reflection of Santayana's unique concept that the doctrines of traditional
orthodox Christianity (i.e., Catholicism), mythical though they may be,
can be retained in a contemporary way of life (i.e., in a life of reason). He
has repeatedly pointed out a lesson of history: Liberalizing, compromising or reductively rationalizing religious doctrines and dogmas will result in the disempowering of religious symbols, the "paganization" of
orthodoxy and a return to a Catholicism of the Renaissance. Here, Santayana is associating the onset of influence from the translation of Greek
and Roman texts and the resulting "humanistic" dilution of religious
belief. Responding to a diluting influence such as this he warns that

> the modernist view, the view of sympathetic rationalism, revokes the
> whole Jewish tradition on which Christianity is grafted; it takes the
> seriousness out of religion; it sweetens the pang of sin, which becomes
> misfortune; it removes the urgency of salvation; it steals empirical real-
> ity away from the last judgement, from hell, and from heaven; it steals
> historical reality away from the Christ of religious tradition and per-
> sonal devotion. The moral summons and the prophecy about destiny
> which were the soul of the gospel have lost all force for it and become
> fables.[107]

Again we are up against the "double moral grid" of Santayana since,
indeed, such an outcome, short of any respect and love that may exist for
the poetic and moral treasure inherent in traditional doctrine, brings one
precisely to the position of the philosopher himself! The non-practitioner
but lover of religion is essentially a preservationist for the thing he loves.
He believes that traditions and dogma have high value for both the "true
believer," where the saints, tales and teaching of dogma are taken literally, and have true authority as well as for the compromised Christian or
unbeliever who can find meaningful symbolic meaning in them. We are
simply admonished to believe what we will but not to interfere for dam-
age will result. This view is of course foundational to the pluralistic viewpoint we noted above and consistent with Santayana's non-reductive
methodology regarding the practice of religion for "others."

CONSIDERING SOME RADICAL PATHWAYS

I have designated above some important aspects of Santayana's legacy
for contemporary religious thought. On the basis of Santayana's philoso-

phy of religion one can also postulate some possibilities for religious *praxis* which could further open the door to spiritual perspectives and opportunities in the twenty-first century. Here we must be imaginative in considering a few radical examples of an extension of Santayana's philosophical vision of spirituality. The most obvious one of a "lay-religion of disillusion" or Santayana's "Ultimate Religion" is clearly a non-radical alternative for many who are comfortable with a spirituality inherent in a more complete intellectual freedom. John Lachs has more than adequately commented on such an alternative for "those with a sympathy for religious values but uncommitted to doctrinaire views," and I have addressed such an option earlier in this book. I now wish to consider some more radical possibilities in order to prompt consideration of other prospects for spirituality within the framework of Santayana's life of reason.

A Pathway of Return to Orthodoxy: A Rationale for the "Cafeteria Catholic?"

In chapter 4 I discussed Santayana's view that apostasy, meaning in his case, a move away from the Roman Catholic church or from a religion of one's birth to a compromising Christianity (e.g., a sect in Protestantism) may be ill-considered. There is both tension and paradox in Santayana's viewpoint. At the same time that he discourages "apostasy" and heresy and lack of compromise, he encourages facing doubts and reminds us that in finding compromise, we may not remember "the graciousness and naturalness of that ancestral accent which a perfect religion [one we were born to] should have." [108] What I propose here is that in the frame of this tension, Santayana's "theology" can open the door of Christian "orthodoxy" to those spiritual or essentially religious individuals who are on the "borders" of organized religion and who find traditional Christian dogma incredulous. In Santayana's language such individuals would be, to one degree or another, *disillusioned*. Such individuals may have departed the fold of formal religion, and like Santayana, may seek some accordance between their life and their religious beliefs. They would not be, by Santayana's uncompromising definition, Christians in a true sense, having sacrificed authenticity along with the rigor of *praxis*. On the other hand, as indicated above, Santayana's perspective is that an individual's departure from the faith of his or her birth is often an ill-considered and even self-defeating exercise. He suggests that "travelers from one religion to another" lose their "spiritual nationality" and find that later religious attitudes are "vestiges of old beliefs." He provides a cautionary note as follows:

> Even the heretics and atheists, if they have profundity, turn out after a while to be forerunners of some new orthodoxy. What they rebel against is a religion alien to their nature; they are atheists only by accident, and relatively to a convention that which inwardly offends

them, but they yearn mightily in their own souls after the religious acceptance of a world interpreted in their own fashion.[109]

It seems that Santayana provides a "window" here for individual spiritual or religious approaches that can benefit from a linkage with traditional elements of Christian doctrine. This can only be a compromise if one denies that they have left the strictures of belief in an authentic Christianity, as Santayana has rigorously interpreted it. For example, we can, I believe, find an opportunity based upon Santayana's philosophy of religion and theology for a reinvigoration of the "community" of orthodox Christianity based upon a rearticulation of its historic symbolism in the light of modern awareness of the history of religions. Santayana then, as a theologian writing from a "non-theistic" vision, offers some prospect for putting Christian orthodoxy, as Kirby-Smith suggests, on a "firmer foundation." This provides some promise for a model of "orthodoxy" that could be beneficial as a religious outlook that lends itself to inclusion of those of a spiritual or religious inclination who may be considered skeptics in regard to the total corpus of orthodox Christian doctrine. However, we must recall that Santayana has also affirmed that a rational restatement of Christianity, in the sense of a "liberalization," could result in a deterioration of the Faith.[110]

There are then vulnerabilities from both sides (i.e., from both incredulous doctrine and rationalization of the traditional doctrine). Santayana attributed the health of the church ultimately to those who would be "literal" believers. At the same time his concern was not so much for apostasy as for those Catholics who would challenge the broad conservative position of the church in regard to its claims for truth. Heresy, acted out, would be, in Santayana's eyes, more dangerous than apostasy, acted out. Based on this position, if one were to put the church on a "firmer foundation" in regard to doctrine, it would seem that it best be done from a personal standpoint without compelling an overall "liberalization" of orthodox doctrine.

How may one gather from Santayana's cautionary note a way to either remain in, or return to, one's "religion of birth" without intellectual or spiritual compromise? One is reminded that Schleiermacher proposed, "I would have you find religion in the religions," flawed though they may be, since he perceived that universal religious concepts are embodied in particular doctrines and practices.[111] Estrangement from organized religion for many constitutes a potential for alienation from the community at large. Such a consideration is supported by recent scholarship that suggests that rituals, and not shared beliefs, are the common bond in religious communities.[112] There are many individuals of course who are not "true believers," who have never heard of Santayana, but who remain within Catholicism or another Christian denomination, or non-Christian religion for that matter, and draw near to the symbols that are a spiritual source of their tradition. Elaine Pagels reminds us, "Anyone who stands within the Roman Catholic communion . . . knows that it embraces members who differ on topics ranging from doctrine to discipline, and the same applies, of course, to every other Christian denomination."[113] Certainly the concept of *fides implicita* (believing what the church believes) has found weaker adherence in our contemporary world of rational individualism. Is this a manifestation of the dreaded modernism of Santayana?

There is a prevalent and growing practice of some magnitude in Roman Catholicism of what is facetiously called "Cafeteria Catholicism" wherein Catholics who find certain dogma or doctrine personally untenable (e.g., prohibition of women in the priesthood, personal confession, prohibition of remarriage after divorce, prohibition of birth control and Mariology) still participate in the church. Such people might be considered, if they are not blatantly vocal in their views or do not vocally support reform, "closet-heretics." The Roman Catholic Magisterium traditionally (and as Santayana would likely suggest, "correctly") opposes such practices, perceiving a potential for weakening of the faith and consequently the Catholic Church. Santayana's view on the value of orthodox Christian doctrine and dogma implicitly encompasses those symbols and ritual practices found in sacred liturgy (e.g., the Mass or Eucharist). Santayana himself was born into Spanish Roman Catholicism and affectionately clung at least to its *Kultur* all of his life. He chose to retain the symbols, doctrine and dogma of Roman Catholicism as a theological language that expressed his own philosophy of religion. He did not "return" to his native belief as a practitioner and never was a "true believer," but in his apostasy he found contentment and "roots" in the religion of his birth.

There is some tension here considering that my proposal is not an extension of Santayana's personal religious choice. Nevertheless, if one finds spiritual or moral value in religious ritual and symbols, respectfully drawing near to traditional practice, Santayana's philosophical interpretation can be a basis for such behavior. Individual spiritual fulfillment and hence happiness and mental health may be served in rediscovering "the graciousness and naturalness of that ancestral accent that perfect religion should have."[114]

An Eclectic Spirituality and a Paradigm for Spiritual Community

Santayana has self-characterized himself and been characterized by others as solitary and contemplative in nature. As a youth he "loved the Christian epic, and all those doctrines and observances which bring it down into daily life [and] . . . thought how glorious it would have been to be a Dominican friar, preaching that epic eloquently, and solving afresh all the knottiest and sublimist mysteries of theology."[115] When one considers his "formula" for the spiritual life, it is expressed in the language of a Christian religious discipline suggestive of a monastic rule. However, its religious or spiritual object and scope is generic, and the discipline can be applied to a more or less degree. At its extreme the exercise of the spiritual life is devoted to the "rare vocation" of the contemplation of "Pure Being."[116] In *Realms of Being (Realm of the Spirit)* the chapters "Distraction," "Liberation" and "Union" provide what may be considered a spiritual guide—a basis for a "rule" of the spiritual life. Santayana puts forward notions regarding the life of the spirit that are reminiscent of Jesuit or Benedictine tenets and admonitions relating to a sought-after spiritual perfection. The contrast is sharply drawn between the life of the spirit, the reality of worldly distraction and the conflict between world and will. He recognizes that "carnal pleasures . . . which are but welcome pains, draw the spirit inwards into primal darkness and indistinction," whereas "labor is therefore a corrective to distraction."[117] We can recall Santayana's notion that we can only be united with the *good* through non-petitionary prayer, in the sense of "recollecting, digesting [and] purifying our conscience."[118] Saint Benedict's axiom of *ora et labora* is not far-fetched in regard to Santayana's notion of a rich and spiritual life. One can readily extend the notion of an individual spiritual life to one of community, one where the realm of the spirit is foremost. There the notion of a community life based upon the life of the spirit and the intellectual framework of Santayana's life of reason can be merely an extension of that life in the individual. The following is intended only to provide a provocative extension of Santayana's spiritual guidelines in the *The Life of Reason* to a broader application.

There are many models of an idealistic religious community, the most obvious ones related to classical Christian monastic communities such as the Benedictines, Franciscans and Cistercians. A more radical model is that of an ecumenical or Christian pluralistic one: a religious monastic community such as the international community at Taizé, France. Even this latter model is likely too confining in its Christian identity and too focused on ritual in common for an easy association with Santayana's religious philosophy. However, the idea of a Platonic or yoga model of an academy, an intellectual and spiritual enclave, could find a rich resource in Santayana's philosophy of the spirit.

In this regard, a more appropriate, but still highly unique model may be found in literature. A contemporary of Santayana, Herman Hesse (1877–1962), published the fictional work that ultimately won for him the 1946 Nobel Prize in literature, *Magister Ludi or The Glass Bead Game* (originally published in German as *Das Glasperlenspiel*).[119] At the core of Hesse's vision was the individual's spiritual path unrestricted by society. In his novel, Hesse depicts the intellectual and spiritual communal "Order" of Castalia dedicated to "The Glass Bead Game," directed at achieving "a mental synthesis through which the spiritual values of all ages are perceived as simultaneously present and vitally alive."[120] Hesse sought a unified vision seeking a morality and transcending the conventional ideas of good and evil and the idea of the "absolute," while he conceived of the "Game" as dedicated solely to the mind and as a symbol of the human imagination. Prior to publication in 1932, Hesse published an essay, "A Bit of Theology," which outlined an order of spiritual progression or individuation from childhood where there was "a state of unity with all being." This spiritual progression was the model for that depicted in *The Glass Bead Game*. The second stage of individuation was one where the despair and alienation of life are encountered and the individual, although subscribing to society's laws, yearns for satisfying his more inherent natural humanity. Not unlike Santayana's depiction of an individual transcending day-to-day life "as an occasional culmination"[121] in the life of the imagination and the spirit, Hesse's individual at this stage, "by an act of the imagination," also occasionally enjoyed transcendence from daily strife to the life of the spirit. The most elevated stage of Hesse's progression is a stage of awareness, only reached by few, where they are "capable of accepting all being," as in the first more innocent stage as a child. At the foundation of Hesse's idea is a heuristic principle represented in the following quote from *Magister Ludi*:

> The Master had never heard him speak so fervently. He walked on in silence for a little, then said: There is truth, my boy. But the doctrine you desire, absolute, perfect dogma that alone provides wisdom, does not exist. Nor should you long for perfect doctrine, my friend. Rather, you should long for the perfection of yourself. The deity is within you, not in ideas and books. Truth is lived, not taught.[122]

The latter stage of Hesse's spiritual progression would be analogous to Santayana's "rare vocation," a stage wherein one withdrew into a life dedicated to contemplation. There are a number of character relationships in Hesse's novel that bring to mind the spiritual aspect of Santayana's philosophy. Of particular interest is that between Joseph Knecht, the principle character, and Plinio Designori where Knecht symbolizes the position of aestheticism and the life of the mind and Designori that of the normality of the day-to-day world. Knecht reflects upon the dangers of excessive aestheticism and intellectual responsibility. The perspective reflected by Hesse's protagonists that the modern world and its conception of progress is on a destructive path recalls Santayana's own view in part arising from the same historical events (e.g., World War I) that influence Hesse. It is in the framework of such a tension that Santayana perceives the reciprocating passage of a human life in accommodation to the practical world on one hand, and on the other, the escape and salvation available in the life of the spirit.

Much more could be said about analogous concepts in Santayana and Hesse (e.g., their mutual attraction to Eastern philosophy and religion, and the potential value of Santayana's spiritual discipline to a radical model of contemplative community life), but space is not available here. My argument is that a broad road of spirituality is opened through Santayana's vision that is congenial to both the religiously *disillusioned* seeking an independent spiritual life, and those who would find spiritual solace by drawing closer to the symbols and discipline of organized religion. It is, then, in the most inclusive vein that Santayana's wisdom guides us toward a harmonious naturalism seeking to worship only the *Good*. As the philosopher posits early in *The Realms of Being*,

> There is no reason why man, or the transitory world in which he finds himself living, should have any prerogative amongst the realms of being. Traditional religion for all its motherly coddling of human conceit, is not without a door to the infinite. Theology must somehow reconcile the special mercies and graces coming to men from God, with the immutability and eternity attributed to him.[123]

SOME CONCLUSIONS

I have tried to choose illustrations in this chapter of the potential scope for theological and philosophical development in the spiritual perspective of Santayana. A depiction of the potential for inspiration and exploration of his project in relation to religion, spiritual life, and religious studies in general is beyond us here, but there are a myriad of opportunities to mine his insights. Religious studies was founded on the basis of the Cartesian and Kantian ideal for precision and certitude and potential access to the absolute. The concept of certainty in philosophical striving has since been subjugated to the reality of the subjective perspective, the unreliability of the rational process and the inherent epistemological limitations of an epiphenomenal human Spirit. In the contemporary milieu of religious tensions and polarizations and the loss of confidence in structured tenets of orthodox religions, the striving toward what Schleiermacher termed "passing beyond the self" seeks new avenues toward fulfillment. It would seem that Santayana's rich philosophy of religion can reveal new pathways in and among the ancient store of the symbols of the great religions and beyond.

NOTES

1. Kenneth J. Gergen, "Social Constructionism and Practical Theology," in *Social Constructionism and Theology*, ed. C. A. M. Hermans, G. Immink, A. de Jong, and J. van der Lans (Leiden: Brill, 2002), 4.

2. For example, Santayana's omission from two relatively recent published major anthologies: Brian Davies, *Philosophy of Religion: A Guide and Anthology* (Oxford: Ox-

ford University Press, 2000); and Walter H. Capps, *Religious Studies: The Making of a Discipline* (Minneapolis, MN: Fortress Press, 1995).

3. Henry Samuel Levinson, "Santayana's Contribution to American Religious Philosophy," *Journal of the American Academy of Religion* 52 (March 1984): 48. I am much indebted to Levinson for pointing out Santayana's contributions over a broad spectrum of philosophy of religion. I can only expand upon and supplement his insightful analysis in selected areas.

4. John Lachs, *The Relevance of Philosophy to Life* (Nashville, TN: Vanderbilt University Press, 1995, 50).

5. David A. Dilworth, "The Place of Santayana in Modern Philosophy," *Overheard in Seville* 15 (Fall 1997): 2.

6. Michael P. Hodges and John Lachs, *Thinking in the Ruins: Wittgenstein and Santayana on Contingency* (Nashville, TN: Vanderbilt University Press, 2000), 88.

7. Henry Samuel Levinson, *Santayana, Pragmatism and the Spiritual Life* (Chapel Hill: University of North Carolina Press, 1992), 285–88.

8. Ibid., 285–86.

9. Ibid., 287. Levinson's characterization of Santayana's fall into disfavor is thorough and as insightful as his argument for including Santayana within the school of American Pragmatism, specifically as a Pragmatist "without scientific method" (see the epilogue, 285–303).

10. Dilworth, "The Place of Santayana," 4.

11. Levinson, *Santayana, Pragmatism and the Spiritual Life*, 292. Levinson suggests that on one hand Santayana was too religious for most naturalists and, on the other, too pragmatic and naturalistic for prominent religious thinkers of the period. I would suggest that it was more Santayana's Roman Catholic "religiosity" and his spirituality that grated on the Pragmatists, one and all products of liberal Protestantism, and in fact, his "atheism" and translation of all religious doctrine to poetry was a step too far for even the naturalists (e.g., William James's negative response to *Interpretations of Poetry and Religion*).

12. Ibid.

13. The Santayana Society, through its meetings and international conferences and its journal *Overheard in Seville* and the publication of the critical edition of Santayana's works has done much to encourage Santayana scholarship and provide a fertile field for a restatement of Santayana's value in contemporary thought.

14. John Ryder, "The Use and Abuse of Modernity: Postmodernism and the American Philosophic Tradition," *Journal of Speculative Philosophy* 7 no. 2 (1993): 92–102. Ryder proposes that Santayana, along with Peirce, James, Dewey and Royce, has a "postmodernist sensibility." For a response and critique of Ryder's position see John J. Stuhr, "Postmodernism: Old and New," *Journal of Speculative Philosophy* 7 no. 2 (1993): 103–9. For additional perspectives on pragmatism and postmodern thought I have earlier cited Robert Corrington, Carl Hausman, and M. Thomas Seebohm, eds. *Pragmatism Considers Phenomenology* (Washington, DC: University Press of America, 1987).

15. John Lachs, *Mind and Philosophers* (Nashville, TN: Vanderbilt University Press, 1987), 16–34.

16. Angus Kerr-Lawson, "Two Philosophical Psychologists," *Overheard in Seville* 21 (Fall 2003): 31–42.

17. Lachs, *George Santayana*, 124–47.

18. Levinson, "Santayana's Contribution," 66.

19. H. T. Kirby-Smith, "Santayana's God," *Overheard in Seville* 20 (Fall 2002): 13.

20. Ibid., 14.

21. In chapters 2 and 4 I discussed the succinct "metaphysical" basis for Santayana's non-theism as lying in his concept of the human unattainability of the knowledge of truth, the infinite possibilities for actualization in the Realm of Essence and that no "necessary" truths (e.g., God) exist in his category of the Realm of Truth. As a result of this position, Santayana has disclaimed the validity of basing the existence of God

upon any metaphysical disclosure. At the same time the lack of certainty of God *not* existing leaves the door open for religious faith. Santayana only chooses to adhere logically to *faith in his own belief.*

22. Santayana, *Realms of Being*, xxxii.

23. Review of Michel Despland, *La Religion En Occident: Évolution Des Idées Et Du Vécu* (Montreal: Fides, 1988) from Steven Engler, "Michel Despland: Philosophy of Religion in History," *Religious Studies Review* 29, no. 4 (October 2003): 343–50.

24. Santayana, *A General Confession*, Schilpp, 7.

25. Richard W. Comstock, "Two Ontologies of Power: A Comparison of Santayana and Tillich," *Harvard Theological Review* 60 (1967): 41.

26. Santayana, *The Life of Reason*, 284.

27. Lachs, *The Relevance of Philosophy*, 8.

28. Ibid., 56.

29. Santayana, *Realms of Being*, 795.

30. Rudolph Otto, *The Idea of the Holy* (*Das Heilige*), trans. John W. Harvey (New York: Oxford University Press, 1958), xviii–xix.

31. Ibid., 8.

32. Kirby-Smith, "Santayana's God," 13–66.

33. Levinson, "Santayana's Contribution," 65. Levinson depicts Santayana's relative optimism in regard to the spiritual maturity of his contemporary philosophers of religion while "they continued to pit belief against belief, to defend or attack 'the coherence of theism.'"

34. Ibid., 100.

35. Ryder, "Use and Abuse of Modernity," 96–97. Ryder draws helpful comparisons between the American philosophic tradition, particularly pragmatism and postmodern thought, and the genealogy of postmodernism.

36. Ibid., 101.

37. Ibid., 94.

38. Santayana, *Realms of Being*, 845.

39. John Stuhr, *Geneological Pragmatism: Philosophy, Experience and Community* (Albany: State University of New York Press, 1997), 103.

40. See Comstock, "Two Ontologies of Power," 39.

41. Clifford Geertz, *The Interpretation of Cultures* (New York: Basic Books, 1973), 5.

42. The theory of social constructionism in relation to religion seems to have been first formally and extensively explored in Peter J. Berger, *The Sacred Canopy: Elements of a Sociological Theory of Religion* (Garden City, NY: Doubleday, 1967).

43. Levinson, "Santayana's Contribution," fn 48.

44. Sources for the six assumptions of constructionist thought, which I condensed in some cases and added to in others are Kenneth J. Gergen, *Social Construction in Context* (London: Sage Publications, 2001), 7–24; Kenneth J. Gergen, *Invitation to Social Construction* (London: Sage Publications, 1999), 46–50; "Theologians of a Kind: Kenneth Gergen," *Science and Theology News: Online Edition* (December 2001), www.stnews.org/Commentary-1984.htm; and Duane Bidwell, "Realizing the Sacred: Spiritual Direction and Social Constructionism," *Journal of Pastoral Theology* 14, no. 1 (Spring 2004): 62–63. A helpful general resource was C. A. M. Hermans, G. Immink, A. de Jong, and J. van der Lans, eds., *Social Constructionism and Theology* (Leiden: Brill, 2002).

45. I cannot affirm Levinson's own reasons for claiming Santayana's role in constructionist theology due to his very brief statement on the subject in his aforementioned essay "Santayana's Contribution to American Religious Philosophy."

46. Santayana, *Interpretations*, v.

47. Ibid.

48. Ibid., viii.

49. Ibid., vii.

50. Ibid., 88.

51. Ibid., 110–11.

52. Ibid., 74.

53. Mark I. Wallace indicates that "Wittgenstein is the progenitor of the constructivist opinion that inherited frames of reference constitute what a culturally situated subject understands to be the nature of things." See Mark I. Wallace, "Losing the Self, Finding the Self," in *Social Constructionism and Theology*, ed. C. A. M. Hermans et. al., 99–100. This view is in close accord with Santayana's attribution of importance to tradition and the religion of one's birth.

54. Hodges and Lachs, *Thinking in the Ruins*, 83.

55. Wallace, "Losing the Self, Finding the Self," 98–99.

56. Santayana, *The Idea of Christ in the Gospels*, 171.

57. Ibid., 171–72.

58. Ibid., 250.

59. Santayana, *Realms of Being*, 845.

60. See chapter 4.

61. Santayana, *The Idea of Christ in the Gospels*, 241.

62. John Robert Baker, "The Christology of George Santayana," *Southern Journal of Philosophy* 10, no. 2 (Summer 1972): 263–75.

63. *Perichoresis* is a term designating the dynamics and character of the three divine persons of the Trinity. From Catherine Mowry LaCugna, *God for Us* (San Francisco: Harper San Francisco, 1973), 270.

64. Santayana, *Realms of Being*, 848–49.

65. Santayana, *Realms of Being*, 846.

66. Ibid., 846–47.

67. Ibid., 847–48.

68. Clifford A. Brown, *Jung's Hermeneutic of Doctrine* (Chico, CA: Scholar's Press, 1981), 117–19.

69. Ibid., 158.

70. Wallace observes that postmodern constructionist theology is "emancipatory" (See Wallace, "Losing the Self, Find the Self," 100). The definition of "emancipation" as freeing from restraint and facilitating individual spiritual freedom and harmony is at the foundation of Santayana's constructionism.

71. Timothy Sprigge, "Whitehead and Santayana," *Process Studies* 28 (1–2): 50.

72. Robert C. Whittemore, "Santayana's Neglect of Hartshorne's Alternative," *Overheard in Seville* 4 (Fall 1986): 1–6. Hartshorne's first critique of Santayana's theory was "Santayana's Doctrine of Essence," in *The Philosophy of George Santayana*, Schilpp, 135–82; followed much later by "Santayana's Defiant Eclecticism," in *Animal Faith and Spiritual Life*, Lachs, 33–43. Santayana's direct response to the first critique is "Apologia Pro Mente Sua," Schilpp, 588–93.

73. Whittemore, 3.

74. Ibid., 3–4.

75. My sources for the theory of process theology are John B. Cobb, Jr., and David Ray Griffin, *Process Theology: An Introductory Exposition* (Philadelphia: Westminster Press, 1976); Robert Kane and Stephen H. Phillips, eds. *Hartshorne: Process Philosophy and Theology* (New York: State University of New York Press, 1989); and Alfred North Whitehead, *Process and Reality* (New York: Free Press, 1978).

76. Santayana, "Apologia Pro Mente Sua," Schilpp, 590.

77. Santayana, *Winds of Doctrine*, 7.

78. Sally McFague, *The Body of God: An Ecological Theology* (Minneapolis, MN: Fortress Press, 1993), ix.

79. Santayana, *Realms of Being*, 566.

80. Antonio Damasio MD, *Looking for Spinoza: Joy, Sorrow and the Feeling Brain* (Orlando, FL : Harcourt, 2003); and Antonio Damasio MD, *Descartes' Error: Emotion, Reason and the Human Brain* (New York: Grosset/Putnam, 1994), passim.

81. Santayana, *Realms of Being*, 550.

82. Ibid., 570–71. Santayana distinguishes between the terms "psyche" and "soul:" "The same thing that looked at from the outside or biologically is called psyche, looked at morally from within is called soul."

83. Angus Kerr-Lawson, "Two Philosophical Psychologists," *Overheard in Seville* 21 (Fall 2003): 31–42. Kerr-Lawson quotes from Damasio, *Looking for Spinoza*, and Daniel Wegner, *The Illusion of Conscious Will* (Cambridge, MA: MIT Press, 2002). I am indebted to Kerr-Lawson's perspective on the subject of Santayana's epiphenomenalism in relation to contemporary neuroscience.

84. Ibid., 33.

85. Gavin D'Costa, *The Meeting of Religions and the Trinity* (New York: Orbis Books, 2000), 1.

86. Knitter, in discussing the idea of interfaith dialogue, differentiates between exclusivism, inclusivism and pluralism, each category inclusive of varying degrees. See Paul Knitter, *Introducing the Theology of Religions* (New York: Orbis, 2002), passim.

87. Herman J. Saatkamp, Herman, Jr., "Hermes the Interpreter," *Overheard in Seville* 3 (Fall 1985): 22–28. Quotation from Santayana, *Persons and Places*, 169–70.

88. The contemporary issue of Christian views on homosexuality is one where Morris Grossman suggests, and I concur, that "Santayana would have been sensitive to Christian strictures against homosexuality." Morris Grossman, review of *The Last Puritan* by George Santayana, ed. Herman J. Saatkamp and William G. Holzberger. *Transactions of the C. S. Peirce Society* 31, no. 2 (Spring 1995): 437–44.

89. Santayana, *Dominations and Powers*, 160.

90. Ibid., 163.

91. Ibid., 166.

92. Ninian Smart, *World Philosophies* (London: Routledge, 2001), 371–72.

93. John J. Stuhr, *Genealogical Pragmatism* (New York: State University of New York Press, 1997), 76. From William James, "On a Certain Blindness in Human Beings," *Talks to Teachers on Psychology: and to Students on Some of Life's Ideals* (New York: Henry Holt, 1928 [1902]). 269.

94. Santayana, *Realms of Being*, xv.

95. Ibid., 843.

96. Santayana, *Christ in The Gospels*, 3–19.

97. Santayana, "Ultimate Religion," 294.

98. Ninian Smart, *World Philosophies*, 371.

99. Ibid., 372.

100. Santayana, *Winds of Doctrine*, 34.

101. Ibid., 54.

102. Ibid., 46.

103. Ibid., 51.

104. Gary Wills, *What Jesus Meant* (New York: Viking, 2006).

105. Hodges and Lachs, *Thinking in the Ruins*, 73. Lachs writes that "Religious languages and practices constitute a form life takes, and 'one can only describe and say: this is what human life is like.'" From Ludwig Wittgenstein, "Remarks on Frazier's Golden Bough," in *Philosophical Occasions*, ed. James C. Klagge and Alfred Nordman (Indianapolis: Hacket Publishing, 1993), 121.

106. Santayana, *The Life of Reason*, 214.

107. Santayana, *Winds of Doctrine*, 50.

108. Santayana, *The Life of Reason*, 213.

109. Santayana, *The Life of Reason*, 179.

110. George Santayana, *Winds of Doctrine*, one-volume edition of *Winds of Doctrine and Platonism and the Spiritual Life* (Gloucester, MA: Peter Smith, 1971).

111. Merold Westphal, "The Emergence of Modern Philosophy of Religion," *A Companion to the Philosophy of Religion*, ed. Phillip L. Quinn and Charles Teliaferro (Malden, MA: Blackwell, 1999), 114–15. There are interesting parallels between Santayana and Schleiermacher: for example, Schleiermacher's enthusiasm for Spinoza, whom he deemed "full of the Holy Spirit," and the formulation of Schleiermacher's *proprium*, the individual's inward differentiation expressing his finite place in the finite whole to arrive at his identity relative to the same goal arrived at through Santayana's "life of reason."

112. Joan Chittister, OSB, "Why Go to Church If You Don't Do What the Pope Says?" www.nationalcatholicreporter.org/fwis,pc102103.htm. Sister Chittister draws in part upon the work of Daniel Lee—for example, *Old Order Mennonites: Ritual, Belief and Community* (Chicago: Burnham, 2000).

113. Elaine Pagels, *Beyond Belief: The Secret Gospel of Thomas* (New York: Vintage Books, 2004), 182.

114. Santayana, *The Life of Reason*, 180.

115. Santayana, "A General Confession," Schilpp, 7.

116. Santayana, *Realms of Being*, 65.

117. Santayana, *Realms of Being*, 704, 706.

118. Ibid., 797, 799.

119. Hermann Hesse, *Magister* Ludi *or The Glass Bead Game*, trans. Richard and Clara Winston (New York: Holt, Rinehart and Winston, 1969).

120. Ibid., ix.

121. Santayana, *Realms of Being*, 737.

122. Hesse, *Magister Ludi*, 83.

123. Santayana, *Realms of Being*, 60.

Selected Bibliography

PRIMARY SOURCES

Santayana, George. *Animal Faith and Spiritual Life*. Edited by John Lachs. New York: Appleton-Century-Crofts, 1967.

————. "Apologia Pro Mente Sua." In Schilpp, *The Philosophy of George Santayana*, 495–605.

————. "Bishop Berkeley." In Lachs, *Animal Faith and Spiritual Life*, 102–14.

————. "A Brief History of My Opinions." *Contemporary American Philosophy* II. Edited by George P. Adams and William Montague. New York: Macmillan, 1930, 239–57.

————. *Character and Opinion in the United States*. New York: Scribner, 1921.

————. "Comparison of Other Views of the Spirit." In Lachs, *Animal Faith and Spiritual Life*, 279–88.

————. *Dominations and Powers: Reflections on Liberty, Society and Government*. Clifton, NJ: Augustus M. Kelley, 1972.

————. *Egotism in German Philosophy*. New York: Scribner, 1915.

————. "A General Confession." In Schilpp, *The Philosophy of George Santayana*, 1–30.

————. *The Genteel Tradition at Bay*. New York: Scribner, 1931.

————. "German Freedom." *New Republic* 28 (August 1915): 94–96.

————. *The Idea of Christ in the Gospels: Or, God in Man, a Critical Essay*. New York: Scribner, 1946.

————. *Interpretations of Poetry and Religion*. London: Adam and Charles Black, 1900.

————. *The Last Puritan: A Memoir in the Form of a Novel*. New York: Scribner, 1940.

————. *Lectures, Essays and Reviews*. Edited by Justus Buchler and Benjamin Schwartz. London: Constable, 1936.

————. Letter to Arthur M. Cohen, February 9, 1948. *Partisan Review* 25 (1958): 632–37.

————. *The Life of Reason: Or, the Phases of Human Progress*. New York: Scribner, 1953.

————. *Persons and Places: Fragments of Autobiography*. Edited by W. G. Holzberger and H. J. Saatkamp, Jr. Cambridge, MA: MIT Press, 1986.

————. *Platonism and the Spiritual Life*. New York: Scribner, 1927.

————. "The Present Position of the Roman Catholic Church." *New World* 1 (1892): 658–73.

————. "Proust on Essences." *Obiter Scripta*. Edited by Justus Buchler and Benjamin Schwartz. New York: Scribner, 1936, 273–79.

————. *Realms of Being*. New York: Cooper Square Publishers, 1972.

————. *The Sense of Beauty: Being the Outline of Aesthetic Theory*. New York: Scribner, 1936.

————. *Scepticism and Animal Faith*. New York: Dover Publications, 1955.

————. *Soliloquies in England and Later Soliloquies*. Ann Arbor: University of Michigan Press, 1967.

————. *Three Philosophical Poets: Lucretius, Dante and Goethe*. Cambridge, MA: Harvard University Press, 1910.

————. "Ultimate Religion." *Obiter Scripta*. Edited by Justus Buchler and Benjamin Schwartz. New York: Scribner, 1936, 280–97.

————. "Why Does Spirit Aim at Its Own Purity?" In Lachs, *Animal Faith and Spiritual Life*, 291–96.

————. *Winds of Doctrine: Studies in Contemporary Opinion*. New York: Scribner, 1913.

———. *Winds of Doctrine and Platonism and the Spiritual Life.* One volume. Gloucester, MA: Peter Smith, 1971.

SECONDARY SOURCES

Alexander, Thomas M. "Santayana's Unbearable Lightness of Being: Aesthetics as a Prelude to Ontology." *Overheard in Seville* 11 (Fall 1993): 1–10.
———. "Beauty and the Labyrinth of Evil: Santayana and the Possibility of Naturalistic Mysticism." *Overheard in Seville* 18 (Fall 2000): 1–16.
Allen, Benjamin Wesley Patterson. "Epiphenomenalism in the Moral Philosophy of George Santayana." PhD diss., Drew University, 1953.
Ames, Van Meter. *Proust and Santayana: The Aesthetic Way of Life.* New York: Russell & Russell, 1964.
Anton, John P. "Santayana and Greek Philosophy." *Overheard in Seville* 11 (Fall 1993): 15–29.
Baker, John Robert. "The Christology of George Santayana." *Southern Journal of Philosophy* 10, no. 2 (Summer 1972): 263–75.
Barosky, Paul. *Walter Pater's Renaissance.* University Park: Pennsylvania State University Press, 1987.
Bell, David. *Husserl.* London: Routledge, 1990.
Bidwell, Duane. "Realizing the Sacred: Spiritual Direction and Social Constructionism." *Journal of Pastoral Theology* 14, no. 1 (Spring 2004): 62–63.
Brown, Clifford A. *Jung's Hermeneutic of Doctrine.* Chico, CA: Scholar's Press, 1981.
Bryant, David J. "The Poetics of Belief: Studies in Coleridge, Arnold, Pater, Santayana, Stevens." *Princeton Seminary Review* 1, no. 9 (1988): 75–77.
Buchler, Justus. "One Santayana or Two?" *Journal of Philosophy* 51 (January 1954): 52–56.
Butler, Richard. *The Life and World of George Santayana.* Chicago: H. Regnery, 1960.
———. *The Mind of Santayana.* Chicago: H. Regnery, 1955.
Campbell, Harry M. "Religion as Illusion in the Thought of Santayana." *Thomist* 4, no. 34 (October 1970)
Capps, Walter H. *Religious Studies: The Making of a Discipline.* Minneapolis, MN: Fortress Press, 1995.
Chandler, Daniel. *Semiotics: The Basics.* London: Routledge, 2002.
Chittister, Joan, OSB. "Why Go to Church If You Don't Do What the Pope Says?" www.nationalcatholicreporter.org/fwis,pc102103.htm.
Cobb, John B., Jr., and David Ray Griffin. *Process Theology: An Introductory Exposition.* Philadelphia: Westminster Press, 1976.
Comstock, Richard W. "Two Ontologies of Power: A Comparison of Santayana and Tillich." *Harvard Theological Review* 60 (1967): 39–67.
Conner, Frederick W. "To Dream with One Eye Open." *Soundings* 74 (Summer 1991): 159–78.
Copleston, Frederick, SJ. *A History of Philosophy.* Vol. I, "Greece and Rome." New York: Doubleday, 1993.
———. *A History of Philosophy.* Vol. VII, "Modern Philosophy." New York: Doubleday, 1993.
Corrington, Robert. *An Introduction to C. S. Peirce.* Lanham, MD: Rowman & Littlefield, 1993.
Corrington, Robert, Carl Hausman, and M. Thomas Seebohm, eds. *Pragmatism Considers Phenomenology.* Washington, DC: University Press of America, 1987.
Cory, Daniel, ed. *The Birth of Reason and Other Essays by George Santayana.* New York: Columbia University Press, 1968.
———, ed. *The Letters of George Santayana.* New York: Scribner, 1955.

————, ed. *Santayana: The Later Years, A Portrait with Letters.* New York: G. Braziller, 1963.

Damasio, Antonio. *Looking for Spinoza: Joy, Sorrow and the Feeling Brain.* Orlando, FL: Harcourt, 2003.

————. *Descartes' Error: Emotion, Reason and the Human Brain.* New York: Grosset/ Putnam, 1994.

Da Silva, Antonio Barbarosa. *The Phenomenology of Religion as a Philosophical Problem.* Sweden: CWK Gleerup, 1982.

Davidoff, Robert. *The Genteel Tradition and the Sacred Rage: High Culture vs. Democracy in Adams, James and Santayana.* Chapel Hill: University of North Carolina Press, 1992.

Davies, Brian. *Philosophy of Religion: A Guide and Anthology.* Oxford: Oxford University Press, 2000.

D'Costa, Gavin. *The Meeting of Religions and the Trinity.* New York: Orbis Books, 2000.

Dennes, William Ray. "Santayana's Materialism." In Schilpp, *The Philosophy of George Santayana,* 419–43.

Dilworth, David A. "The Place of Santayana in Modern Philosophy." *Overheard in Seville* 15 (Fall 1997): 1–10.

Eastman, Maxwell. "Philosopher in a Convent." *American Mercury* 75, no. 35 (November 1951): 35–40.

Edie, James M. *William James and Phenomenology.* Bloomington: Indiana University Press, 1987.

Edman, Irwin, ed. *The Philosophy of George Santayana.* New York: Scribner, 1953.

Edwards, James C. "Contingency, Philosophy and Superstition." *Overheard in Seville* 13 (Fall 1995): 8–11.

Ellwood, Robert. "Is Mythology Obsolete?" *Journal of the Academy of Religion* 69, no. 3 (September 2001): 673–86.

Engler, Steven. "Michel Despland: Philosophy of Religion in History." Review of *La Religion En Occident: Évolution Des Idées Et Du Vécu,* by Michel Despland. Montreal: Fides, 1988. *Religious Studies Review* 29, no. 4 (October 2003): 343–50.

Faurot, J. H. "Santayana's Philosophy of Religion." *Hibbert Journal* 58 (1960): 258–67.

Feshbach, Sidney. "An Orchestration of the Arts in Wallace Stevens' 'Peter Quince at the Clavier.'" *Analecta Husserliana* 63 (2000): 183–94.

Fisch, Max Harold. *Classic American Philosophers: Peirce, James, Royce, Santayana, Dewey, Whitehead.* New York: Appleton-Century-Crofts, 1951.

Fisher, John J. "Santayana on James: A Conflict of Views on Philosophy." *American Philosophical Quarterly* 2, no. 1 (January 1965): 69–70.

Flamm, Matthew Caleb. "Santayana and Schopenhauer." *Transactions of the Charles S. Peirce Society* 38, no. 3 (Summer 2002): 413–31.

Friess, Horace L., and Henry M. Rosenthal. "Reason and Religion and the Emancipated Spirit: A Dialogue," In Schilpp, *The Philosophy of George Santayana,* 353–76.

Gaskin, John C. A. *Hume's Philosophy of Religion.* London: Barnes & Noble.

Geertz, Clifford. *The Interpretation of Cultures.* New York: Basic Books, 1973.

Gergen, Kenneth J. *Invitation to Social Construction.* London: Sage Publications, 1999.

————. *Social Construction in Context.* London: Sage Publications, 2001.

————. "Theologians of a Kind: Kenneth Gergen." Interview. *Science and Theology News: Online Edition* (December 2001), www.stnews.org/Commentary-1984.htm.

Gobar, Ash. "The Phenomenology of William James." *Proceedings of the American Philosophical Society* 114, no. 4 (August 1970): 294–308.

Gouinlock, James. "Ultimate Religion." *Overheard in Seville* 16 (Fall 1998): 1–12.

Grossman, Morris. "Interpreting *Interpretations.*" *Bulletin of the Santayana Society* 8 (Fall 1990):18–28.

Hammond, Michael, Jane Howarth, and Russell Keat. *Understanding Phenomenology.* Oxford: Basil Blackwell, 1991.

Harap, Louis. "A Note on Moralities in the Philosophy of Santayana." In Lachs, *Animal Faith and Spiritual Life,* 359–65.

Harrison, Charles T. "Santayana's 'Literary Psychology.'" *Sewanee Review* 61 (1953): 213.

Hartshorne, Charles. "Santayana's Defiant Eclecticism." In Lachs, *Animal Faith and Spiritual Life*, 33–43.

———. "Santayana's Doctrine of Essence." In Schilpp, *The Philosophy of George Santayana*, 135–82.

Hartshorne, Charles, and Paul Weiss, eds. *The Collected Papers of Charles Sanders Peirce*, vol. 1. Cambridge, MA: Harvard University Press, 1931.

Hermans, C. A. M., G. Immink, A. de Jong, and J. van der Lans, eds. *Social Constructionism and Theology*. Leiden: Brill, 2002.

Hesse, Hermann. *Magister Ludi or The Glass Bead Game*. Translated by Richard and Clara Winston. New York: Bantam Books, 1972.

Hodges, Michael P., and John Lachs. *Thinking in the Ruins: Wittgenstein and Santayana on Contingency*. Nashville, TN: Vanderbilt University Press, 2000.

Holzberger, William G., ed. *The Complete Poems of George Santayana*. Cranbury, NJ: Associated University Presses, Inc., 1979.

Houser, Nathan, and Christian Kloesel, eds. *The Essential Peirce: Selected Philosophical Writings*. Vol. 1 (1867–1893). Bloomington: Indiana University Press, 1992.

———, eds. *The Essential Peirce: Selected Philosophical Writings*. Vol. 2 (1893–1913). Bloomington: Indiana University Press, 1998.

Howgate, George W. *George Santayana*. New York: Russell & Russell, 1938.

Husserl, Edmund. *Cartesian Meditations: An Introduction to Phenomenology*. Translated by Dorion Cairns. The Hague: Nijhoff, 1960.

———. *Ideas Pertaining to a Pure Phenomenology and to a Phenomenological Philosophy*. Translated by F. Kersten. The Hague: Nijhoff, 1982.

Kane, Robert, and Stephen H. Phillips, eds. *Hartshorne: Process Philosophy and Theology*. New York: State University of New York Press, 1989.

Kelly, Eugene. "Pragmatism and Platonism in Santayana's Philosophy of Religion." *Religion and Philosophy in the United States of America* 2. Essen: Verlag Die Blau Eule, 1987, 427–46.

Kerr-Lawson, Angus. "Pragmatism and Santayana's Realms." *Overheard in Seville* 12 (Fall 1994): 17–21.

———. "Santayana's Epiphenominalism." *Transactions of the Charles S. Peirce Society* 21 (Spring 1985): 200–221.

———. "Two Philosophical Psychologists." *Overheard in Seville* 21 (Fall 2003): 31–42.

Kirby-Smith, H. T. *A Philosophical Novelist: George Santayana and the Last Puritan*. Carbondale: Southern Illinois University Press, 1997.

———. "Santayana's God." *Overheard in Seville* 20 (Fall 2002): 8–14.

Kirkwood, Mossie May Waddington. *Santayana: Saint of the Imagination*. Toronto: University of Toronto Press, 1961.

Knitter, Paul. *Introducing the Theology of Religions*. New York: Orbis Books, 2002.

Kronegger, Marlies E. "A. T. Tymieniecka's Challenges: From a Spiritual Wasteland to Transcendence." *Analecta Husserliana* 43 (1994): 84.

Lachs, John, ed. *Animal Faith and Spiritual Life: Writings by George Santayana with Critical Essays on His Thought*. New York: Appleton-Century-Crofts, 1967.

———. *George Santayana*. Boston: Twayne, 1988.

———. "Matter and Substance in the Philosophy of George Santayana." *Modern Schoolman* 44 (1966): 1–12.

———. *Mind and Philosophers*. Nashville, TN: Vanderbilt University Press, 1987.

———. *The Relevance of Philosophy to Life*. Nashville, TN: Vanderbilt University Press, 1995.

LaCugna, Catherine Mowry. *God for Us*. San Francisco: Harper's, 1973.

Lamprecht, Sterling P. "Santayana Then and Now." In Lachs, *Animal Faith and Spiritual Life*, 305–25.

Lane, James W. "The Dichotomy of George Santayana." *Catholic World* 140 (October 1934): 20–28.

Lears, T. J. Jackson. *No Place of Grace*. Chicago: University of Chicago Press, 1982.

Levey, Michael. *The Case of Walter Pater*. Plymouth, UK: Thames and Hudson, 1978.

Levinson, Henry Samuel. "Charity, Interpretation, Disintoxication: A Comment on Gouinlock's 'Ultimate Religion.'" *Overheard in Seville* 16 (Fall 1998):13–18.

———. "Meditation at the Margins, Santayana's Skepticism and Animal Faith." *Journal of Religion* 67 (July 1987): 289–303.

———. "Pragmatic Naturalism and the Spiritual Life." *Raritan* 10 (Fall 1990): 70–86.

———. "Religious Criticism." *Journal of Religion* 64 (January 1984): 36–53.

———. *Santayana, Pragmatism and the Spiritual Life*. Chapel Hill: University of North Carolina Press, 1992.

———. "Santayana's Contribution to American Religious Philosophy." *Journal of the American Academy of Religion* 52 (March 1984): 48.

———. "What Good is Irony?" *Bulletin of the Santayana Society* 8 (Fall 1990): 29–34.

Logan, Beryl. *A Religion without Talking: Religious Belief and Natural Belief in Hume's Philosophy of Religion*. New York: Peter Lang, 1993.

Lucretius. *The Nature of Things*. Book III. Translated by Frank O. Copley. New York: Norton & Company, 1977.

Moreno, Daniel. "The Pathetic Fallacy in Santayana." *Overheard in Seville* 16 (Fall 2004): 16.

Martin, Robert K. *The Homosexual Tradition in American Poetry*. Iowa City: University of Iowa Press, 1998.

McCormick, John. *George Santayana: A Biography*. New York: Knopf, 1987.

McFague, Sally. *The Body of God: An Ecological Theology*. Minneapolis, MN: Fortress, 1993.

Meyers, Jeffrey. *Edmund Wilson: A Biography*. New York: Houghton Mifflin, 1995.

Moran, Dermot. *Introduction to Phenomenology*. London: Routledge, 2000.

Munitz, Milton K. "Ideals and Essences in Santayana's Philosophy." In Schilpp, *The Philosophy of George Santayana*, 185–215.

Munson, Thomas N., SJ. *The Essential Wisdom of George Santayana*. New York: Columbia University Press, 1962.

Murphy, Richard T. *Hume and Husserl: Towards Radical Subjectivism*. The Hague: Nijhoff, 1980.

Otto, Rudolf. *The Idea of the Holy (Das Heilige)*. Translated by John W. Harvey. New York: Oxford University Press, 1958.

Pagels, Elaine. *Beyond Belief: The Secret Gospel of Thomas*. New York: Vintage Books, 2004.

Passmore, John. *A Hundred Years of Philosophy*. New York: Basic Books, 1966.

Pedarske, Daniel T. "Santayana on Laughter and Prayer." *American Journal of Theology and Philosophy* 11, no. 2 (May 1990): 143–52.

Peirce, C. S. "A Guess at the Riddle." In Houser and Kloesel, *The Essential Peirce*, 1:245–79.

Pelikan, Jaroslav. *Jesus through the Centuries*. New York: Harper & Row, 1987.

Perry, Marvin. *An Intellectual History of Modern Europe*. Boston: Houghton Mifflin, 1992.

Reynolds, Thomas. "Considering Schleiermacher and the Problem of Religious Diversity: Toward a Dialectical Pluralism." *Journal of the American Academy of Religion* 73, no. 1 (March 2005): 156.

Rosensohn, William L. "The Phenomenology of Charles Sanders Peirce: From the Doctrine of Categories to Phaneroscopy." *Philosophical Currents*. Edited by David H. DeGrood. Amsterdam: B. R. Grünner B.V. 10, 1974.

Rowse, A. L. "Santayana: A Prophet of Our Time." *Contemporary Review* 260 (June 1992): 320–23.

Rudd, Margaret Thomas. *The Lone Heretic*. Austin: University of Texas Press, 1963.

Ryder, John. "The Use and Abuse of Modernity." *Journal of Speculative Philosophy* 7, no. 2 (1993): 92–102.

Saatkamp, Herman J., Jr. "Santayana: Hispanic-American Philosopher." *Transactions of the Charles S. Peirce Society* 34, no.1 (Winter 1998): 51–68.

Saatkamp, Herman J., Jr., and John Jones. *George Santayana: A Bibliographical Checklist, 1880–1980*. Bowling Green, OH: Bowling Green State University Press, 1982.

Schilpp, Paul Arthur, ed. *The Philosophy of George Santayana*. LaSalle, IL: Open Court Publishing, 1971.

Schleiermacher, Friedrich. *The Christian Faith*. Edited by H. R. Macintosh and J. S. Stewart. Edinburgh: T & T Clark, 1948.

Schneider, Herbert W. *A History of American Philosophy*. New York: Columbia University Press, 1946.

Seaton, James. "Santayana Today." *Hudson Review* 52, no. 3 (Autumn 1999): 420–26.

Shaw, Marvin C. "Santayana's View of Myth and the Meaning of God." *American Journal of Theology and Philosophy* 1, no. 3 (September 1980): 83–87.

Siegfried, Charles Haddock. "William James' Phenomenological Methodology." *Journal of the British Society for Phenomenology* 20, no. 1 (January 1989): 62–76.

Singer, Irving. *George Santayana, Literary Philosopher*. New Haven, CT: Yale University Press, 2000.

Smart, Ninian. *World Philosophies*. London: Routledge, 1999.

Spicker, Stuart F. "William James and Phenomenology." *Journal of the British Society for Phenomenology* 2 (October 1971): 69–74.

Spiegelberg, Herbert. *The Phenomenological Movement*. The Hague: Nijhoff, 1982.

Sprigge, Timothy, L. S. *Santayana: An Examination of His Philosophy*. London: Routledge & Kegan Paul, 1974.

———. "Whitehead and Santayana." *Process Studies* 1–2, no. 28 (1999): 43–55.

Stegnor, Daniel. *The Illusion of Conscious Will*. Cambridge, MA: MIT Press, 2002.

Stevens, Wallace. *The Collected Poems of Wallace Stevens*. New York: Knopf, 1955.

Stuhr, John. *Genealogical Pragmatism: Philosophy, Experience and Community*. Albany: State University of New York Press, 1997.

Sullivan, Celestine J. "Philosophical Inheritance." In Schilpp, *The Philosophy of George Santayana*, 65–91.

Ten Hoor, Marin. "George Santayana's Theory of Knowledge." In Lachs, *Animal Faith and Spiritual Life*, 220–36.

Thompson, Manley H. *The Pragmatic Philosophy of C. S. Peirce*. Chicago: University of Chicago Press, 1953.

Tiller, Glenn. "Peirce and Santayana: Pragmatism and the Belief in Substance." *Transactions of the Charles S. Peirce Society* 38, no. 3 (Summer 2002): 363–92.

Vivas, Elisio. "Life of Reason to the Last Puritan." In Schilpp, *The Philosophy of George Santayana*, 315–50.

Wachterhauser, Brice R., ed. *Phenomenology and Scepticism: Essays in Honor of James M. Edie*. Evanston, IL: Northwestern University Press, 1996.

Wakin, Edward, and Father Joseph F. Scheuer. *The De-Romanization of the American Catholic Church*. New York: Macmillan, 1966.

Whitehead, Alfred North. *Process and Reality*. New York: Free Press, 1985.

Whittemore, Robert C. "Santayana's Neglect of Hartshorne's Alternative." *Overheard in Seville* 4 (Fall 1986): 1–6.

Wilshire, Bruce. *William James and Phenomenology: A Study of "The Principles of Psychology."* Bloomington: Indiana University Press, 1968.

Wolfson, Harry Austryn. *The Philosophy of Spinoza*. Cambridge, MA: Harvard University Press, 1962.

Woodward, Anthony. *Living in the Eternal: A Study of George Santayana*. Nashville, TN: Vanderbilt University Press, 1988.

GENERAL REFERENCES

The Catholic Encyclopedia. New York: Appleton, 1909.

Edwards, Paul, ed. *The Encyclopedia of Philosophy.* New York: Macmillan/Free Press, 1967.

Eliade, Mircea, ed. *The Encyclopedia of Religion.* New York, Macmillan, 1987.

The Internet Encyclopedia of Philosophy, www.iep.edu/.

Kim, Jaegwon, and Ernest Sosa, eds., *A Companion to Metaphysics.* Cambridge, MA: Blackwell, 1995.

McGrath, Alister E., ed. *The Blackwell Encyclopedia of Modern Christian Thought.* Oxford: Blackwell, 1993.

The Penguin Dictionary of Philosophy. London: Penguin Books, 1996.

Reese, William L. *Dictionary of Philosophy and Religion.* Atlantic Highlands, NJ: Humanities Press, 1996.

About the Author

After a career in science and business, Edward Lovely received his PhD in philosophy of religion from Drew University. He teaches philosophy at Fairleigh Dickinson University and William Paterson University, both in New Jersey, and his research interests are in philosophy of religion and American philosophy.

Index

absolute, 201–203

Absolute Truth, 63, 72, 134–135

acceptance, 187–188

action, path toward, 60–63, 70, 73

actuosa essentia, of universe, 136–137

Agassiz, Louis, xiii

Alcibiades, 37

Anglican Church, 169, 179n243

angst, 136, 187

animal faith, 63, 76n55, 85, 113; basis
   for, 66; defined, 60–61; essences and,
   88–90, 101, 102, 147; ideal and, 147;
   memory and, 115–118; ontological
   parity and, 56, 60–63;
   phenomenological character of
   Santayana's philosophy of spirit
   and, 88–90, 105–106, 115–118;
   philosophy of religion and, 129, 134,
   136, 153; presentation and, 51;
   skepticism and, 36–37, 46, 57, 109,
   132, 136. *See also Scepticism and
   Animal Faith*

anthropomorphic gods, 42, 50

anti-modernism, 31n80, 163–166,
   178n212, 190

Anton, John P., 36, 46

apodicticity, 102, 104–106, 133

Apologia Pro Mente Sua: A Rejoinder
   (Santayana), 36, 51

apostasy, 166, 207, 208

Aquinas, Thomas, 10, 21

Aristotle, 21, 22, 77n65; essence and, 96;
   influence of, 39, 41, 46, 66, 70, 96,
   139, 167, 187

Armstrong, Karen, 25

Arnold, Matthew, 16, 17, 30n72

atheism: objections to, 166;
   Santayana's, x, 3, 17, 19, 132–133

atomization, 42

attributions, paucity of, 40

Baker, John Robert, 195

Beal, Boyleston, 30n62

being, equality in, 54–63

belief, path toward, 60–63

Berenson, Bernard, 3

Berger, Peter L., 192

Berkeley, George, 40, 78n109

Bidwell, Duane, 192

Boston, Catholicism in, 18

bracketing, 108–110

Brentano, Franz, 40, 60

"A Brief History of My Own Opinions"
   (Santayana), 21

Brodrick, Michael, 149

Buchler, Justus, ix, x, 27n4, 36, 40, 72,
   74n2, 95, 145

Butler, Richard, 8, 9, 10–11, 23, 29n31,
   29n39, 32n95, 167

Cafeteria Catholic, 207–209

Cartesian Meditations (Husserl), 113,
   114–115

charity: philosophy of religion and,
   141–143, 162–163, 188, 203;
   spirituality and piety synthesized
   with, 141–143, 188

chess game, in *The Realms of Being*, 106

Christ, 51, 92; prayer of, 24, 152;
   resurrection of, 153; in Trinity,
   194–196. *See also The Idea of Christ in
   the Gospels*

Christianity, 140–141, 143, 152; in
   Anglican Church, 169, 179n243;
   balance of liberalism and orthodoxy
   in, 204–206; Darwinism and, 15–16;
   diluted, 185, 204, 206; dogma,
   31n80, 194–196; Existentialism and,
   136; humanism and, 16; politicized,
   202; Schopenhauer scuttling, 51. *See
   also* Protestantism; Roman Catholic

229